Swept Up by the Spirit

Journey Of Transformation

Gary Garner

Swept Up by the Spirit

ISBN 978-0-9856705-2-8

Cover Photograph

The cover photograph is of downtown Augusta, Georgia, at sunrise in late October. The Savannah River separates the states of Georgia to the right, and South Carolina to the left.

The city is still shrouded in near darkness as the sun breaks the horizon. Soon the city will be bustling with activity—industrial, commercial, retail, educational. As in most moderate-sized cities, business is the first priority. Many of the events described in this book took place within or near this sprawling scene. Broad Street and other primary streets in downtown Augusta are easily detectable, as are some buildings that are significant to this book.

The darkness of this scene typifies the darkness over humanity that only increases with man's exclusion of the Lord and His help.

The photo came about after a clear vision from the Holy Spirit just for this book cover, and an aerial shot was required to capture it. Upon hearing my description of this vision, friends from our church, Damon and Valerie Comparetta, commercial aerial photographers, volunteered to try to capture the scene as I had described it to them. Their photo is nearly identical to my vision, including the plumes of smoke from an industrial plant in the distance.

I believe that the Lord wanted this cover to be used to accentuate the power of His light to overcome any darkness and also to under-score His presence in everyday, workday settings. Most of the events in this book occurred while work of all kinds was in progress. We are reminded that regardless of the setting, He is the King of Glory, who wants to meet us anywhere, anytime, and most especially in our darkest moments. In the pages of this book, may His light begin to dispel any darkness threatening you, the reader.

> *Through His tender mercy a great light from on high dawned upon us as we sat in darkness and the shadow of death and led us into His way of peace. Luke 1:78-79*

Acknowledgements

As a first time author, I have many to thank for their support and help. If you are among those not listed, know that I realize who you are, and am most appreciative. So many encouraged me on this mission.

My most profound thanks to Jesus, the wonderful, merciful Savior who twice delivered me from near death, then placed me on this most incredible journey, the Holy Spirit, who has enabled me to experience near unimaginable blessings, protection and capacity for each occasion—whatever it held.

The members of Holy Family Catholic Church prayer group who introduced me to this wondrous adventure of God and man interacting here and now.

Fr. Walt Foley, the first example of all-out living of expectant faithfully walking in the Spirit.

The pentecostal men of Mount Paran Church of God who fleshed out this experience of faith in such a powerful but normal manner— their approach to life.

Daryl Hilbrands for being a prime example of a man single-minded for Jesus taking Him everywhere—always "on duty".

The speakers and attendees of the National Charismatic Conferences who validated this awesome new life on a worldwide ecumenical level..

The Alleluia Covenant Community for exemplifying Acts 2 lifestyle, in this age and the readiness to pay the price to answer the call. My ongoing thanks and gratitude for allowing our family to join them.

Don and Karen Lansing for risking the Alleluia " come & see" with us. The Alleluia leaders, especially Bob Garrett , Dan Almeter, and the rest of the community and their consistent encouragement, for their belief in the use of our gifts to build the Kingdom.

Wayne Waldrop for a decade long exhortation to write the stories and compile the book that he saw in the Spirit. Jim Cordell and Tom Hartney's ongoing encouragement to see it through to completion.

The many random readers of the stories and their helpful comments and encouragement to get the book finished; for the few professional editors and writers and their helpful critiques.

Damon and Valeria Comparetta's photographic skills and efforts and Barbara Harshman's computer artwork for the cover.

Dora Lockhart, a close friend and witness to many of the experiences, who for three years skillfully, and with her heart, edited the entire manuscript, over and over. Her love for the Lord and desire that this life changing truth get out, were evident throughout—and called me on.

Of course, my wife Nancy who has typed every word and corrected many, many, phrases time and again; for her supportive dedication to this daunting task, like the many other large projects throughout our life together, go far beyond words of thanks or gratitude. Her commitment to me and to what the Lord seemed to be doing made possible the completion of the project.

And finally to the Holy Spirit who allowed me to get involved in the events and replayed each one with total clarity in my mind , dictated the contents of the book, and brought the book to print— *with God, all things are possible.*

Come Holy Spirit-Let Your Fire Fall

*May the Holy Spirit inspire the words and events to your
reading and fan each of us into brighter flames for His
Glory and the building of His Kingdom.*

*Let us not hold out, or hold back against God's higher call,
let us go where He takes us and put everything into this
greatest of journeys—and trust Him with the results*

Amen, Glory !
Gary Garner

DOUG AND LESLIE,
YOU BLESS US WITH YOUR
SPIRIT LED LIFE IN ALLELUIA
IN BOTH LOCATIONS.
MAY YOUR JOURNEY BECOME
EVEN GREATER AND YOU BE
STIRRED EVEN HIGHER IN THE
SPIRIT —AND THE LORD LEAD
EVERY STEP OF THE WAY.
WITH ALL OUR LOVE,
GARY AND NANCY   NOV
                      2012

Contents

Introduction

This book is totally factual, told in the first person, recounting many of my experiences with the Holy Spirit, spanning my Christian life. I'm simply telling you what I saw or experienced as an eyewitness.

It begins in my condition of unbelief, total lack of faith, and worldly mindset, and tells of two incredible encounters with the Holy Spirit—and then describes the transformation that the Lord orchestrated in my life. Many other people, including my wife, Nancy, and our family, were also radically changed by the Lord as these events occurred.

The stories in this book could be those of anyone—man or woman—who has suddenly entered the dominion of the living God and recognized it as *the pearl of great price*. They recount struggles between good and evil for each person's free will, and man interacting with God and His Holy Spirit, spontaneously, but with increasing expectancy and awareness. The power and energy in these experiences has all been possible through the Holy Spirit, the Helper, the Paraclete that Jesus promised the followers at Pentecost. My own part was simply to try to be available and "on duty." Many times, I wasn't alert and missed what the Spirit had planned. I may well have missed far more than I experienced.

The events recorded in this book deal with divine encounters, satanic attempts, revelations, Holy Spirit leadings, growth, wisdom and knowledge, transformation, Holy Spirit manifestations, healings/miracles, and much more. Any list would be incomplete and the stories keep coming. It was my intent and effort to record each of these experiences in print, accurate down to each word of dialogue, and invite the reader into the experience and the wonderful discovery of the Holy Spirit's active presence and intervention in everyday situations. As the book progresses, you will notice my awareness and understanding developing—a life-long process.

The stories are told just as they happened. Some of the occurrences described may seem preposterous. They unfolded without plan or warning, in the midst of the everyday routines of people living their lives—people with real problems to be dealt with and real needs to be met. These events occurred as I was going about a full work schedule as an independent contractor.

In writing the book, I've tried to be open and personal, allowing the reader to see some of my many frailties and weaknesses. It seems that's the way the Holy Spirit wanted these stories shared. Hopefully, you, the reader, can read this book in the same way, with openness, and allow the Holy Spirit to use it to build up His people and His kingdom here on earth. (Come, Holy Spirit!) Perhaps you will find yourself or your situation in some of these stories.

It is my hope that the book will speak to all readers, particularly to go-getters and people of action—and especially to those who have been praying for a change of heart in another person towards God.

These stories recount our own experience of God's subtle ways—the ways He reveals His will and reshapes our minds and direction as He draws us into that will through the Holy Spirit and the circumstances that He puts in place or in motion. We believe He works in this way for all those seeking His will for their lives. Divine encounters and the miraculous have a way of strengthening faith in those already being led by the Holy Spirit, and I hope these stories will greatly encourage all such readers.

These accounts run the gamut: some are joyful, some sorrowful, some both, but they're all real and alive and personal. More importantly, in each one, Jesus is dealing with our hearts and our faith. He is beckoning us to trust Him with everything, and to believe that He can and will deliver, and to consciously and intentionally be transformed to live in His world all the time. He will supply the power for everything through the Holy Spirit. Glory!

Walking with the Lord in the power of the Holy Spirit, in pursuit of His perfect will, is the best life can get for anyone. It's dynamic, it's fulfilling. It's His "ultimate" for each of us—and anyone can do it! God has made sure of that.

> *Now, Lord, consider their threats and enable your servants to speak your word with great boldness. Stretch out your hand to heal and perform signs and wonders through the name of your holy servant Jesus.*

> *After they prayed, the place where they were meeting was shaken. And they were all filled with the Holy Spirit and spoke the word of God boldly... God's great blessing was upon them all. Acts 4:29-31,33 (NIV)*

Part I:
First Encounters

The Voice

After fourteen years of owning my own small custom furniture-building business, with all of its challenges, it was time for a new course. The demands of our growing family of five were calling me to have more regular hours, more regular paychecks and some more time at home. With some sadness and reluctance, my wife Nancy and I agreed it was time to close down our business so that I could go to work for a larger company.

Our family moved to Tennessee in the early part of 1968, to a still small but bustling town named Hendersonville, eighteen miles north of Nashville. I had taken a position with Davis Cabinet Company, a longtime manufacturer of fine, solid wood furniture. The plant was located in the downtown area of Nashville. Our home was about a half-hour drive from the furniture plant, nearly a straight shot, first on I-24, then I-65 N and on to Gallatin Road. My business had always been within three miles of home, so a "drive" to work was new for me.

Having been somewhat addicted to golf, I had brought the habit with me to Nashville. Along with two or three men from the plant, I usually played once a week after work. I played just well enough to remain "hooked" and coming back week after week. Once a week was plenty, though; any more would have been too costly in many ways.

One particular day, October 17, 1969, was to become a milestone in my life. Having completed my work day, I joined Bob, the personnel director, and we went to the nearby course to get in as many holes as possible before dark. Bob and I had been the most consistent participants of the group, and today it was just the two of us. We had similar levels of talent—or lack of—and enjoyed playing together. It wasn't an overly competitive kind of thing, just enough to make it interesting, and to push each of us to try a little harder. These golf outings were good therapy for both of us after a hectic and grueling week in a loud, dangerous old plant with 400 workers. We were both in responsible positions that had a high level of stress. The constant production noise of the bustling plant, the roaring old machines, the whining and screaming of other equipment, along with the pungent smells of wood, lacquer and sweat were draining on the senses; so were the workers we managed. The golf course, late Friday afternoon, with few golfers left, was very peaceful, a great place to savor fresh air and quiet, and a good way to transition into a weekend with the family. After an enjoyable time together, walking the course, carrying our bags, and hitting a few decent shots, darkness called time on us. We put our clubs in our cars, said, "See you on Monday," and left in separate directions.

The eighteen-mile drive home was like hundreds of others I'd made. The silence was so welcome, I didn't even turn on the radio. I was about halfway home on I-65, just before my turnoff, when I was surprised to hear a voice. In the quiet of the drive, the *Voice* spoke, and with calm, distinctive authority, said, "Buckle your seatbelt." Nothing else. It was so clear, it seemed audible. I'm not certain that it was—but I think it was. For sure, it was not something to question or delay obeying. I was driving a 1963 Pontiac LeMans, a compact car about the size of a Mustang. It was a nice little sporty, five-speed car, our very first car with seatbelts. I was aware of the seatbelts but had not used them, denying any need. I had a natural resistance to restraints and requirements.

The *Voice*, however, had so captured my attention that I immediately began to reach for the big steel buckle. I found it right away, pulled it over and locked it. I remember the heavy, metallic clunk, and checking the tension to make sure it was tight. Having done this, the message gradually slipped from my mind. For whatever reason, I didn't worry or wonder about what it might mean. I did, however, wonder about the *Voice*, compelling like none I had ever heard.

Just about this moment, my exit sign appeared, for Two Mile Pike, and I turned off to the right, heading toward Gallatin Road. Coming to the end of Two Mile Pike, I was faced with the usual wait at the traffic light before turning north toward home. About seven more miles and one more right turn, and I would be on my street. Thoughts of the weekend projects ahead began to replace thoughts of weeklong responsibilities of the furniture plant; now I could take care of the things that needed doing at home.

Waiting for the light to change, I became aware of the beauty of the evening. It was about 7:20 pm, Friday night, high school football night, and heavy traffic was headed toward Nashville. A steady stream of headlights, two lanes wide, was quickly moving down the hill—you could sense the energy of the people passing by. The stars were exceptionally bright; the sky was full of them. Finally, the light changed to green. Turning left, I began the long uphill grade of about 300 yards. I remember getting three fourths of the way up the hill— and then nothing.

The next thing I was aware of was seeing the stars again, but this time I was looking straight at them, suddenly realizing that I was lying on my back. It felt like gravel under me—increasingly uncomfortable. Getting up was not a consideration. I had no "get-up" left in me. It seemed as though I had been out, unconscious; things were just now starting to come into focus. I became aware of a siren in the distance, far off, the intensity of the sound waxing and waning, but always getting closer. An old fear of being carried away by an ambulance flashed across my mind. I knew it was coming for me.

A group of people had formed a circle, about twenty feet or so away from me. I guess they were concerned and wanted to help, but didn't know what to do, so they just stood and made comments in low voices to each other, like, "Look at that car," or, "Look at his face," or, "He isn't going to make it." Strangely, I could hear their comments as if they were standing right next to me. Only one young man ventured up to speak to me. The siren kept getting louder, and then the EMTs were there, rolling out the stretcher. This was my first time in an ambulance or going to a hospital; I certainly had mixed feelings about the whole thing. I was so out of it, though, that the entire event was just a passing blur. I do remember that long ambulance pulling away under full power, heading for the hospital—it was scary, but also encouraging.

Nancy arrived at the hospital and found me on one of the steel tables in the emergency room. Little by little she began to piece together the story of what had happened. She was told by witnesses that just as I had approached the peak of the hill, in the inside northbound lane, there were two cars coming in the opposite direction. Gallatin Road was a four-lane highway, with a 70-mph speed limit, and no median separation—just a stripe between the lanes. The locals referred to it as "suicide alley." Two southbound cars were racing, a Corvette on the outside, with just a driver, and a GTO in the inside lane, carrying five young men. Eyewitnesses said the two cars were traveling about 100 miles per hour. As the racing cars approached the top of the hill from the other side, the GTO came upon a stalled car that was blocking the lane. With nowhere else to go, the young driver of the GTO had jerked the wheel to the left to avoid running into the back of the car, then straightened his car in the inside lane of northbound traffic. Immediately his car and mine collided, head on in my lane, at the very crest of the hill. Both cars stood up on their back wheels from the impact. My motor block was driven back to the front wheels by the sheer force. The man driving behind me later said he had to unbuckle me from my seat belt to take me out and lay me on the ground.

The scene Nancy came upon at the hospital was certainly one of confusion, hurried activity and apprehension. Five of us had been brought to the local hospital, taking a toll on its facilities and staff. As time went by and the story unfolded, Nancy found out that the driver of the Corvette had just kept going, never stopping. All five young men in the GTO, who had just graduated the previous year from a local high school, had various injuries. The two in the front seat were hurt pretty badly, but their injuries were not life threatening. The impact had catapulted the one sitting in the center of the backseat over the front seat and down under the dash. He was the most injured of anyone, and had been rushed to Vanderbilt Hospital. Soon afterwards we learned that he was dead on arrival, his skull crushed by the motor block.

The extent of my own injuries was unknown for awhile. As we waited on doctors and x-rays, a very gifted Asian plastic surgeon came to sew up my wounds. For a long time that evening he calmly sewed away, putting nearly a hundred stitches just in my face. Most of the damage had been done by my steering wheel, which had slammed into my face, cutting me severely. My palate was split in half and several teeth were knocked out or broken. A few ribs were also broken. The next morning, the doctors would find that I had a traumatic lung collapse (as from a bomb explosion). The belated discovery of the collapsed lung put the hospital staff into quick action. Ten years later we learned that my back had also been fractured by the collision. In the crush of multiple patients and injuries, the doctors had not x-rayed or found that injury.

Certainly the main factor that saved my life that night was being restrained by the seat belt. The impact would almost certainly have thrown me through both windshields. If the cars had not collided, headlight to headlight, into the full strength of my car frame, their car would likely have torn right through mine; our combined speed at impact was around 150 miles per hour.

During the recovery period from the accident, even though I had no faith, I had some sense that God had saved my life, and I wondered if someone would come and explain it to me. I thought someone (who understood) might come and "tell me what had happened" and what it meant—but no one did. I think a couple of my visitors to the hospital were supposed to (one was even a minister), but they just couldn't bring themselves to step out and tell me, especially about my need to be open to God. I even tried to draw a few people from church into talking about the possibility that God had saved me from death. They mostly responded, "Just be glad you're alive," or "I guess it just wasn't your time to go." After awhile, I decided to leave it alone. Gradually, over time, the belief that God had saved my life began to fade. I rationalized that maybe it was just one of those good coincidences, or just fate, or maybe just "good luck." After all, I had been hit head on at an incredible speed by a bunch of kids playing games, and lived to tell about it. Maybe that was enough! But what about the *Voice*? What was that, and where did it come from?

Reflecting on these events, numerous times, maybe the most surprising element to me was that God would have shown such mercy to an unbeliever. I was barely churched at the time, and that was purely on a social level. In reality, I had no idea who the Lord was. Even Nancy didn't know what church was really about. A cradle Catholic, she knew she was supposed to be at church every Sunday—and, for sure, she was—but that was the extent of her faith. Like me, she had grown up with no real faith lived out at home or at work, day to day. But God was gracious. I was alive to play another day. Our fourth child would be born a year and a half later. Without God's mercy that night, Hell would rightfully have claimed me.

The wreck was one of the most horrendous events of my life, but God's grace and mercy had rescued me. My hospital stay was limited to eleven days; my recovery was complete, with virtually no permanent damage. I was back at work in three weeks, but I returned with no more compassion or sensitivity to the needs of the workers under me. I had learned little about life and still saw my job strictly as supervising manufacturing.

To this day, I have never seen anything, heard anything, or felt anything of the actual collision. The whole block of time, maybe ten to fifteen minutes, was removed from my mind. This was probably God's merciful way of protecting me, especially from any fear of driving. I now believe that Satan intended this wreck to finish me—but God granted me a reprieve that night.

Driving over the exact spot of the wreck many times during the next two years, I would revisit that night in my mind. It remained a significant mystery yet to be revealed; other activities and life gradually dimmed the memory. Only the compelling *Voice*, saying, "Buckle your seatbelt," remained sharp and clear—but unexplained.

The next several years saw me slide more and more into worldliness and the pursuit of materialism, into increased darkness. Even after God had spared my life, I failed to recognize Him on His mercy visit and now began to distance myself further from Him.

You were following the course and fashion of this world—were under the sway and tendency of this present age; following the Prince of the power of the air.

We were then by nature children of God's wrath and heirs of His indignation, like the rest of mankind.

But God, so rich is His mercy! Even when we were dead by our own shortcomings and trespasses, He made us alive. Ephesians 2:2-5

The Imposter

Our family moved back to Marietta from Nashville in January of 1972. We had lived on the south side of Marietta most of our lives, but now we were moving up. I had been given a promising new position with a different manufacturer, as plant manager and vice president, so we were moving to the thriving new east side of town. Our house was brand new, as was the subdivision. Most of the residents were middle income and above. The neighborhood had a pool and tennis courts for members to enjoy; it was definitely a step up for us. Our young family was very excited about it. We even added a new sports car to complement my new position. We liked the way the good life was coming together for us. A good work ethic, strong will power and the pursuit of excellence—we had what it took and we were on the way. Nashville was a memory—as was the wreck.

Our newfound prosperity was soon challenged, however. As the year 1973 dawned, Nancy and I were feeling the stress of uncertainty and financial concerns. All of the members of management in my new company had agreed to a 20% pay cut to try to salvage the company, but after a struggle it had just gone under, seriously undercapitalized. With four growing children, ages two to fourteen, and a rather expensive lifestyle, we had a real need for financial stability. With no higher education or degrees to back our abilities, our options were limited. Our lifestyle was the main consideration— a risky basis for choosing a new vocation.

Landing a job as a plant manager for a furniture manufacturer was my most promising option, to produce the kind of income we desired, but would require us to relocate, probably to North Carolina. We dismissed that idea since we had moved just a year earlier and were still adapting to our new home. Trying to think clearly and objectively, Nancy and I decided that my best opportunity in the Atlanta area, with my design and woodworking background, would be as a designer and building contractor of nicer homes. To us, it didn't seem to matter that I'd never worked in house building, per se; we both had faith in my talents and ability to adapt. We saw this option as a natural fit. The four years of manufacturing experience in Nashville had allowed me to develop abilities in leading people to produce good work, which would be a significant aspect of this new career. And all of the economy experts were saying that the future of building in Atlanta was a sure thing—can't miss.

We still felt a little like we were heading into deep water, but went ahead and started the new business. For about a year and half, it seemed that this was indeed working out to be a good plan. After building two "spec" houses, which sold right away, I landed a "state of the art" contract house—nine thousand square feet plus deck and patio on four acres in prime Dunwoody. This house was a real showstopper and was getting lots of good attention. It was a wonderful business experience; things couldn't have gone better. My confidence in succeeding in this power-wielding business was growing by leaps and bounds. We were on the way! When the world discovered us, clients would be lining up, waiting. We had tapped into the Golden Goose.

Just as this great house was reaching completion, and without warning, the one thing that seemingly couldn't happen did. The bottom dropped out of the housing market. Watergate finally took down Nixon, Gerald Ford replaced him, and Jimmy Carter would follow, all in quick succession. The nation was in shock. Mortgage rates soared to 14% and higher, and then the Federal Reserve put a halt to virtually all mortgage lending. Across the country, in two weeks' time, contractors and supply companies, as well as lenders, were brought to a near standstill. The whole construction scene, as well as mortgage banking, was thrown into total chaos. Our third and fourth spec houses were now virtually not sellable—no mortgage money was available, and my fast-developing new business was really in trouble. My lone investor wanted out immediately, demanding his small investment returned, and we had no cash reserve. The large contract house I was building was privately funded and suffered no effect, but everything else that we had going ground nearly to a halt.

We would eventually sell our last two spec houses at a sizable loss and spend the next four years building large contract houses in upscale neighborhoods, while underfunded and overstressed, trying to avoid disaster. The funding for the current house would pay for expenses on the former house, keeping most of our payments well in arrears. Most of the building contractors were forced to operate this way. Keeping this merry-go-round of money moving was imperative—actually, it was basically kiting. If the cash flow stopped, you were dead in the water.

Our personal situation was dangerously challenging since we were not incorporated and were personally liable for all business debts. Almost before we realized it, we were in the midst of a battle for financial survival, and desperately trying not to lose our family home. How quickly fortunes can turn.

After moving back to the Atlanta area, I had pretty much stopped attending church. Now that timeslot in my week was usually spent playing football or softball with other men in our subdivision. Several of them were good athletes and competitive, and it provided a stimulating diversion to the pressure-cooker world of home building. My spiritual life had become such a nonentity that now, when asked what denomination I was, I would respond with "agno-protholic." I would then explain that I grew up Protestant, my wife was Catholic, and I didn't know if I believed anything (agnostic). Therefore, agnoprotholic seemed fitting, and even Nancy described me by that term. Strange looks often followed when people would hear this—I think it may have chilled them.

Occasionally, I thought of the car wreck, but had pretty much dismissed the "buckle your seatbelt" experience as just another odd, inexplicable happening. I was really busy with the "real world," and any thought I might have had that God had spared me that night just faded away. I wasn't thinking about much of anything, except about building expensive houses and paying costly old debts. I did think of the *Voice*, which I could still clearly remember hearing.

In late summer of 1976, a pivotal time began in our lives. The building business was making a slow, gradual recovery, although over half of the builders were said to have gone bankrupt from the 1974-75 recession. Now trying to stay afloat with only contract home building, we pressed on.

I was due to start building a large house for a doctor and his family right away, as soon as we finished our present house. We had selected a nice lot, very buildable, near Sandy Springs, and the doctor, Joel, was ready to close on it. Then the national mortgage lending problems of the previous two years blindsided us. The property had some liens against it, and couldn't be cleared anytime soon. Through no fault of ours, the lot couldn't be closed on. The bank told us to just forget that lot and look elsewhere for another.

Searching the surrounding area for an appropriate lot became my immediate project. It had to be located in a good, upscale area, near the interstate highway and hospitals. Soon, I found a lot that looked like it might be the one. It was located in a well established, sought-after subdivision near the Chattahoochee River. The lot was totally wooded, on a hillside next to a dry creek bed.

After visiting the lot a couple of times, admiring its beauty and its view, I was convinced this was it. (It had a distinct Frank Lloyd Wright look about it.) I was ready to show my clients this new lot to see if it met with their approval. Joel and his wife, Carla, loved it right away for its beauty, their only question was, "Do you think the incline might be a little steep?" I had already convinced myself it was great—I had to get the house moving. So with my assurances, they were put at ease and asked me to proceed and get a closing date set. They undoubtedly had total trust in my judgment about the lot and house. Later, I would feel the enormous weight of that trust many times.

The date was set and the lot was closed on; I had completed the house plans and the construction loan had been obtained. We were ready to start. I was nearing completion on my other house, a few miles away, and my attention was split between the two.

Making final preparations to begin grading and setting the foundation, I was met with a startling surprise. The leaves had now all fallen from the trees and I was jolted by how steep the lot looked with the trees bare, now that I could really see it. The house site was actually fifty-five feet above the street. In spite of this realization, operating with more confidence than was warranted, I began the house, disregarding the incline. I had already built and sold two houses on steep lots.

I would soon come to realize that those lots had been only about half as steep as this site. Because I really had to get this house started to keep the cash flow moving, I had allowed myself to be quite deceived about the difficulty of the lot. Gradually, it became apparent to me why a building lot with such natural beauty and views had gone unsold and not been built on—until I had claimed it. The other builders in the area had considered the lot unbuildable.

As the grading contractor, Slim, began to grade for the house site, his loader hit rock. A very big rock. The entire crown of the hill where the house was to be located was one huge vein of rock. I arranged for a grading contractor with a D-9 loader (highway construction size) to try to remove the rock. After a half hour, doing everything he knew to do, the rock did not budge. The contractor just loaded up his equipment and left. In my urgency to get started, I had overlooked having the lot tested for rock. The vein of rock added an unexpected weight to my work and my woes, as well as cost and time to the project.

Winter arrived fast and hard that year; it would become one of the coldest winters to date in the area, dropping to zero at one point. It not only got brutally cold, it stayed cold. We got the concrete foundation and walls poured with the major efforts of a seventy-five-ton winch truck (tied off to trees at the top and back of the lot) to pull the mixers up the muddy driveway bed. At one point the winch truck pulled down a tree that it was tied to. Nothing about this house was going to be easy.

All of us on the job soon found that without a front-end loader, materials couldn't be delivered up to the house site. Loaders were not readily available in our area due to the slowdown of building because of the recession, and because the subdivision was nearly "built out." I had most of the lumber and plywood delivered and unloaded at the street, and we hand carried it to the top, up the rough hillside. I helped carry much of the material in hopes that my subcontractors wouldn't walk off the job. The lot was looking more like Mt. Everest than like a Frank Lloyd Wright site.

The harder the lot became to deal with, the harder it was to get my regular subcontractors and keep them happy. To them, the project looked daunting. As the building progressed, their spirits and energy were being depleted; each day became an ordeal. All of the extra challenges were compounding the demands of building of this big, special house. I had to keep it moving, regardless, to keep the cash flow coming in and old accounts paid. I still believed the house would come out fine, but I wasn't sure about myself. I was talking a beating mentally and physically, and the end was nowhere in sight. I could feel myself starting to doubt my decisions—they were getting harder to make, and they weren't all that good. My ever-present confidence was slipping—badly.

Finally, it was time to have the sheetrock delivered, and we needed a driveway to get it up to the house. By now, I was really pressing, not thinking clearly, sleeping very little and worn out, tired to the bone. After a lot of private vacillating about the path of the driveway—straight up the steep left side next to the property line, or longer and curved, out toward the front and back to the left (which would require taking out trees, bringing in fill dirt, and building up a bed), I decided on straight. I had some dubious feelings about that, but convinced myself that I was overreacting and needed to bite the bullet and go for it.

Because of the height and length of the driveway, the concrete would have to be pumped by a pump truck. Becoming more paranoid as the time drew near, I chose to go with 4,000-pound mix concrete (which is used for highways) and not the usual 3,000-pound mix, and pour it six inches thick, rather than the usual four inches thick. The driveway was going up a rock-filled hillside, so this all made sense to me. I was unusually uptight when we started the pour—then the pump truck broke down, almost immediately. The replacement pump truck didn't get there until midday for the concrete finishers to begin pouring. Even though they poured until after dark, they would have to come back the next day and finish the last section down to the street. When we finally finished, I was totally worn out and mentally drained, and looking up that long, straight concrete strip, a spirit of dread came over me. I felt almost sick. Usually, completing a driveway pour gave you a nice sense of accomplishment and relief. Not this time.

The following day, Bill, the concrete finishing contractor, came by to take a look at the driveway, and he wanted to drive up it with a vehicle. Dreading the worst, I tried to put him off, saying, "Let's give it another day to cure." I knew it was plenty solid, as that 4,000-pound mix had been literally smoking as it came out of the mixer the last two days. Knowing the concrete was fully set, Bill said, "Mr. Gary, let me take your little truck and try it out." He could tell I wasn't going to try it myself.

Realizing it was time to find the courage and have a vehicle try the driveway, I agreed and gave Bill my truck keys. Then, trying hard to look nonchalant, I turned my back on the driveway, stuck my hands in my back pockets, and slowly walked down the street, actually afraid to watch. My "little truck" was an El Camino with a

454 engine, and I heard it accelerating up the hill, then a loud "skwonking" of tires. Looking back over my shoulder, there it was, my high-powered truck halfway up the driveway, at a standstill, burning rubber, tires just smoking. The dread I had been feeling was suddenly replaced by this new, numbing reality. I just wanted to leave, run away and hide.

As I stood there, not wanting to accept what I had just seen, Bill slowly backed my truck down to the street. Leaning out of the window, he said, in a hopeful manner, "I'll make it this time, Mr. Gary," and took off again. This time he almost overshot the turnaround up at the house. I didn't feel any better. Then, as he turned the truck around and prepared to come back down the drive, I was looking at the whole undercarriage of my truck. As he started slowly down, I stood there almost expecting the truck to start flipping end over end. Of course, it didn't, but I almost did. Fear is an awful tormentor.

Before Bill got down to the street, I knew the driveway would have to come out, completely, and be replaced by a longer, curved driveway. The thing I had feared the most had come upon me, and I felt weighed down by Joel and Carla's complete trust and my responsibility for their dream house.

I believe it was at this time that the momentum shifted. I had tried to hold back the stresses and pressures of the last three years and had hoped the slow, steady progress would deliver me from this cold, dark sense of oppression. Now, all of a sudden, the driveway was the newest obstacle. And what an obstacle it was. It seemed almost bigger than life—insurmountable.

Along with all of my other problems, I was ever mindful that Nancy knew nothing about the business finances. I handled them all, and had kept everything to myself; she was completely unaware of our serious dilemma. We had continued to draw the same moderate salary from the business throughout the troubled times. She knew only that the building business in general had been bad for everyone involved over the past three years. She hated for us to be in debt to anyone; she always had. Our dire situation was going to be hard for her to accept. Also, our daughter, Sherre, was due to start college the next year at the University of Georgia. That was now totally out of the question.

Having no faith life at all, I felt totally alone in the midst of this mountain of troubles. Throughout the long series of hard blows from the mortgage and housing collapse, up until now, I never once thought about praying, never even considered it. I valued being self-reliant and independent, and now I was in the process of being overwhelmed and facing possible devastation and humiliation. Fear and hopelessness were filling my mind.

Now a new "player" was about to move to the forefront, and he would force the issue. It is said that Satan (whom I didn't know or give credibility to) counterfeits all that God does. A different voice from the *Voice*, an imposter voice, one that was chilling and unnerving, began to talk at me. This imposter voice would say, "Cash it in—you're a loser—you always have been and always will be—do something good for your family—cash it in—you're worth more dead than alive." This voice didn't sound like the *Voice* that had told me, "Buckle your seat belt," but it was almost as calm.

I didn't know the imposter voice, but I understood the "cash it in" part. I had an insurance policy for $300,000 that I had taken out three years earlier. I had given consideration to "cashing it in" (the policy was old enough) to pay off all the debts and give Nancy and the kids a new start. Of course this $300,000 was good only as a death payment. To cash it in the only option was suicide. Having never experienced depression before, I was shocked at how overwhelmingly it now dominated my mind. I had trouble shaking the thoughts, even for a short while.

As the days went on, the imposter voice visited more and more, always with the same reasoning message, "Cash it in—you're worth more dead than alive. Do something good for your family, cash it in." As time went on, this voice sounded more like a counselor; it was becoming less threatening to me and more familiar. I was getting less and less sleep through the night, and more torment. As the imposter visits increased, my remaining self-confidence drained away. Anytime I was driving and passing a tractor trailer or a bridge abutment, I would have both hands gripping the steering wheel tightly for fear of a deadly impulse to obey that voice—and cash it in.

It was in the midst of all of this horrific turmoil that Nancy surprised me by asking if I would be interested in going to a retreat that weekend at St. Ignatius Retreat Center, on the Chattahoochee River, about four miles from our home. It's almost unfathomable that I considered and accepted her offer, but I did. I was desperate for some kind of breakthrough, and she was, also. We were living as two strangers under the same roof, focused on different problems. Something had to give, and soon. Our last five years of living in the fast lane had taken a serious toll.

So we went to the retreat with different equipment and different expectations. Nancy went with *Sylvia Porter's Money Book* to read between sessions. I took nothing but problems. I had little interest in the retreat but was planning to walk around outside as much as possible, hoping to sort out my thoughts and make some sense of everything. I was sinking fast and needed something to grab hold of.

After the third break, Nancy began to tell me about an old dog-eared paperback book that she had pulled from a pile of books on one of the tables. The book was titled, *Charismatic Movements in the Catholic Church*. She was curious about it because she had heard some talk about "the movement" and hoped to write it off in her mind as a sham or fraud. Instead, she had been unable to quit reading this little book and now needed to talk to someone who really understood what was written about this strange phenomenon.

Nancy thought of Fr. Walt, the new priest at church. He had been ordained a priest the year before, even though he was fifty years old. Before that he had spent sixteen years in Africa as a religious brother, traveling the wilds on a motorcycle. Now, in suburban Atlanta, he drove a pickup truck or rode his motorcycle. He impressed her as different from any other priest that she had known. He even carried his own Bible around. Fr. Walt just might know about this "movement." Nancy called the church and asked him to come and talk to us. Without hesitation, he said, "Sure, I'll be over in a few minutes."

In less than a half hour, he arrived at the retreat center. Except for the collar and all black clothes, with his windbreaker and down-to-earth manner he could have been Joe Anybody. But he wasn't. He was different. He seemed laid-back and intense at the same time, but mostly, he seemed totally peaceful with who he was and what was happening right then. Fr. Walt was like a man on a mission, but getting his orders as he went. He just backed up against the wall, slid down it, and sat on the floor amongst the six or eight of us. He had the capacity to gain your total trust, seemingly without trying.

As he fielded our questions, giving his honest responses, I could tell Fr. Walt was the "real deal" and he really believed in what he was about. He was a man's man who was out there facing life straight up—no hype and no excuses. Yes, he was definitely different—but a magnetic different. What was this difference?

None of the group knew enough to ask really meaningful questions, and he could easily see that. After a half hour, Fr. Walt told us that there was a group of folks involved in the charismatic movement who met at the church every Thursday night. He was part of the group and would be there. As he prepared to leave, his parting words burned deep into my heavy-laden mind, "Any of you can come and see for yourself." With that, Fr. Walt turned and walked toward the door, having done what he was sent to do.

He, Jesus, said to them, "Come and see." John 1:39

Prayer Requests
and Praise Reports

Nancy and I talked a little about Fr. Walt over the next few days. We were both intrigued by him. He had a presence like no one we had met before. We knew no one with whom to compare him. Whatever he had—he had it! But we didn't talk about the "Charismatic Movement," or the Thursday night prayer meeting held at the church. Not a word.

I really wanted to go and check it out, probably just to get it off my mind. (What about this Fr. Walt?) I didn't want to admit it to Nancy, though. I thought to her it might look like a weakness. I hoped she, too, would want to go, and would want me to go with her—but she hadn't mentioned it. She had been exceptionally quiet.

Finally, early Thursday evening, with a doubtful look, Nancy asked me, "Do you think we ought to go to that prayer meeting, just once, and see if there's anything to it? Fr. Walt said he would be there."

In my most restrained, serious manner, intentionally sounding disinterested, I said, "If that's what it will take to make you happy." She lit up a little and got into action. "All right," I thought, "We're going to check this out."

Over the five days since Fr. Walt's "come and see" invite, I had anticipated Nancy's request and given some thought to going and what to expect. I envisioned a group of fairly old people, mostly women (some probably knitting), sitting in a circle, some even rocking back and forth, out of touch with reality. I guessed that Fr. Walt would be there just to give the group some credibility and lift their spirits. This could likely be one of those things you never needed to do a second time.

As Nancy and I entered the church and approached the room, we were met by joyful music that filled the air. Then, there they were, sitting in the circle, but that was all that resembled my preconceived idea. This group was young, most were in their twenties and thirties. A fairly even number of men and women were there, and they seemed vibrant, lively and hopeful. Energy just radiated from the group. They seemed expectant of good things. I had never entered a gathering with such a level of joy—and they all seemed to have it!

Fr. Walt recognized us walking in, but made no reaction to our coming. We just sat down in the back row, folded our arms over our chests, and hung on. We prepared ourselves for a ride. Aside from Fr. Walt and a couple of women Nancy recognized (but didn't know and had carefully avoided in the past), we were total strangers to them all.

The happenings throughout the meeting seemed to be free flowing and spontaneous, without a program or plan. Glory and praise songs (*that* was new) flowed one into another, interrupted from time to time by an impromptu Scripture reading or praise report. A strange but beautiful melodic singing would come forth from time to time. This too would start and end naturally. Although everything seemed spontaneous, at the same time, all appeared somehow to be orchestrated. Something highly unusual was afoot. The participants all seemed totally comfortable and peaceful with the activities. Nancy and I were the only ones in the room looking uncomfortable, sitting there as cautious observers.

There was even more to Fr. Walt than we had guessed from our first encounter with him at the retreat center. He was calm, collected, and fully present, but also seemed well connected to the "other world." Surely he must have spent lots of time there. Maybe he had experienced serious challenges that had changed his outlook on life.

Cathy, the lead woman in the group, a vivacious young mother of six, looked as if she had just been dunked in a "joy bath" and wanted all of us to get in, too. Her exuberance was contagious, and she was caring and compassionate. A few others were clearly on to something exceptional; they seemed barely able to contain it and exhibited a need to share whatever it was with everyone. They all looked intelligent and capable, and I wondered why they were there. If they were in big trouble or had serious needs, it wasn't obvious.

At one point in the meeting, there was a startling occurrence. A man we'd never seen before opened his Bible and emphatically read, *"Unless the Lord builds a house, the builder builds in vain."* Then he snapped his Bible shut. Nancy and I almost fell out of our chairs—especially me.

The group eventually moved on to prayer requests for all kinds of things, minor as well as significant. They seemed to believe that nothing was beyond God's reach. They also gave "praise reports" about how God had answered their prayer requests from the previous week. Then, with a closing song and closing prayer, the gathering was over for the big group. The leader said that anyone needing individual prayer could stay on and be "prayed over." That was definitely a new term to our ears.

Nancy and I had gotten a glimpse of another world, and we left quietly stunned. Plenty to think about—but we didn't talk about it—not throughout the entire next week. I replayed in my mind several times, *"Unless the Lord builds a house, the builder builds in vain."* Why that verse out of the whole Bible? And who was that guy? And why did it seem like he was reading it just for me?

The next Thursday night rolled around and even though we hadn't talked about going back, Nancy asked, rather hopefully, "Do you think we ought to give the prayer meeting one more try?" My response was a half-interested sounding, "Yeah, I guess so—they probably deserve that."

With that settled, I couldn't wait to get there and hear "how they had done" with their prayer requests from the previous week. They had looked like they really expected to get what they asked for. Amazing.

We arrived and hunkered down in our seats. We thought we knew a little more about what to expect this time. Though similar, it was just as fresh as the first time. There was energy and power throughout that was both enlivening and peace giving, unlike anything else we had ever experienced. We both found ourselves observing the happenings with more open minds. Our tension was lifting just a little and we were less self-conscious.

We began closely observing the participants and listening intently. These people had needs, but they also had real hearts for giving. We were becoming more aware of their gifts and their love of God. Some of them even told of speaking to strangers, and encouraging and praying over them. I was amazed how many times the name of Jesus was mentioned—and He was deeply thanked. I couldn't have said "Jesus" if I'd had to, but His name just flowed from their mouths.

By the end this meeting it was obvious to us that Jesus was the key to these people's hope. He was their doorway to a life of promise and had gained their trust. They spoke of Him and prayed to Him as a friend. At the time, I wondered why they put so much emphasis on Him. As for me, I had walked away from Jesus twenty-five years earlier. If He knew me at all, He surely remembered that.

Again, their prayer requests and praise reports were enthusiastically brought forth and, in many cases, God's response to their prayers had exceeded their requests. It certainly appeared that these people were on to something that worked, at least for them. I was moving away from doubt and just wondering: what is all this?

Over the next three weeks, the deadly imposter voice visits continued, with more frequency and urgency. Nancy and I began to talk about the prayer meetings and about our business difficulties. I began to let her in on where we were financially. She cringed, but handled it well. She is a great crisis player, and her response was, "We're in this together, we'll work it out as we always have before."

As I mentioned earlier, sleep had become a big problem for me. For some time, I had been able to only get an hour or two of sleep each night, never knowing when that would be. Sometimes, I would go to bed and go right to sleep, only to wake up in an hour or so, unable to get back to sleep. Other times, I might lie awake until three or four in the morning, or later, before ever going to sleep. However or whenever the sleep came, I spent the rest of the night tormented, tossing and turning, wrestling endlessly with the problems— especially about money, the house and the driveway—and trying to turn off the imposter voice. Mornings would usually find me wound up in my bedcovers from all the thrashing during the night.

Nancy knew about my problem with lack of sleep but didn't know all of the causes. The imposter voice continued to assault me, telling me, "Cash it in—you're worth more dead than alive. Do something good for your family—cash it in." I told no one, not even Nancy, about the voice, but it was intensifying.

By the fourth and fifth prayer meetings, I found myself depending on the prayer and praise and the people's faith to get me through the week. I don't believe either Nancy or I had yet said anything in the gatherings, but we surely were listening, watching and learning. Something was happening. The slightest glimmer of hope was returning to a long, hopeless season. Maybe there was something here even for us.

The sixth meeting was upon us and we were scurrying to leave the house and get there on time. We hadn't missed a meeting since our first visit. My prescription for tranquilizers had run out the night before (I was taking two a night to try to knock myself out and sleep), and we needed to get by the drugstore to pick up the refill. Nancy had called it in but in our hurry, we decided to wait until after the meeting and get it on our way home.

By this meeting, we were feeling more comfortable, like card-carrying guests. The group had been looking us over as well. Two of the core group women were registered nurses, and they told us later that they had thought I had terminal cancer. My lack of sleep and lack of eating, along with all the stress, had done a number on my body, as well as my mind. I looked like a refugee from a prison camp.

The meeting was glorious and uplifting like the others, much like a nice rain after a prolonged drought; like flowers, our heads were beginning to lift. As always, with the meeting drawing to a close, the leader asked for any prayer requests. The requests came forth readily, as did the praise reports. Apparently, for them this was the way it worked. It seemed almost too easy; there must be more to it, I thought.

The meeting concluded, the group gave their hugs and goodbyes (I still didn't let any of the men hug me), and no one was staying back for private prayers. Only the core group of about eight had not yet started to leave. Then, I heard someone speaking in a halting, unsure manner, "Would you people pray for me that I could sleep?" I was the most surprised person there, because I was the one who was asking. I had not intended to ask, it had just tumbled out.

Almost as if the event were scripted, the group converged on me, Fr. Walt leading the charge. They pulled a chair forward and sat me right down, moved Nancy up next to me, and all circled round and laid hands on my shoulders, neck, head — any place they could reach. They all began to pray or sing in the spirit (prayer language), surrounding me with their love and concern for our well being. Their love was palpable and building as they prayed. I had never experienced anything remotely similar — and they didn't really even know me.

Their prayers seemed to be lifting me up toward the ceiling, like a jet engine under my chair. I thought for a few seconds that we were all going through the roof, but I felt so good and peaceful that I wouldn't have minded if we had. Wow! I had never felt anything like this! Their prayers took only a short while, ten minutes or so; then a quiet and peace took over. I don't remember any words that were said. Sensing the presence of the Holy Spirit, we all left quietly.

As we got into our car, Nancy reminded me of the tranquilizers to be picked up from the drugstore. I decided we had to show some degree of faith, so I rather boldly said, "If we believe God heard those people's prayers, we need to do our part. We'll wait 'til tomorrow to pick up the prescription and give God tonight to do something." It wasn't much, but it was my first intentional act of faith. Remembering the prayer requests and answers at the prayer meetings over the past several weeks, I didn't want to be caught doubting. They had asked God to help me sleep, so I needed to expect just that. And you know, deep down, I guess I really did expect it.

Going to bed a little earlier than usual, I wondered if sleep would come fast, like with the sleeping shot in the hospital after my wreck. Lying flat on my back (unusual for me), I placed my covers in a nice, orderly way and prepared to see if God would answer their prayers. Almost instantly I was gone. Sleep came.

Upon opening my eyes, I was engulfed in a glorious April day with all its beauty—and with a rested mind, body and spirit. The sky showing through our window was bright blue (the first blue sky I could remember that season). Sunlight was pouring into the room and songbirds were filling my ears with their songs of celebration. I didn't remember having heard a bird all spring. I was immediately aware that my body had not moved from its position the night before; the sheets and covers were unaltered as well. I had been motionless for almost eight hours, while refreshment had been poured into my whole being.

Then, surprisingly, I noticed that a critical, negative spirit that had been present throughout my adult life had been lifted. I was seeing things without paying attention to their flaws—and actually feeling gratitude. A peace about my entire situation had replaced my anxiety. There was even a feeling of freedom emerging. As the group at the prayer meeting would say, "Praise the Lord!"

Lying there in bed for just a few minutes, savoring this wonderfully refreshed, energized feeling, it suddenly dawned on me. If God could do all this in response to a simple request for sleep, from people I hardly knew, He could solve all my problems if I just turned it all over to Him. And there it was! Just that quick. The Lord had shown me the way out of this hopeless blackness. I somehow understood that Jesus had stepped in to become my Savior, and that He had taken my problems as soon as I asked for His help.

Going downstairs and giving Nancy my exuberant report, it was hard to tell which of us was more shocked. My condition was so different from that of the night before, neither of us was prepared to understand or take it all in. We were in a state of wonder at what God had just done. In a moment in time, I had been visited and rescued by the Lord himself. We both just stood there overwhelmed by His mercy.

I went right on to work as usual, but I was different. My workmen could see the difference right away, and were quite curious. I explained what had happened the night before. I told many people over the next couple of days about the prayer session, and the people praying over me and what God had done. I even spoke the unspeakable name "Jesus" a few times. My bondage was being broken. I had to tell people about this miracle. Suddenly, I was a living example of an inspired evangelist—and I didn't even know what the word meant.

God had done His part, now I had to do mine. My situation remained full of stress; the ever challenging "driveway house" with all its difficulties, the awareness that the driveway would have to be totally replaced, and the financial problems. But now, I knew deep down that we would be able to handle it all. I was seeing with new eyes, a new heart and even a new mind. That pitch black tunnel I'd been locked up in for months now had a pinhole of the brightest light I'd ever seen at the far end. I had a clear sense from the Lord that I needed to just walk straight toward the pinhole of light and in time

He would remove all the obstacles and bring me out of this dark tunnel into His great light. I didn't know much yet, but even then I knew that God had granted me mercy. This time I wouldn't miss it! I was hanging on for dear life. With His help, we would make it.

I had barely escaped death and Hell and heaping untold misery on my family. Instead, I had been rescued by the living God Himself. Even then I was pretty sure who the *Voice* was that years earlier had told me, "Buckle your seat belt." My mind could not even begin to process such mercy.

> *For I know the plans I have for you, says the Lord. Plans for welfare and not for evil, to give you a future and a hope. Then you will call upon me and come and pray to me, and I will hear you. You will seek me and find me; when you seek me will all your heart. I will be found by you, says the Lord, and I will restore your fortunes... Jeremiah 29:11-14*

Greater Works

In the days that followed my being prayed over, I felt somewhat like a person waking up from a coma. The big difference, though, was that the person waking was a different one than the one who had been asleep. It was as if a totally new person now lived in my body, a person with different thoughts, values, goals, knowledge and priorities. I had difficulty believing I could have been so blind and unaware for forty years. I could already see my big mistake: that I had been totally self-absorbed, choosing to shut God out of my life.

The prayer group members rejoiced in what had happened to me and how their prayers had been answered. They explained that I had been "born again" and "baptized in the Spirit" that night. This was totally new territory for me. I had never known anyone before the prayer group members that had experienced such a drastic change. Also, this term "baptized in the Spirit" sounded really important to the prayer group members. I had never heard the term before visiting their group.

I began to realize that I had, by God's grace, entered into a whole new way of life and into the dominion of the Father, Son and Holy Spirit. They had lifted me from Satan's dominion of darkness and placed me into God's marvelous light. This Jesus, whose name for decades I had been unable to even say, was becoming a very special friend. Wow!

Awake, o sleeper, and arise from the dead and Christ shall give you light. Ephesians 5:14

The manifestations of the new life became apparent right away. I never again heard the imposter voice saying, "Cash it in," never had another sleepless night, never picked up the tranquilizers from the drugstore, or took another one. I began reading Scripture (I soon got my first personal Bible) and couldn't get enough of this "newfound truth." Finding the wisdom and direction for the tough things we still faced was amazing. It seemed as though the Bible had been written just yesterday to deal with my needs and problems. Key passages just leapt off the pages. I've since come to know that many new believers have experienced this. It's just His normal provision.

If any of you lacks wisdom, let him ask God, who gives to all men generously and without reproaching, and it will be given him. But let him ask in faith, with no doubting. James 1:5-6

Nancy was rather awestruck and concerned about my new demeanor and outlook. I was sleeping well again, all night, and was optimistic, as in earlier times, before the depression. Now, however, I had an abiding joy that I had never before experienced. For years, Nancy had prayed that I would just attend church with her and the kids (her father never had with their family). Now I couldn't stay away from church. I had swung from one extreme to the other. It would be a couple of months before she was "baptized in the Spirit" herself, so it was somewhat perplexing to her, what had happened to me. However, because of the others in the prayer group, especially Fr. Walt, she knew not to worry, and that it was real. We were on this fast, new ride together into uncharted territory. God's country, for certain!

My head was now spinning and clearing at the same time, spinning with all the great new revelations from Jesus and the Holy Spirit, and clearing because I was being given practical wisdom for life's hard challenges. I knew my first big hurdle to clear would be the driveway: plowing up, hauling off and replacing it. Real, lasting peace of mind and my future in the building business were waiting on the other side of the new driveway. I sure didn't want to, but I had to look this monster in the eye and face it head on.

As I prepared to tackle the driveway, one of the additional challenges was the presence of the affluent homeowners in the subdivision itself. Several of the neighbors were top executives of international corporations and drove past the house almost daily. This was certainly a success-oriented group of individuals, and my pride was definitely going to take a hard hit. I had recently heard that other people in the area had been observing the driveway and had been coming there on Sundays to challenge it—to see if their cars could make it to the top. They thought it was great sport.

This humbling experience felt very different from earlier times, when I had basked in the pride I'd felt after successes and hearty affirmations. I was beginning to get a glimpse of the meaning of the Proverb, *"Pride goes before a fall,"* and if I hadn't felt the Lord's peace and constant assurance, I would have been overwhelmed and completely alone with this grueling challenge.

The Lord, however, poured out special grace for the daunting project. I made arrangements for my faithful loader (bulldozer) operator, Slim, and his battle-tested old machine, for dump trucks to come and haul the broken-up concrete away, and then to bring back fill dirt to the property, and for the saw man to handle the trees that had to be taken out. The pump truck and concrete trucks were scheduled, and the concrete finishers would be ready. It was a lot to accomplish and we would need continuous grace throughout to pull it off.

Beginning to learn the value of prayer for all projects, I got prayed over for wisdom, courage and peace for the ordeal, and scheduled it to begin first thing on Monday morning. This had weighed so heavily on me for the past several weeks; I was fully ready to embark on it, as arduous as it was going to be. Of course, I was totally responsible for this house and my clients. Their trust in and dependence on me remained solid. I felt the weight of their trust at all times. They would be living here in a few months using the driveway. They never mentioned to me the additional costs for the changes.

Early Monday morning, the quiet of this prominent bedroom community was rudely interrupted as Slim arrived in his lowboy, carrying the loader. The dump trucks soon followed. Losing no time, Slim had the loader down on the ground, moving into action. Soon the morning air was filled with the sounds of the big loader straining and creaking against the imposing, heavy concrete. Then came the dull, crunching sounds of the concrete breaking under the strain and giving way to the powerful machine. Slim's wonderful ability with his loader, the machine that had carved each lot for every house I had built, was now put to a different test. For years, I had marveled at his handling of that powerful old loader. Maneuvering and directing it deftly, almost like a conductor of a fine symphony, he was always graceful and careful, never damaging anything. Now, Slim was turning his ability toward artful demolition. I felt shameful to even ask him to come do such work; I could barely watch. He had cracked the loader's bucket weeks earlier while battling the rock at the house site, and that time he had to take it to be welded back together. This concrete wasn't likely to be much friendlier to the bucket. Fortunately, Slim had long since learned that "you do what you have to do," and was about the job at hand.

With a keen eye and judgment and dexterity, Slim pressed on with the task of pitting machine and steel against brute, heavy-duty concrete. Sometimes straining to lift, sometime biting and tearing with the loader's four-way bucket, sometimes using the bucket with its teeth like sledgehammers coming down hard, Slim went after the work—unrelentingly. All the noise of the machine straining, the beating and banging and scraping of metal against concrete, the huge, heavy slabs of concrete dropping into those steel dump truck beds, and the heavily loaded trucks straining to drive away slowly, up the steep street, almost overloaded my senses. With the smell of the diesel fuel and dust along with the sight and the sounds of the demolition, I felt at my limit—totally maxed out. I was a builder, not a demolition contractor, definitely not of anything that I had built myself. My contribution to the entire scene was to stand there and stay in prayer. Except for God's grace and Holy Spirit-given courage, I doubt whether I could have even stayed there and watched.

By the end of the day, the driveway was almost all relocated to the dump. I'd had no idea how this would all go, so I was greatly relieved and considerably relaxed. It seemed that along with the broken-up concrete, a lot of my stress and some of my pride had been hauled off to the dump. There was still too much of both left, but this was a great start. Perhaps even the demolition was building something new. Something that could surpass everything I had ever built.

The saw man had cut down the necessary trees and Slim adapted from a demolition expert on Monday to the shaper and molder of a new, curved driveway bed up the hillside on Tuesday, moving truckloads of fill dirt into place and packing and shaping them tight and solid with his heavy old loader. Slowly, a picture of a beautiful lot, house and driveway began to emerge. Everything was going to be all right. "Thank you, Jesus. Thank you, Lord," I thought.

The almost endless parade of loader and trucks up and down the hill, then pump truck and concrete mixers and finishers, went on the entire week. The rebuild of the driveway went smoothly, without a hitch; everyone's work on the whole project was exemplary. Frequently, subdivision residents had to wait in their cars on the street for the equipment to move out of their way. I sometimes got to stand on the street, by the driver of a nice, luxury car, apologizing for the wait and confessing my failure with the first driveway and the saving grace God had given for building the new one. And, also, telling them what a difference Jesus was making in my "new life." Since they were a captive audience, I wasn't going to miss the opportunity. A new abiding peace and sense of humility were replacing that old noxious pride and deadly fear—it felt so refreshing and life giving. Hopelessness seemed to be running down the hill into the storm drain!

The Lord carried the completion of the house by His Holy Spirit in so many ways, and it finished beautifully. The family would live there permanently, raising their children and adding two additions to the house over the decades (it was over 4,000 square feet original-ly). And, yes, driving along the new driveway felt like a drive in the park—actually, a little like driving along the Blue Ridge Parkway with its scenic views. In exchange for the driveway troubles, I per-sonally built a quadruple sunburst teak wall and steps in the foyer.

The Lord used the "driveway" house as an anvil to reshape and begin to mold me into a new image. The experience was brutally hard, but just what I needed. I will be forever grateful, as it was the beginning of the end of the old man and the coming forth of the new man. I am continuously humbled by His mercy that kept me alive—then brought me to life—and saved our family. All praise and glory to Him!

It was a beautiful spring in Atlanta and new growth was blooming everywhere. Our new life seemed right in step. Each day brought new grace and growth, and new developments (I guess I was sufficiently ready for the "new man"). Nancy got baptized in the Spirit, and within a few months, I was put into a leadership position in the prayer group. Things were changing at rocket speed. I learned about Saul (Paul) on the way to Damascus. I could relate. Could I ever!

The financial trouble still surrounded us, but it didn't dominate our lives. Paying off old debts became far more satisfying than buying anything new. Each day that pinhole of light at the end of the black tunnel got just a miniscule bit larger. The Lord even arranged a new client, a referral from the driveway house, a design-and-build project on the very next lot (a much more buildable lot). That family had recently been transferred to Atlanta and was ready for us to start. A second house to design and build would also come from the driveway house. It would be in the next subdivision over, and they also were ready for us to begin. We would actually build both houses simultaneously, over the next year.

Without intention or expectation, I quickly found myself ministering hope to people (frequently strangers). The wonderful, life-giving virtue of hope that had almost disappeared from my life had now become mine—to have and to pass on. Incredible! It seemed almost as though these people were being sent to me to get help. The more hope I gave to others, the more I had.

Undoubtedly, this great escape from death—twice—had been entirely due to God's grace and mercy. The awareness that the Holy

Spirit had been poured into Nancy and I so that we could do good works now called us to shift gears and add His business to ours. We didn't know what this would mean, but we knew there was Kingdom business to tend to and that the clock was running. As we had been rescued, now we were to help in the rescue of others. Come, Holy Spirit!

> *For by grace you have been saved by faith; and this is not your own doing, it is the gift of God—not because of work, lest any man should boast, for we are His workmanship; created in Christ Jesus for good works, which God prepared beforehand, that we should walk in them. Ephesians 3:8-10*

Be Transformed by the
Renewing of Your Mind

In order to better communicate this transformation that had been put in motion, we should revisit the six weeks prior. On our first visit to the prayer meeting, Nancy and I had been invited to look in upon a world vastly different from the one we had both known for a lifetime. We had no clue how different! These meetings were like a doorway to light and hope and the things of God. At this point they were beyond our reach, but we could see that others in the group had reached them and had been profoundly affected!

When we first arrived, I came looking for answers: how to get some sleep, how to stop the tormenting voice, how to get out of the pit—and how to find peace. My suicidal promptings had made me want to get off the merry-go-round, get away from people, phones and answering machines, and just disappear for awhile. Yet I really had no way to escape or get any kind of respite. My worst fears were of failing, losing everything, being humiliated—and failing Nancy and the kids. Coming to that first meeting, I had zero expectations. I was almost afraid to hope and felt quite skeptical. I came burdened—burdened to the breaking point—with no relief in sight. I was like a hollow tree, weighted down with heavy limbs, totally vulnerable to the next strong wind.

I kept all of my problems to myself, and said nothing about them to anyone. Sleeplessness was taking its toll and the imposter voice gradually stepped up. He persisted in telling me to "cash it in." I told no one. The people in the prayer group had no knowledge of our dilemma. Some sensed we had come with big problems, but they gave us space. I struggled at each session to pay attention—thoughts of my problems were constantly replaying in my head while this utopian world of light and hope was being displayed by all of the people around us. Somehow, it didn't bother me that they were so joyful while I was "dying." It was just good to be in an uplifting setting. Nancy, who is very practical and results oriented, was being encouraged by the good reports that resulted from their prayers.

The peace that was resident among the people in the group was awe inspiring. I had never, ever felt such peace; it seemed to flow out toward us. Without our realizing it, our stress would begin to decrease as we quietly sat there. I soon came to learn it was *the peace that passes all understanding*. It should be the most sought-after commodity anywhere.

Different members of the group said that their peace came from their trust in Jesus. Before coming, I had wondered to myself if I would find these people overly religious, but I quickly dismissed that thought. Instead, I was affected by their authenticity. They spoke of Jesus' suffering and death on the cross as if it had happened to a close family member.

The group read about Jesus returning to heaven and about a Sunday celebration named Pentecost that was coming up in a few weeks. They described it as though it was as special as Christmas. I didn't recall ever hearing of it. I had heard of Pentecostals (my old church had derisively referred to them as "holy rollers" and even snake handlers), but these prayer group people were Catholic and certainly didn't inspire any mockery in us. Within a year, I would learn how much the Pentecostals had helped the charismatic Catholics understand and receive the baptism in the Holy Spirit.

47

As they read the Bible, I was drawn to the account in the book of Acts: *"Not many days from now you will receive power from on high…"* and *"When the day of Pentecost had fully come…"* It seemed directed to me. Anything from the Book of Acts began to get my attention, but what really grabbed me were those *"tongues of fire"* that *"came to rest upon them."* And they were empowered, right then and there! Wow!

Several in the group shared how the Holy Spirit had helped them with little everyday things, like providing a parking space or an item in a store or help from a friend. They had offered brief prayers and then the Holy Spirit just seemed to make things happen. Nancy and I had always thought of these as nice coincidences or good luck. They explained that "luck" was no longer in their vocabulary. They said the Holy Spirit was as active today as back at Pentecost. I was shocked. Fr. Walt would share about a hospital visit to pray for someone (his hands would begin to feel hot, and he took that as a sign to go), and Cathy or someone else would share about an everyday occurrence in a grocery store or on the street "sharing Jesus" (simply what He had done for them), or even praying for someone. The term "laying hands on people" came up over and over. They said that it was as important as the prayers themselves. I was surprised that people, especially strangers, actually allowed themselves to be touched. It seemed that the members of the prayer group were personally concerned about everyone's salvation. Some even seemed to feel other people's pain and misery. That was the other end of the spectrum from my "look out for number one" world view.

The members explained that this need to reach out and these Holy Spirit-led encounters had never happened to them in the past, but now that they were "baptized in the Spirit," these events happened frequently. The Holy Spirit was telling them what to do and then enabling them to do it.

As we sat there for an hour and half each Thursday night, week after week, trying to process what was happening in us and in all of them, it was truly a strange phenomenon. I would arrive in one world, full of cares, struggles, fears, and uncertainties, and be transported into this other world of love, joy, peace, goodness—if I could stay focused on what was happening in "their" world. Soon the serenity and hope of "their world" was carrying me from Thursday to Thursday. I was living on their hope, or so it seemed. After our third visit, I considered the prayer meeting to be a top priority. We needed to get to the bottom of all this. For a long time, Nancy and I had desperately needed a solution to our troubles. And now it seemed that the answer might be before us—but it was all so incredible. We were almost afraid to step out and risk getting disappointed.

The leaders spoke of the infilling of the Holy Spirit as the equipping to do some work; gifts were entrusted to be used by the person to accomplish the work He sent them to do. For the past twenty-five years, I had really appreciated good woodworking equipment; I had collected it since my teenage years. Working with quality sharp equipment that was reliable had great appeal to me—I loved to use it and depended upon it. So I really listened to their accounts of doing "the work" by the power of the Spirit. This sounded like something lots of men could get into in a serious way. I wondered how many knew about this. Did people ever talk about it during church?

This exuberant bunch considered the Holy Spirit equipping to be the ultimate—light years beyond what the world could offer, the power to accomplish anything. But far more than just one who equips, they spoke of the Holy Spirit as a person, One to know intimately. Jesus referred to Him as the "Spirit of Truth." One of the new ideas we heard from group members frequently was, "Then I just knew things I'd never known before—then I just knew. The Spirit revealed it to me!" They believed that their spiritual eyes had been opened. The Bible explained this clearly.

> *Now we have received, not the spirit of the world, but the Spirit who is from God, so that we may know the things freely given to us by God... We have the mind of Christ. 1 Corinthians 2:12-16*

They were getting their minds totally reprogrammed—with revelation knowledge!

They did an in-depth look at the Scriptures pertaining to spiritual gifts. I was fully alert. I needed to understand this.

> *Now there are varieties of gifts, but the same Spirit... But to each one is given the manifestation of the Spirit for the common good. For to one is given the word of wisdom through the Spirit, and to another the word of knowledge... to another faith... and to another gifts of healing... and to another the effecting of miracles, and to another prophecy, and to another the distinguishing of spirits, to another various kinds of tongues, and to another the interpretation of tongues. But one and the same Spirit works all these things, distributing to each one individually just as He wills. 1 Corinthians 12:4-11*

When, at the end of the sixth meeting, to my total surprise, I asked for prayers, the Holy Spirit, the people, and Jesus moved into action. My old man was evicted and this new man brought to life. Neither the departure of the old man nor the transformation into the new man will be completed during my lifetime, but it began with a bang! Even then, I sensed it would be a journey like no other. When we walked into that first prayer meeting I had no thought that we were embarking on a whole new life. I was forty years old; too old, I would have assumed, to begin a completely new life. In fact, that's exactly what happened. I've been allowed to live two vastly different lives. I would come to learn over the years that it was "The Plan." Jesus told Nicodemus, *"You must be born again to enter the kingdom of God."*

After being prayed over and awaking rested, hopeful and peaceful, it began to dawn on me that all I had heard and felt during the previous six weeks was suddenly a reality—for me. I was no longer a visitor, allowed in by Fr. Walt's "come and see" invitation, looking through this incredible doorway to life. I had now been led through the doorway and invited by the Lord Himself to share in His indescribable abundance of blessings. It was so real, so freeing. My mountain of unresolved burdens and cares was miniscule compared to this new freedom!

Recalling these life-changing times, I am struck by how quickly it all happened. Many conversions come about much less rapidly, but mine was overnight, and even by the next day there was undeniably strong evidence of the new man emerging. I had run from and denied the Lord throughout my adult years and now, in a moment—in response to my first prayer request—the Lord had drawn me to Himself. I had asked for sleep and He gave it, and a whole new life as well. He had given me hope, peace, purpose, and His Holy Spirit, to help me work out all of my existing problems and go to work building His kingdom. Even deep spiritual truths that had passed by my tormented mind in a whirl over the past six weeks were now being made clear by the Holy Spirit.

One of the spiritual gifts enumerated in Scripture is that of faith. I believe that is one of my strongest gifts. There are many fruits of the gift of faith, but one is that we are able to move quickly into action, without faltering, when inspired by the Spirit. From day one of my transformation I knew (by faith) that this was it, my life was hidden in the Lord, wherever He led or took us. We were going. This was *the pearl of great price* and we weren't letting go. In all areas of life, I had always appreciated what was real, genuine. Now, the ultimate "real" had entered my heart and mind. Very early on I fully believed the Scriptures.

> *And without faith it is impossible to please Him, for he who comes to God must believe that He is and that He is a rewarder of those who seek Him. Hebrews 11:6*

Fr. Walt handled his Bible like a treasure chest. He encouraged everyone in the group to learn to use this storehouse, and to look up Scriptures and read them out loud. He even believed it was okay to pray and then break open the Bible and read for guidance whatever your eyes fell on. I still do that, because it works for me. Right away, I became hooked on the word and consumed it whenever I could. The inspired word became a lifeline out of the black tunnel I was in.

> *For this reason we also constantly thank God that when you received the word of God which you heard from us, you accepted it not as the word of men, but for what it really is, the word of God, which also performs its work in you who believe. Thessalonians 2:13*

Scriptures read in the meetings began to burn in my mind; some seemed meant especially for me. There were hard, perplexing ones—plenty of them, like John the Baptist's statements that, *"I am not worthy to untie the thong of His sandal,"* and *"I must decrease and He must increase."* Also, Jesus' statement, *"If anyone wishes to come after Me, let him deny himself and take up his cross daily and follow Me."* As tough as these words sounded, even then, I knew they were true and that I was called to conform to them. I seemed to be discovering what had been strategically placed for me to find. It seemed surreal, but was in fact so real. Some other Scriptures rang a special chord:

If anyone is in Christ, he is a new creature; the old things passed away; behold, new things have come... Therefore, we are ambassadors for Christ, as though God were making an appeal through us; we beg you on behalf of Christ, be reconciled to God. 2 Corinthians 5:17,19-20

Old hymns that I had heard decades earlier began popping up in my mind out of nowhere, like jonquils in the early spring after the longest, cruelest winter. They had been unwanted and buried under many worldly pursuits and interests all those years. Now, without thinking, I would catch myself humming or singing, even hours at a time, "What a Friend We Have in Jesus," or "Blessed Assurance, Jesus Is Mine," or "Just As I Am, Lord, Just As I Am." Priceless old treasures were coming forth, like Lazarus from the tomb.

We learned so many things in those early months. Things we had never thought of before. The Holy Spirit is the ultimate instructor, who also prepares us to learn. We learned about gossip and slander, sarcasm, negative humor and the unbridled tongue. Members of the group said that they were trying very diligently to control their tongues, so that all of their words would be uplifting and encouraging.

These new adjustments in my mindset were also beginning to influence my business. I had always worked hard at being honest, and considered myself such. One day a tile supplier sent me an invoice with a note. He reminded me that my account with him was ninety days old and unpaid. Like many suppliers, his business had suffered from the recession, but he didn't mention that. He simply wrote, "When you take the money you drew from the bank as payment for my tile and use it to pay another overdue account, you're stealing from me!" Wow! I almost went through the floor, convicted on the spot. The Lord had given him the word that I needed to hear. His account got paid next and I never again rationalized that kiting was okay. My mindset had been changed. The Lord is about transforming all areas of our lives toward righteousness, in accord with His standards.

Seek first His kingdom and His righteousness and all these things will be added unto you. Matthew 6:31

I also learned when the Lord sends someone to speak correction or admonishment to me, I better receive it well—and act upon it posthaste! I don't want a second visit.

The name Satan and references to demonic spirits came up frequently in the Bible and in different sharings. Fr. Walt had firsthand knowledge of evil spirits and how they worked from his many years of service in Africa, dealing with the people and the culture. He assured us of their reality and the need to never deny their presence but to learn how to discern and deal with them, to "read" the spirits and recognize that they are always out to steal, kill or destroy. He explained that they are often very subtle but always around us.

When I confessed to the prayer group what my main problem had been, that I had been suicidal and severely tormented, it was faith building to them. They told me that the imposter voice was that of an evil spirit—likely, the fear of failure. Being part of the Lord's rescue from such a devastating situation gave them new incentive to step out and use their spiritual gifts. Our God is the God of redemption, and second and third chances.

Over the years, I've heard so many accounts of transformation of very fine brothers and sisters from destructive patterns of addiction or sinful lifestyles into exemplary lives of faith and holiness dedicated to the Lord. I have a close friend who, prior to the infilling of the Holy Spirit, was plagued by a vile spirit of profanity. This spirit was frequent and controlling, trying to poison his mind and his communication. Immediately after he received the baptism of the Holy Spirit, the spirit of profanity left, never to return. I've known others who had been addicted to drugs or alcohol, and through the Spirit, were delivered right away.

I never used profanity, drugs or alcohol but was increasingly enamored with the world. I had an appreciation for many alluring, beautiful things and liked to attribute this to my artistic and creative nature. The Scriptures in I John 2:15-17 clearly spoke to me:

> *Do not love the world nor the things in the world. If anyone loves the world, the love of the Father is not in him. For all that is in the world, the lust of the flesh and the lust of the eyes and the boastful pride of life, is not from the Father, but is from the world. The world is passing away, and also its lusts; but the one who does the will of God lives forever.*

Upon my "Great Awakening," one of the first things the Spirit brought to my mind was my seven-year collection of glossy Playboy magazines, stacked neatly in my office. Nancy had graciously bought me a subscription as a gift just prior to my first visit by the *Voice*. All eighty-four magazines were quickly boxed and taken to the attic. I was now embarrassed that they were even under our roof. Soon we disposed of them altogether.

The people in the prayer group were a great help to us. Right away, they became our circle of friends. They literally loved us out of isolation. Hardly anyone else understood what we were going through. Some were afraid to find out. These trusted new friends went to great efforts to give us a crash course and get us up to speed. Nancy and I will forever be appreciative of their part in our transformation. Because of my dramatic rescue from darkness and death, many suspected we would be put into quick and heavy service out in the world. My contacts in the construction and business world greatly needed what we had been receiving in the prayer meetings. I was forewarned that as incredible as the Good News is, many will reject it. Still, we are to present and offer it. The Bible says that, *"God would have that none be lost."*

The imposter voice never fully gave up on me. He occasionally talks at me about smaller things, trying to peddle his lies, as he probably does with most everyone. He was never again able to speak into my ears about "cashing it in." That deception was immediately cleared by the Lord and gone. Like abortion, suicide is all about self-concern, and is never a solution. The imposter's voice never again sounded like a counselor to me, but rather a devious enemy. I also was quickly learning that *"Greater is He who is in you than he who is in the world."* What a gem for a lifetime!

Within a year, at conferences, we were meeting people from all over the world. They told of experiences and groups like ours that had gone through very similar transformations, sounding like they were put through a corresponding crash course. The Lord was calling

His people into a work that would require the empowering of the Holy Spirit and putting on the "new man" each day. I was already being challenged by the Great Commission Scriptures.

> *And He said to them, "Go into all the world and preach the gospel to all creation... These signs will accompany those who have believed: in My name they will cast out demons, they will speak with new tongues; they will lay hands on the sick, and they will recover."*
>
> *And they went out and preached everywhere, while the Lord worked with them, and confirmed the word by the signs that followed. Mark 16:15-20*

With the world in such a devastated condition spiritually and being pillaged more each day, perhaps we had been called forth for just such a time as this. After all, I understood the plight of those who didn't know God; I had been there just weeks earlier. I also knew that only the Holy Spirit could redirect their misguided minds and make known to them their very life and purpose.

> *And do not be conformed to this world, but be transformed by the renewing of your mind, so that you may prove what the will of God is, that which is good and acceptable and perfect. Romans 12:2*

Part II:
Yes, Lord—Send Me

Sent Out

The Holy Spirit had used the two-month crash course with the prayer group to position us for an entirely new and dynamic life. I had even received some "on the job training," joining in with some of the more experienced in praying over members in the meetings. It was an "other world" feeling for me, but the others seemed to easily accept me as a "prayer." They had watched this progression over and over with many others. I believe they also perceived my life-or-death outlook about this new life, the urgency I felt to share what had been literally lifesaving to me.

My mind was filled with potent Scriptures and I was praying for spiritual gifts to be activated so that I could be about the work. The gift of faith came alive overnight, as did the call to evangelize. Suddenly strangers were not only approachable, but their needs were sometimes known to me even before I got to them. The wisdom and knowledge gifts were activated right away.

I quickly became aware that the prayer group setting would be expanded and I would be going out into the world. The meetings became the locker room, where we got prepared and ready, but the game was mostly played out in the world. I had never heard of the church taking it to the world, but that's exactly what the Great Commission said:

And He said to them, "Go into all the world and preach the gospel to all creation. He who has believed and has been baptized shall be saved; but he who has disbelieved shall be condemned. These signs will accompany those who have believed: in My name they will cast out demons, they will speak with new tongues; they will pick up serpents, and if they drink any deadly poison, it will not hurt them; they will lay hands on the sick, and they will recover." So then, when the Lord Jesus had spoken to them, He was received up into heaven and sat down at the right hand of God. And they went out and preached everywhere, while the Lord worked with them, and confirmed the word by the signs that followed. Mark 16:15-20

Until this season of my life, I had not known that God uses ordinary lay people to do His work, yet now I saw it everywhere. My old belief that God calls people to do His work only as ministers, missionaries, priests or nuns was seriously off base—far short of His ways. It was also becoming apparent that He cared for those on the highways and byways as much as He did for those in church. Every single one was special to him.

Now to see fired-up lay people as sharp tools in His hands, called into His work, and as a new Christian to be sent myself into His missions—it almost took my breath away. It was so real and alive! Laying hands on and praying over almost anyone for His touch, healing or blessing seemed beyond belief—but the nudge was there, and when I acted upon it, so were the results. It would soon become the new way of life. I felt, at the same time, both inadequate and totally sufficient. I've since come to learn that that's a healthy perspective. We remain totally dependent on His grace.

Suddenly, as everyday life unfolded, extraordinary happenings were breaking out, drawing us in, and allowing us to be personally involved alongside the Holy Spirit. My construction workload remained the same, but now the Lord was fitting in lots of Kingdom opportunities. Whatever time or expense the Kingdom work required of me, He made up for it, one way or another. I didn't know a lot of Scripture yet, but this one pierced my heart early on, *"To him who has been given much, much is expected."* Life-saving mercy had been given to me twice already; now He wanted some particular things from me. He seemed to want to use me and what He had given me—frequently. The prayer group members told me that the Holy Spirit had given me an extra measure of holy boldness. I was encouraged.

The Great Commission, *"Go into all the world..."* convicted me personally and was quickly becoming what I was about. It seemed that if I was open to and expecting to be used by the Holy Spirit, it almost always happened. Isaiah's prayer, *"Send me, Lord,"* became my prayer as well. Almost immediately, Nancy and I became far too busy with the happenings in the present to worry about what would happen in the future. Worries were replaced with opportunities, and as opportunities were acted upon, the worries just melted into trust. We were putting our cares in the Lord's hands, and leaving them there. Much like a plane lifting off the runway, the height and speed of this trip defied the imagination. What I had resisted for a quarter century was quickly becoming my main concern!

Hallelujah!

Then I heard the voice of the Lord saying; "Whom shall I send, and who will go for Us?" Then I said, "Here I am, send me!" And he said, "Go, and tell this people." Isaiah 6:8-9

Harry —
God's Messenger

Harry was a neighbor of ours who lived four houses away in our subdivision. We didn't really know him; only saw him from a distance. His wife's name was Marsha. She had lived in the same house with her former husband, a big, vile-acting motorcyclist. That rocky marriage ended and she remarried Harry; they now lived in the house. Harry and Marsha had a different lifestyle than we did, so we had very few encounters during the years we lived there. Kings Cove was a moderate-sized subdivision of spacious new houses that were bought mostly by young couples in their thirties. The following event happened after both of our families had lived there for several years.

Nancy and I were in our second year of walking in the Spirit. We had really been impacted by the number of experiences recounted in Scripture of Jesus and His healings — the laying on of hands and healing of the sick, the blind, the lame. We continued to become more and more aware of His incredible healing ministry; it seemed to manifest itself wherever He went. We also began to pray over more and more people in the prayer group or share group and out in ordinary places as well. We were praying for healing and expecting God to do big things — and He was!

The experience with Harry occurred during the first year or so of being really active in praying over people and having expectant faith. One Friday night before a share group, we had a request from one of our Christian neighbors. She had heard that Harry was in the hospital with what they thought were gallstones. Marsha had told her this at the mailbox. The neighbor told Marsha that she would ask our group to pray for Harry, and then passed that on to us. We prayed for Harry in our meeting, and asked the Lord to touch him and heal him, and that was that—at least, we thought.

The next morning, Saturday, I began to be really "quickened in the Spirit" to go and see Harry at the hospital. I didn't want to go see Harry (this was definitely out of the comfort zone), but there was an urgency to go and see him, and talk with him. Nothing about this was a social visit; instead I thought it must be like what Fr. Walt experienced with his Spirit-led hospital visits to pray over people. This was definitely not like being in the prayer meeting—this was to be man to man. Finding out from the neighbor which hospital Harry was in, I told Nancy that I was going to see him. She was surprised, since we didn't really know either Harry or Marsha, and I didn't do hospital visits. Also, I usually had a full schedule on Saturdays and didn't use the day for socializing.

As I entered the hospital, somewhat apprehensively, and was waiting for the elevator, the door opened and there stood Marsha, ready to step off. With a very surprised expression, she said, "What are you doing here? Do you have somebody in the hospital, too?"

I said, "No, I'm here to see Harry."

She changed color a little bit, became slightly pale, and said, "I don't know if you want to do that. I don't know if Harry wants to see you." Then, after looking at me in the most intense way, she just left it and walked away. Her comments confused and perplexed me, but the Holy Spirit's anointing was getting stronger. I was beginning to really sense my mission. I didn't understand what she was saying, but I knew I had to see Harry, so I headed for his room. He was a large man, 6'4" or so. I had heard that he had, in years past, played football in the NFL. He was about fifty at this time. He was looking right at the door as I walked in and seemed very surprised; curious as to why I was there.

I began to tell him that I really didn't want to come, it was not a social visit, but the Lord had sent me there this morning to talk to him. I was hoping that he would be open to hear what the Lord wanted to tell him. I assured him I wouldn't waste his time, or mine, but would get right to it. Obviously, he had time. He said that Marsha would be gone for a good while.

I began to tell him of my experience of trying to run away from the Lord, wanting to be independent and doing my own thing, and how it had almost killed me. In fact, I just gave a step-by-step account of my testimony and how my life had been transformed. Before long, really incredible things began to happen; I could see tears welling up in his eyes as what I was telling him began to resonate in him. Something was happening with him—I didn't know what, but it looked important.

He then told me that he would have thought of me as the least likely person to come and tell him this. He confessed he had been very resentful toward me based on an experience a few years earlier. It was the only occasion that I remembered Harry and Marsha coming to one of the subdivision parties. Ours was a socially active subdivision with highly energized, upwardly mobile-minded folks— there were lots of weekend parties, with music and dancing. Nancy and I were not yet Christians and had been going to some of these. We weren't drinkers, but we were into the social part of it—we enjoyed people. I wasn't a dancer (at all), but this particular night, I found myself involved in some sort of a fast dance with Marsha. The others stopped dancing and seemed caught up in just watching us. It was totally out of character for me, it was almost like I was watching someone else. I was the most surprised of anyone—almost embarrassed. Nancy was not thrilled by it. But Harry had been extremely irritated by it all, to the point that, over the next several years, anytime he would see me driving or walking through the subdivision, he would turn to Marsha and say, "There goes your friend, the Dancer."

Before coming to visit him at the hospital, I had no clue about Harry's long-time resentment toward me—none at all! Now I began to understand Marsha's comments back at the elevator.

Somehow, the Holy Spirit was cutting through all of this. As I continued to share with him about how God had changed my life and saved me from myself, Harry burst into tears, confessing that he, himself, had run from the Lord his whole life. Harry accepted the Lord right there, on the spot that morning, and gave his life totally to Jesus. I just led him through a sinner's prayer (an impromptu, Spirit-led confession of sins, repentance, asking for forgiveness and a new start in life following the Lord). This was my first experience of seeing someone literally enter into a conversion experience as I shared the Good News with them.

We had just about finished, and Harry looked like a whole new person, younger, bright and radiant, when Marsha returned. She was totally overwhelmed by the change in his attitude and looks, and could hardly believe him as he told her in full detail what had happened. His conversion was even more mind boggling than I would have guessed. I found out later that they were into reading tarot cards and practicing occult activities. People had been frequently coming to their home to participate in this. Nonetheless, Harry had a total conversion to Christianity that morning. Praise God!

The next day, Nancy and I came back with a group of about a half dozen people, some with guitars, and gathered around his bed. We had a great time singing praise songs and lifting up the Lord and rejoicing. Harry was just beaming, like a bright light, fully entering in. He looked right at home with it all. Marsha looked like it was starting to touch her even though she hadn't yet "gotten it." She was very confused by the change in Harry's spirit and outlook. She seemed a little dazed, but the sheer brightness of Harry was washing over her as well. She knew for certain it was good. It was glorious to behold this transformation.

In the ensuing days, I would frequently go and visit Harry in the hospital and pray for his healing. Soon the tests showed that it wasn't gallstones, but terminal abdominal cancer. The doctors were giving him a very limited time to live. I don't know how many times I visited, probably eight or ten over the course of six weeks. Harry became physically weaker and weaker while getting spiritually stronger and stronger; his light burned brighter each time I saw him. It wasn't long before he was in intensive care and had become blind. When I would walk up to his bed, upon hearing my voice, he would put out his great big paw and take my hand and squeeze down firmly, and in a soft but certain voice say, "God's messenger, God's messenger." You could tell that Harry was realizing how close he had come to missing it all, and was deeply grateful for God's mercy. I would just feel like kneeling down, but didn't. I probably should have (and maybe would today).

It was really tough, seeing the large body of this big "new creation" rapidly deteriorate, and Marsha so perplexed and overwrought. Her relationship with Harry had likely been the one good relationship of her tumultuous life (you could feel their deep love for each other), and now his life was quickly ebbing away. Marsha knew there would likely never be another Harry.

As Harry drew closer to going to Glory, you could tell he was looking forward to it. Knowing that the time was approaching, Marsha's parents, who were nonbelievers, came from New York to visit. Harry had a son, about twenty-five years in age, from his first marriage. This son's name also was Gary, and Marsha's parents would refer to Harry's son as Gary, and flippantly call me, "Gary come to Jesus." I knew they definitely didn't mean it to be a compliment, as they considered me to be rather fanatical, probably a Jesus freak. This jolted me at first, but through the years it has been a great encouragement that they saw me as "Gary come to Jesus." I came to treasure that tag they had put on me.

I know Harry is with the Lord. It was my first great experience of praying for healing, in a life-and-death situation, and seeing life win out over death. Even though his body died, new, glorious, eternal life replaced it. I also learned that someone doesn't have to really "like" you in order to receive the truth from you. Truth delivered in love is strong enough to carry the day. After he came to love Jesus, Harry liked me just fine.

Nancy and I ran into Marsha sometime after Harry went to Glory. She looked a lot better, much more peaceful. You could tell that Jesus had wiped away her tears. She looked like someone who was finding herself—her real self.

God is Good—and His ways are certainly higher than our ways.

Today when you hear His voice do not harden your hearts.
Hebrews 4:7

Daryl—
The New Man

I first ran into Daryl on a Tuesday morning at a men's prayer breakfast at Mt. Paran Church of God, north of Atlanta. Mt. Paran is an awesome church, very Pentecostal, very orderly, with a ministry group for every kind of pain, suffering, abuse or addiction.

After being baptized in the Spirit, I was quickly learning that if it happened at Mt. Paran, it was likely right on. I began going to the Tuesday morning men's prayer breakfast there each week. There were usually forty to fifty men from various denominations and diverse walks of life. I had never been in a church, or around one, where the men took their rightful roles. They did it by the book—and in the Spirit!

On Tuesday mornings I would usually finish my time there at the altar rails as others began to leave. I had lots to repent of and get right; by this time, it was mostly just the Lord and me. On this particular morning, believing that everyone else had left, and pretty much caught up in prayer, I became aware of a commotion. A few men were literally dragging a handicapped man, whom I had never seen before, around the sanctuary, beseeching the Holy Spirit to heal his limp legs and have them start working. It was such an uplifting commotion my entire attention was drawn to them. I just stayed in place at the altar rail, praying with them. It turns out that the man they were praying over was named Daryl. He would soon become a great friend of mine and of our family.

Daryl seemed very tall (he was 6'5", but looked taller). They were holding him under his arms, propping him up and dragging him with his feet trailing behind. He was sweating—working hard and in full agreement with what was going on. It was quite a sight. They made several rounds in the sanctuary before stopping. Daryl didn't start walking but we all got a lesson in faith and hope. Daryl was grateful and appreciative of all their efforts and their faith and not at all dismayed that he felt no change. He thought more of developing their faith than he did about walking. He had long since accepted this impairment in life, and was working hard to see it as a blessing.

Being so taken by the experience, I followed up that morning and made sure to get to know Daryl. He was obviously an important piece in my puzzle; I could just sense it. He was a slender, athletic man, in his mid-thirties, with laser-like eyes that could look right through you. Within minutes I knew he was a strong, mature man of God—at peace with God and himself. Clearly, he had been deeply immersed in the Spirit for a good while and was well ahead of me in understanding and experience. As we talked, his story began to unfold. He spoke sparingly and softly but with great authority. He didn't waste or mince words and I learned to pay attention to anything he was saying.

He had been a motorcycle rider, rebellious and doing his own thing with no real regard for God—or God's plan. Apparently, he had been "living on the edge" for awhile and it had gotten him into trouble. He recalled riding down a quiet road, no one in sight, and no memory of what happened next; everything just went black. When he woke up, Jesus was there with him in the emergency room. He had been in a wreck that had paralyzed his legs. He still had no idea of what happened or how it happened, but he awoke from it as a "new creation." Jesus' presence in the room transformed him on the spot. After only a few minutes of listening to Daryl, it was obvious that he now had a "Kingdom" mind. He literally had little else cross his mind and distract him—he was as transformed as anyone I've ever known. It was as though Jesus had brought him to the emergency room, performed a divine lobotomy, and had given Daryl a Kingdom mind.

He was paralyzed from the waist down but had a very strong upper body. He drove an old "98 Olds", modified for hand controls, with a whip antenna pulled down over the top of the car. His folded-up wheelchair was tucked behind the driver's seat, and he handled it almost like an old Western gunslinger would a revolver. He would reach back with his left arm, grab the chair, and with one quick move to the left, snap it in the air and set it down next to the car. Then in one motion he would swing himself into it. It made your shoulder ache just watching him—and then the rest of your body as well.

The car was full of Christian tracts, tapes, Gideon Bibles, and any other type of equipment that Daryl could use to evangelize. He was truly a rolling ministry, always packed and ready to go. Daryl went all over evangelizing in the power of the Holy Spirit; nothing seemed to deter him. He was God's man on a mission—on duty! He was living in the present moment in pursuit of the souls of men.

Daryl would soon become a frequent visitor at our home. Everyone loved him. He had an open invitation to come, anytime. He never wanted to be a burden on anyone, and he never was—at all. We would just hear the back door open and the slightest noise as his chair rolled across the floor. You knew it was him. He was always extremely calm and collected. He had played a lot of sports (basketball, for sure) and had likely done a lot of risky things. Most people considered Daryl a "man's man," but the Holy Spirit had given him such a deep gentleness, women of all ages felt very comfortable and peaceful around him, very much like he was a favorite brother or uncle.

Daryl was always thinking of helping others, even taking people into his apartment as ministry cases. We met one such case, a young man named Jamal. He was built like a football running back, in his twenties, and troubled by grand mal and other seizures that came without warning. Daryl had taken him in to his apartment several weeks earlier, trying to minister to him and help him to get his life on track with Jesus.

One day, Daryl was serving as a volunteer at the soup kitchen and had brought Jamal with him. Just as the doors opened and the crowd started in, Jamal had a severe seizure and went rolling under the table that held the big coffee urns. These seizures would render him totally oblivious to what was going on, and he came up from under the table like a wild bull, headed for the door to the outside. As he ran past, Daryl snatched Jamal's belt with one hand, hoping to stop him. Hanging on, Daryl was yanked out of his chair and was airborne, landing flat on the floor as Jamal ran out the door, headed for Peachtree Street.

It only took a minute or so for Daryl to regroup and get himself back into his chair. All that was hurt was his pride — and that had almost no hold on him. He took off rolling, as fast as he could, chasing after Jamal, fearing what might happen to him in mid-day Atlanta traffic. He caught up with him a couple of blocks down Peachtree as the seizure began to wear off and end. And like a good shepherd, Daryl gently brought him back.

Not all of Daryl's ministry was to the hurting or the down and out. One day, while visiting our home, he disappeared into another part of the house. We found him sitting very erect in his wheelchair, staring intently at a painting that was hanging in our living room. It was inspired by the movie "Suzy Wong." The woman in the painting was about half life size, reclining on a bed. Fully clothed and gorgeous, she was also seductive and provocative. I had asked my artist sister to paint her for us. This painting was the most valuable object in our home. It was so special that we had decorated the room around it—all the colors and even the furniture.

Before Daryl spoke, I knew what was coming. In a low but authoritative voice he said, "Brother, she's got to go." The Holy Spirit had spoken through His prophet. The next day Suzy was returned to my sister and her art collection.

This would be the beginning of many changes to come. Our life could no longer revolve around the love of materialism, even very fine art. We had to hear this from someone who really cared about us—and our transformation.

There were numerous great experiences with Daryl. Anyone traveling God's highway with him was blessed. Nancy and I had probably been given this season with Daryl so we could learn many valuable lessons by his example. Pursuing full-time ministry, Daryl moved to California. After a few years, he called, wanting to come to our home for a few days' visit and bring his new wife, Elena, and her two children. They came and they all looked great. It was especially good watching them interact as a family. He was obviously an excellent husband and father, and the family treated each other with deep love and great respect. He had a radiance, a look of fulfillment that we hadn't seen in him before. His wife and kids looked well cared for and content.

Through the years, we have continued to hear from him. Daryl and his family started an orphanage for Mexican children in the southern California/Baja area. His newsletter gives praise reports for everything that God has done, is doing, and will do. Their orphanage/school is growing, prospering, thriving, and bringing new hope and life to those formerly rejected kids. Each newsletter from them increases our faith and makes us want to "step it up." Three decades later, I have come to realize that the Holy Spirit was teaching me so many truths about life, real life, through Daryl.

Daryl is a marvelous example of the transformed life and grateful heart, sharing with others—with everyone that he can—everything that he can. Truly, any limitations he has have been far surpassed by his unlimited spirit and faith and love for the Lord and His work.

He would be too humble to admit it, but I believe Daryl exemplifies Paul's Scripture:

I have been crucified with Christ; and it is no longer I who live, but Christ lives in me; and the life which I now live in the flesh I live by faith in the Son of God, who loved me and gave Himself up for me. Galatians 2:20

Asking Jesus to Heal

As I previously mentioned, soon after being "baptized in the Spirit," we began to be aware of physical healings happening through prayer. Nancy and I experienced a major awakening in coming to accept that healings could and would take place in our time—they were not just historical events that had been recorded in the Bible. Jesus, who we were learning to trust in all other situations, wanted to answer prayers for healing of all types of sickness, disease, and debilitation. A year or two earlier, most of us in our prayer group would have considered experiences of this type to be either totally out of the question or somehow contrived—our minds had been shaped by unbelief, even skepticism and disbelief, developed in a secular culture. That's all we had seen modeled and lived out throughout our lives. Now, speakers at charismatic conferences were encouraging us to believe that the gift of healing would be made manifest through the prayers of believers, and those healings were to be fervently sought, without doubting. Scripture tells us, *"Keep on asking and it will be given you; keep on seeking and you will find; keep on knocking."* This opened up a whole new understanding for us, a world of faith we had never imagined. It seemed extraordinary; yet, with our own eyes, we were witnessing these healings.

The insightful books on healing by Francis MacNutt and others further unveiled for us this dynamic relationship of trust that could exist between God and man, and told us more about healing through prayer. How could anyone who was fortunate enough to be at one of the healing seminars, and see healings take place right in front of them, not be in awe? Remaining in prayer and waiting while someone's leg, which has always been two inches shorter than the other leg, grows two inches before your eyes—this quickly changes your outlook and brings you to believe in healing through prayer. Jesus and the Holy Spirit were the ones being called upon and glorified; undoubtedly, this was the work of the God we served, and He wanted to bring about healings for us. Our level of faith and trust in other important areas quickly increased as well. We could see that the Lord was interested in and cared about all of our needs—and was going to act on them. As we approached Him, He was literally drawing us to Himself, and healing our whole lives. It was a glimpse of heaven come to earth. Perhaps the most amazing part about healings through prayer was that He allowed a broad range of believers to participate in praying, from the gifted and experienced Francis MacNutt to the recently transformed novice believer. The Lord tells us all to ask. And He heals!

> *Is anyone among you sick? He should call in the church elders—the spiritual guides and they should pray over him, anointing him with oil in the Lord's name. And the prayers of faith will save him that is sick, and the Lord will restore him. James 5:14-15*

In our first prayer group, our prayers over people did not result in the blind suddenly seeing or the lame suddenly walking, but the healings we saw were meaningful for us and made life more bearable and pleasant for those who were healed. They really built our faith. Some of those early healings were simply the Lord removing pain, headaches (even migraines), backaches, and the like, when we prayed and asked Him. Sometimes the relief came right then, other times it might be a day, or days, before the healing was realized.

As we became more attuned to pray for people, and our expectant faith increased, the healings occurred more frequently and for more serious illnesses. Before long, when we encountered pain, sickness, or disease in someone, our first response was to pray, and we expected the Lord to heal whenever we asked Him. Frequently, He did just that.

One of the more memorable occasions was when a woman with severe arthritis got instant release from her long suffering and debilitation as soon as prayers were offered and hands were laid on her. She seemed anxious to go home, earlier than she usually would, and told us the next day that she had joyfully done housework into the wee hours of the morning. She was that thrilled to be able to again grip firmly and painlessly with her renewed hands. She even took a gallon jug of milk in and out of the refrigerator, over and over, just to get to use her hands again.

Another time, a woman brought her mother to us. For a long time the mother had been plagued with severe back problems; she could barely sit, stand or walk without extreme pain. Through the laying on of hands and the prayers, she received immediate release and total freedom. She found it hard to believe that her back had actually been healed. She was speechless to have received such a life-changing gift after so many years of suffering. She had regularly attended church all her life, she was very devout, but she had never heard of present-day healing through prayers. She could hardly wait to tell her priest back home about this wonderful new thing God had done for her.

An elderly man, who was deaf, was brought by his daughter to the prayer group to be prayed over. After expectant prayers had been offered up for him and hands laid on his ears, we all prepared to leave. Suddenly, the man was able to hear voices and conversations of people behind him, and he clearly understood all that was said. He had not been able to hear at all for years. What a wonderful time he and his daughter shared that night! Her faith and his trust had given him the gift of hearing.

A regular member of the prayer group had been diagnosed with cancer and was scheduled for surgery. We prayed over her the night before her next visit to the oncologist. The Holy Spirit then had us tell her to request one more x-ray. She did, and nothing was there—she was free of cancer and healed. No surgery was needed! Her cancer was gone, but the faith of all of us grew immeasurably that day.

Throughout the years we've heard many of these types of reports, of women or men with clear evidence of a disease, who, after being prayed over, had new scans or x-rays that showed no more sign of the disease. Jesus is the Great Physician and wants us to ask Him to heal. Each time we ask for a healing, especially for something major, we move more toward Jesus, and our faith and trust increase. We've also found the healings from the Lord to be every bit as permanent and complete, sometimes much more so, than those received through conventional medical practices and treatments.

One night, as a "Life in the Spirit Seminar" began, a young couple arrived. We had never seen them before. John and Teresa were both sharp and vibrant, but John was carrying Teresa in his arms and laid her in a chaise lounge. All her life she had been plagued with a serious spinal defect.

John and Teresa arrived this same way for the next two weeks before the Holy Spirit clearly prompted us to lay hands on her and pray for her healing. We promptly responded and she felt touched.

The following week, they walked in together—and have ever since. Jesus had healed her back.

Over the years we have witnessed many healings as the result of prayer, and there were probably many others happening around us that we just didn't hear about. Most of these might not be considered miracles, but all were healings that were helpful and appreciated, and some were downright life changing.

My own healing from sleeplessness, fear and hopelessness as a result of my own first prayer request, and others prayers, was life changing—180 degrees. It didn't sound like any disease but was equally debilitating, and potentially, far more dangerous.

We often don't know the seriousness of a prayer request, or how to pray. That's one reason praying in the Spirit (tongues, prayer language) is so important. The Spirit, who knows everything, prays through us. (There is more about this in a later chapter on spiritual gifts.)

We have learned that there is great value in laying on of hands and praying audibly as soon as a need becomes known. The intentionality and boldness and stepping out in faith seem to especially resonate with the Lord. Interrupting other activities to pray, regardless of the surroundings, often bears great fruit. We learned to not let any fear of what people might think, or doubt of success, deter us from open and fervent prayer. Our part is to ask.

We've also learned that not all of those prayed for receive a physical healing, but prayer always makes a difference, especially for those like Harry who were taken on to Glory—the ultimate healing. Some of this we won't fully understand on this earth; such mysteries are not for us to comprehend yet.

The Lord has brought us quite a distance. Before walking in the Spirit, we had thought all healings as the result of prayer had happened only in Biblical times. Now we were eyewitnesses to healings that looked very much like those in Scripture. Jesus was teaching us and deepening our understanding.

Jesus is the same yesterday, today and forever. Hebrews 13:8

Inasmuch then as we have a great high priest who has already ascended and passed through the heavens, Jesus, the Son of God, let us hold fast our confession of faith in Him.

Let us then fearlessly and confidently and boldly draw near to the throne of grace—the throne of God's unmerited favor (to us sinners); that we may receive mercy (for our failures) and find grace to help in good time for every need—appropriate help and well timed help, coming just when we need it. Hebrews 4:14 & 16

With God all things are possible. His ways are higher than our ways. It seems that our part is to pray and beseech Him with all our heart, soul and spirit, and then trust and embrace His response just as wholeheartedly.

And we know that God causes all things to work together for good to those who love God, to those who are called according to His purpose. Romans 8:28

Three Men Down

Not long after Harry went to Glory, we received a distressing phone call. A neighbor, who with his wife, lived down the street from us, was in the hospital in a serious condition. Stuart was a long-time Bible-believing, Scripture-speaking, gentle giant of a man in his mid-thirties. Stuart and Ann, his wife, had made several mission trips to the Caribbean, working with impoverished children and youth. They were unwavering in their faith, and very active in their church. We were asked to pray, fervently. The doctors thought Stuart had a sizable tumor in his abdominal area and were girding for the worst.

With a lot of trepidation, I decided to follow the prompting of the Spirit and go to the hospital to see him. The situation sounded extremely serious, and Satan was accusing me of being totally inadequate for the occasion. Stuart was a much more mature Christian than I was; he had been walking with the Lord very earnestly for several years. He could probably quote the "entire" Bible. What did I have to bring him? I thought I could have made a good case for trying to avoid this one. The Holy Spirit does not indulge me in such rationalization and excuses. He just says, "Go." I would go out of love, respect and obedience—but I sure felt empty handed.

Walking into the room, I found Stuart in the bed, flat out, looking huge and helpless. He told me the surgeon had cut him open and found a football-sized tumor attached to his spinal column. The doctors told him it was inoperable, sewed him back up, and gave him two weeks to live. He made sure that I knew that his only hope was in the Lord—and that his faith remained strong, and was getting stronger.

As I was trying to process this stunning report, which was much worse than I had feared, and handle my own uncertainty, Stuart shifted into another gear. He was still lying flat on his back but had now zeroed in on the moment, fully focused and "at his post." Looking me right in the eye, he firmly said, "Brother, you think you're here to minister to me, but I'm here to tell you, I'm here to minister to you!"

With that, he raised his head and shoulders up off the bed and said, "Brother, holy boldness you've got—get meekness." As he said that, big tears began to spill out of his eyes and run down his cheeks. In quick succession, two more times, he said, "Get meekness." Each time he said it, large tears ran from his eyes and streamed down his face. Stuart was definitely not "off duty." He was knocked flat and his life was threatened—but he was still very much on duty, delivering the mail!

Well, I was finished before I had even started. The Holy Spirit had nailed me! I left as quickly and graciously as I could—trying hard to look hopeful—but feeling pretty overwhelmed and perplexed. I had known for awhile that gentleness was lacking in my life, but I wasn't expecting to be called on it in this way. I felt I had been blindsided and was now just trying to land on my feet. Nothing about this visit was what I had expected or wanted to see or hear. Hospital ministry can make you feel weak in the knees if you're not ready—and I was still pretty new at it.

Very soon afterward, we got another call. A middle-aged man named Bill, who lived diagonally across the street from Stuart, had fallen from a tree while trying out a new chain saw. The fall had broken his neck and he was paralyzed, with little hope of recovering the use of his limbs. The prognosis was grim and our neighborhood was reeling under all of the terrible news. We were used to sharing the pleasurable things of life, not devastating tragedies.

A couple of days later, we got a third call that jolted us. A man who lived half a block away had been diagnosed with five blocked arteries in his heart. Gene, who was forty, was going to have quintuple bypass surgery early the next week.

Wow! Three brothers, all relatively young, living within a block of each other in our subdivision, were all down at one time with life-threatening situations. Prayer, lots of prayer, was definitely needed.

Nancy and I had known for several years that our subdivision had a lot of sharp, worldly people, busy with ambitious lives. There were a few committed Christians scattered across the subdivision— but very few. Most were in full pursuit of the "good life" (materialism) for themselves and their families, and paid little attention to the Lord and faith. Since our own radical conversions a couple of years earlier, we had fallen from favor with some of the subdivision neighbors and had basically been ignored by others. Some perhaps considered our faith a threat to their lifestyles. Now, prayer by many friends and neighbors, including the worldly ones, was needed. It was time to step out. That seemed to be what the Holy Spirit was calling for. It definitely didn't look easy. The same faith that we saw in the prayer meetings would be needed—but what a different setting.

We called Stuart's wife, Ann, suggesting a prayer meeting at their home. We knew Stuart and Ann would be fully in favor of it, but we didn't know about the others. We suggested that the three wives of the fallen husbands be there to sit in proxy for (in place of) their spouses. It was our hope that our neighbors would come and we could all lay hands on the wives and pray over them for their husbands' healing.

All three of the wives readily agreed to the proposal. The prayer time was set and calls went out across the neighborhood. At the appointed time, a considerable number of men and women came to Stuart and Ann's home. A few other neighbors indicated a desire to pray for them, but just couldn't bring themselves to be part of the home gathering. They went instead to a restaurant and prayed together at the same time for the men and their wives.

The chairs were placed close together, facing toward each other, and we asked the three wives to each sit in a chair. All of the rest of us gathered in a circle, standing or kneeling, and laid hands on their heads, shoulders, backs, wherever we could touch, and prayed for their husbands, that they each be healed. We all knew that we were dealing with life and death and disability, and prayer was our only hope. The prayer time was very reverent and spiritual and it only took about fifteen minutes. Then we stood up, hugged the wives, promised to keep praying, and dispersed. It was a challenging situation but a very holy time, and we left hopeful. We had done all we knew to do, put aside our comfort and what others might think, considered the fallen men and their families, asked for the Lord's help—and just trusted.

During the next few weeks, we heard the following reports. A new scan of Stuart showed no trace of the inoperable, football-sized tumor that had been threatening to kill him, and he was back home, headed for a full recovery. Gene's bypass surgery went great; he was home making a complete recovery, with no complications. Bill was regaining movement and starting to walk very slowly. The doctors were amazed but now expected him, in time, to make a full recovery, with no permanent paralysis.

God had done it! He answers prayer. Prayer changes things, especially group prayer, and it seems especially so when it's hard to "step out."

As for my "getting meekness," it would be several years before I really wanted it and asked for it. I had to grow in understanding of what the Holy Spirit had said through Stuart. It took that amount of time for me to fully realize that meekness/gentleness is not weakness at all—but is God's power under control! What could be better than that? (God's patience with us is amazing.)

Reflecting on these frightening experiences that became wonderful tributes to God's power, I'm reminded of the fruits of the Spirit that were so evident throughout. They were manifest in so many loving, caring concerned people—and the Lord sure delivered!

The fruit of the Spirit is love, joy, peace, patience, kindness, good-ness, faithfulness, gentleness and self control. Galatians 5:22-23

Coming In

One night, about a year into our new journey, midway between Easter and Pentecost, I had a surprise encounter. I had recently experienced my first Good Friday and the cross, Easter, and the resurrection as a new believer, and with great expectancy I was looking forward to celebrating Pentecost "in the Spirit." Anything having to do with Pentecost had my full attention.

Judy K. walked briskly up to me one evening at our weekly prayer meeting. Usually a very upbeat person, she was more upbeat than normal. Judy was forty years old and a diminutive woman, just 4'10" and about ninety-five pounds. She had carrot red hair, sparkling eyes, and was full of the Spirit. She and her husband, Joe, were leaders in the group.

Judy said that she had a word for me from the Lord. She was ready to deliver it and made sure that Nancy was within hearing distance. By this time, I had become pretty familiar with the prophetic gift being used, sometimes quietly in my spirit and sometimes through others. Judy was used in this gift as the occasion required. I stilled and braced myself, since the Lord had given me directions this way from time to time. The prophecy flowed out from Judy as if on teletype.

"You must eat My body and drink My blood, and with this all of your questions about confession and the infallibility of the pope will be answered."

Given my past year's involvement with Catholic Charismatics, the word clearly pointed to the Catholic Church. I had never considered joining—not at all—even after being very active there for the

87

past year. Nancy was a lifelong Catholic and our kids were being raised Catholic. (I had signed an agreement to this at the time of our marriage, which was normal when a Catholic married a non-Catholic. I was not overjoyed with it at the time.) I was from a background in which Catholics were considered quite suspicious. Did they worship Mary, or the pope? Were they Christian or a cult—or worse? In the past year, I had moved beyond all those old questions as I became involved in the prayer group, share group, and men's prayer groups, and was even attending church regularly with my family, something I had never done in the old days. I now knew that the Catholic Church was plenty on target, but for me to become Catholic would be a major stretch. The charismatic element felt really "right on" to me now, but the worldwide universal Catholic Church—that was something else. The words *tradition* and *doctrine* still tripped me up a little.

Through the empowering of the Holy Spirit, my faith life had been moving like a rocket during the past year. I didn't want to take any chance on compromising that. Even so, the delivered word was sharp and concise and had cut right through to me. It felt clear and strong enough to act upon based on sheer obedience, but I received it, took it to the Lord, and pondered it for a few days.

Several factors came to my mind:

- I believed in the gift of prophecy and in heeding its message.
- This was the church that the Lord had used in my rescue and awakening.
- I was big on loyalty—especially to people who had helped me.
- I was already very involved in the Catholic Charismatic Movement.
- Nancy would be thrilled, and it would be great for our family.

- And maybe the Lord could use me to help bring the Holy Spirit into the mainline Catholic Church.

Nancy and I, along with Joe and Judy and others, had recently returned from our first large Catholic Charismatic conference at Notre Dame. Fr. Rick Thomas, a Jesuit firebrand from El Paso, had brought a group of unlearned peasants from Juarez, peasants who had experienced miracles. Their personal witness and testimonies really stoked our fire. With hundreds of Catholic priests and bishops and over 25,000 in attendance, and tens of thousands of arms raised in the air in worship, the Catholic Church was looking far more "on fire" than I would ever have imagined. I knew I would never be the same again. This all seemed to validate Judy's prophetic word to me.

All of that, along with Nancy's hearty approval, pointed to "Yes, Lord."

When I told Fr. Walt, he just said, "I thought it was about time. When do you want to come in?"

Without thinking twice, I said, "Well, Pentecost would be my first choice, of course." Fr. Walt said, "Fine. I'm baptizing two babies that day and we'll just add your First Communion and Confirmation to the service." Pentecost again moved to front and center in my life. And it was only three weeks away.

For the past year, I had considered myself a virtual Pentecostal, while spending most of my time and energy with Catholic Charismatics. Mt. Paran Church of God, a Pentecostal church, had meant so much to my development. I could have felt right at home as a member there. They were tracking with the Holy Spirit and were really proactive believers. I had been meeting with many of their men two mornings a week, and at other times as well.

The Spirit quickly showed me that through the Holy Spirit gifts He had given, I could definitely be more useful and have the most impact on the Catholic Church. The Charismatic Renewal was still a well-kept secret to most of this gigantic church. Physical healings through faith, prayer and laying on of hands also seemed a total mystery to many Catholics, and even to many priests. So, on Pentecost, I would become a Roman Catholic.

Pentecost weekend arrived and so did a "Nor'easter," or so it seemed. Unusual for June in Georgia, but by Friday night we had strong, steady winds. Saturday's weather became very stormy, with the wind gaining strength. That night, Nancy and I attended a Pentecost mass for Charismatic Catholics, and the electrical storm got so bad we were concerned for the building. The windows were literally rattling.

Sunday afternoon, we were very mindful of the stormy weather. The service was to be a backyard mass and would include baptisms and the confirmation service. By this time, the clouds were fast moving, dark and ominous, the wind had gained more strength, and the summer temperatures had dropped at least twenty degrees. The wind was so strong it was nearly impossible to control the flapping pages of the lectionary. To top it all off, several doves were quietly walking around us, unusually close, but apparently unperturbed.

Fr. Walt handled the service and the stormy conditions as though they were just routine. He always seemed prepared for whatever came along.

The three of us came into the Church.

And then the clouds suddenly blew out and away, blue sky replaced them, the wind totally abated and the temperature went back to normal. Apparently the Holy Spirit proclaimed this "coming in" event completed. I wondered if this could be expected at every Pentecost. Why wasn't everybody enthralled by the Book of Acts?

Later, I would remember being enamored with Pope John XXIII, about the time of my "seat belt wreck" eight years earlier. I was even reading a book about him. His famous directive, "Open the windows of the church that the Holy Spirit may come in," called for and ushered in the great move of the Holy Spirit in the '60s—and it defined his papacy as well. At the time that I read the book, my only interest in him was that he seemed an extraordinary man. I wasn't interested in him from a faith perspective. I now realized that I had been led to that book just to begin the marinating of my mind, in preparation for the days to come.

Six months after I came into the church, another very special man was installed as pope. This pope, John Paul II, became my man to emulate. He would take the faith to the world like no man had since Jesus walked the earth. He was so courageous, so evangelical, so ecumenical, so tuned in with the Spirit, and yet so humble. He even gave us a great lesson on how to suffer and die graciously. He made so many people grateful to be Catholic and so many others deeply appreciative just to have served the same Lord!

Over the years many pieces of this puzzle would be put into place. I had acted mostly out of obedience to the Lord's word, after reasoning that the apparent call made sense at that time. Later, I would come to really appreciate what I had moved into. My "yes" to this seemingly hard call to become Catholic had opened up untold blessings that were revealed in due time. A deep appreciation for the liturgical, the traditional, and the courageous believers throughout the centuries would find their place in my heart and soul. I was like a minute speck on this great canvas, the Church. I would come to realize that many professing Catholics had a deeper, more abiding faith than I had first believed.

Now a longtime communion minister in the Church, I find that serving His Body or Blood is still new and alive each time, like "His mercies are new every morning." Kneeling at the altar rail just before we serve, it is rare that I don't ask myself, "How did I ever get here?" After my long pursuit of the worthless, I am now allowed to handle the most precious: the real presence of Jesus. Again I remember that Jesus said, *"I am the bread of life" (John 6:35).* And his difficult to accept words, *"Truly, truly, I say to you, unless you eat the flesh of the Son of Man and drink his blood, you have no life in yourselves" (John 6:53).* Peter could only say, *"Lord, to whom shall we go? You have the words of eternal life" (John 6:68).* Until I personally ate His body and drank His blood, I couldn't really understand Jesus' "hard words."

When I joined the Church in 1978, I had no comprehension of how important that "coming in" would ultimately be. Just as I had needed to come into the body of Christ the previous year, I now needed to come into the organized church and get connected. I could no longer operate outside it. We needed to build His kingdom together. Millions of devout Catholics were already in place serving the church, but much more was needed of the release of the Spirit

As the Book of Hebrews tells us, *"And let us consider how to stimulate one another to love and good deeds, not forsaking our own assembling together, as is the habit of some, but encouraging one another; and all the more as you see the day drawing near." Hebrews 10:24-25*

It would be quite some time before I would realize the many and exceptional strengths of the Catholic Church in standing against the evils of our world culture, and how centered on Jesus and the cross it is. Now I can much better understand what I was called into, and the major work to be done.

I've come to know that the Lord is in no way denominational. He has myriads of followers in many places, worshiping and serving in different styles and forums. Many of the very best, most committed, Spirit-led people whom I know are not Catholic. The overall church of the believers is so powerful when it works together and lives out Jesus' prayer for unity: *"I do not ask on behalf of these alone, but for those also who believe in Me through their word; that they may all be one; even as You, Father, are in Me and I in You, that they also may be in Us, so that the world may believe that You sent Me." John 17:20-21*

We are so blessed to be able to stand shoulder to shoulder with uncompromising Christian brothers and sister of all areas of committed faith. Being what each is called to be and serving as He asks— that is what is important. I'm definitely not the most Catholic-looking person around. But I'm living my spirit-filled Catholicism as I believe the Lord leads. After all, He called me in when I was sky high in the Spirit, and He never told me to let up.

In the early years of faith, I became engrossed in the stories of the great healings and miracles attributed to the famous healing evangelist, Smith Wigglesworth. These accounts included many documented "raisings from the dead," and served as a launching pad for me to believe God would act miraculously. I would read about Wigglesworth and then expect to be used myself.

Late in his life, Wigglesworth dramatically prophesied over David DuPlessis (then the head of the Holiness Pentecostal church) that the Holy Spirit would use DuPlessis to unite the Pentecostal and Catholic Churches—a unity beyond all logic and difficult to fathom. At the time of fulfillment, DuPlessis acted on the prophecy and the results were the outpouring of the Spirit on the Catholic Church in what is known as the Catholic Charismatic Renewal—a spiritual joining of two of the most powerful Christian churches on the face of the earth.

It's uplifting to reflect on the lives of the martyrs and saints and all those who've gone before and made this possible. On our one trip to Rome, Nancy and I stood quietly in the Coliseum, that famous bastion of suffering, humiliation and death created for the depraved entertainment of the powerful and wealthy. I wanted to feel the blood of the martyrs, and I did. And it was strengthening. Surely, the martyrs and saints from many backgrounds felt a real oneness as they laid it all down and headed for Glory together.

When the Lord called me to join the Catholic Church, He had a plan in motion of which I hardly had a glimpse. Five years would pass from the time I joined the Church before I would begin to see how much more He had planned. A whole new understanding of ecumenism was yet to emerge in our lives, an understanding that only a small percentage of Christians have seriously considered. We would get to experience it up close and personal, on a daily basis, and would find it beautiful to behold—just like Jesus' prayer!

The glory which You have given Me I have given to them, that they may be one, just as We are one; I in them and You in Me, that they may be perfected in unity, so that the world may know that You sent Me, and loved them, even as You have loved Me. John 17:22 and 23

As You Did to One
of the Least of These

Soon after receiving the "Baptism in the Spirit," I was pulled toward evangelization, one-on-one style, almost anytime and anywhere. It became a burning call upon me—but it also seemed very natural as well. This wasn't so with Nancy; to her, as to many Christians, evangelizing seemed foreign and very difficult. Nancy was more into organizing and participating in group activities with structure. We gave each other the space to do what God seemed to be asking of each of us. The burden I had for people was mostly spiritual, but Nancy had a growing concern for their physical life, their practical needs. One day Nancy told me that she had been really moved by a Scripture in Matthew—it kept convicting her as Scripture can surely do. She couldn't get it out of her mind.

I was hungry and you gave me no food; I was thirsty and you gave me nothing to drink; I was a stranger and you did not welcome me and entertain me; I was naked and you did not clothe me; I was sick and in prison and you did not visit me with help and ministering care.

Then they also in their turn will answer, Lord, when did we see you hungry or thirsty or a stranger or naked or sick or in prison and did not minister to you?

And He will reply to them, solemnly, I declare to you, so far as you failed in doing it for the least of these, you failed to do it for Me.

Then they will go away into eternal punishment, but those who are just and upright and in right standing with God into eternal life.
Matthew 25: 42-46

Nancy and I had both been discovering and searching the word of God and its revealed truth for today's living. We were almost certain that there were no poor in our subdivision or area. We didn't know anything about going and looking for them in depressed areas.

Almost as quickly as Nancy became convicted by the Scripture, the Atlanta Constitution drove the point home. They ran a full-page article on St. Luke's Soup Kitchen, located in downtown Atlanta. The article had photos, names, contact phone numbers—the works. Now that excuse was removed. We knew where to go. What next? We both sensed that if we touched this one, we could get pulled in. But we knew that all is in the Lord's hands and we wanted to pursue His plan, whatever it was. We had no knowledge of living on the street, but knew the world could be hard on anyone.

We talked it over and Nancy decided to bite the bullet and try volunteering (even as scared as she was). She had always been uncomfortable when we were approached by street people or panhandlers. She thought more about what got them into such a condition than about reaching out to them. With much trepidation, she embarked on this new mission at St. Luke's. After a brief introduction and instructions, she began, stationed in the kitchen area behind a counter, "hanging back" and serving sandwiches. The woman in charge was wonderful and understanding, the volunteers were gracious and helpful, and Nancy began to see that with time and effort she could probably fit in. Certainly, into the work.

Going back the next week was easier, and right away, she became a regular. Nancy soon looked like an old pro, moving about the tables filled with "guests," refilling their soup bowls and coffee cups and even gently touching some on the shoulder as she gave an encouraging word. She was beginning to see that these people had real lives—just as she did—only much harder. Most of the people were devoid of self-respect, and that just filled up their wounded eyes. They might not make a whimper, but were silently crying out for understanding and acceptance. Soon Nancy's mother, Fran, and I would join her one morning each week, making the mission trip into the broken, inner city world. The reports that Nancy had brought back from St. Luke's had torn at our hearts also—and sympathy won out. Once anyone stepped out and gave it a try, it was hard to stop going. In a strange way these people and their problems became our people and our problems. If we weren't willing to help, who was?

The soup kitchen seemed a microcosm—all the inhumanity of the world visited on one small group of people. Having nowhere to go home to seemed to us the most daunting of prospects, yet these people lived nowhere. They just kept surviving and moving around, almost seeming to be their own worst enemies. Rejection, low self-esteem, frustration and anger gave them little rest, gnawing at them mercilessly. We felt guilty having a nice home to return to. Sometimes the street people would remind us of that guilt and tell us that we came downtown to help them just to ease our own consciences, and then go back to our nice comfortable life in the suburbs. That hurt—but there was some truth in it. Working a half day in a soup kitchen seemed about the equivalent of a full day of physical work. Contending with the demons was very energy draining; the spiritual struggle for the lives of these people was unending.

Some of the people clung to life tenaciously. Regardless of disease or addiction, depression or fear, they hung on. Many seemed to filter into the crowd and willfully get lost, almost disappearing, nothing notable about them. This probably had been the story of their lives. Some few we came to know, in a limited way. Most wouldn't let us know them. This book has separate stories about some individuals who did allow us into their lives.

Many didn't mingle with others, often resenting being grouped with people of such low estate, almost blind to their own condition. Some were hard-core racists, unwilling to even sit next to other people, while others showed each other due respect regardless of color. We soon learned that each had to be dealt with separately— not grouped together or profiled. We also learned that not all of them had brought this upon themselves. Some had never had much chance in life at all. We often wondered if, given the same circumstances, we would have done as well. Some had not always been poor or homeless, a few had fallen from rather lofty positions. Alcohol and drugs had claimed many victims; depression and defeats had also. A few were deeply embarrassed about "being on the street."

Some individuals seemed fearful or even paranoid during their whole time at the soup kitchen. We could only wonder how they managed out on the hard and dangerous streets. They all needed more of the love of Jesus; however, few would really let Him in. For most, their woundedness far overshadowed their ability to receive love and be healed. One couple came regularly, the woman always walking about eight feet behind the man who, we found out later, routinely abused her. Her formerly attractive face now bore witness to that frequent maltreatment. She may have felt unable to go through life alone, even with this heavy cost of companionship, or she might have been unable to get free from him at any cost.

We came to know that once anyone had been on the street for a period of time, it was extremely hard for him or her to get off. Every day out there lessened their chances of a comeback (made them less hirable), and each day diminished their self-confidence and ability to work. About all that was available for men was day labor, such as digging ditches or unloading trucks. Many didn't have the physical strength or stamina to do that type of work. Worst of all, with each day, Satan increased his stranglehold on each of them, and his bondage of them. Occasionally, we heard of a death among the group, usually either from torching a building while trying to stay warm, or getting tanked up on cheap wine or Aqua Velva and unknowingly freezing to death. Occasionally, Satan would pit one against the other over something petty and one would die from it.

As long as we lived in Atlanta, we continued to serve at the soup kitchens. There was a second one, at 910 Ponce de Leon Avenue, much smaller but quite good. Called "910" by the guests, it had been started and was run by a Christian couple, Ed and his wife, Murphy, both ordained Presbyterian ministers. This was the "call" on their lives. Their ministry focused more on redeeming the people and pointing them to Jesus and a new life. Their facility also had showers and a clothes closet for the guests. Those who looked trustworthy, who tried hard and did well, could even become resident workers in the ministry and live there full time. They had both successes and disappointments with these select few. Some would recover their lives; others would make progress and then fall back into the old life. These setbacks were painful for everyone, especially for the others who were trying hard to make it.

The most challenging place that we served was a night shelter in downtown Atlanta. It was located in the gym of Central Presbyterian

Church, across the street from the Capitol. After hearing about this ministry, Nancy and I signed up to serve a night. We came with little knowledge of what to expect. At the designated time, 5:15 pm, we arrived and met the two leaders, a husband and wife, for a brief instruction before the doors were to be opened for the guests, the first 150 people in line outside. As the doors opened, the people filed in and went to pick up a mat to sleep on. Each person would then bring his or her mat (about 3.5 feet × 6 feet in size) and lay it on the gym floor right next to the other mats. Among the total number were about a dozen women, who were herded to a small upstairs room to keep them separated from the men. Even with all the hardship, dirt and deprivation, the sexual tension was very present—perhaps even more so in that setting. I sensed that that was usual for this place.

Quickly, we received our first spiritual wakeup—the 150 maximum had been reached and due to the fire code, no more would be allowed in. We stood at the door looking into the eyes of the remaining twelve or fifteen who had been at the end of the line. Being turned away on this biting cold winter night, just at dark, with nowhere else to go, must have felt like the ultimate rejection. We felt very guilty staying inside and closing the door on them. If only they had gotten there a little earlier. We wondered if that was a pattern for them, also.

All that we had learned while working in the soup kitchens would be needed here; we had this group for the whole night. The rules allowed anyone to leave at anytime, but no one could leave and return. It was a real lock out. No one could enter throughout the night.

With the guests inside, the instructors quickly thanked us for coming and told us that they had to leave. There were three seminary students who were to be the other volunteers; they straightaway holed up for the night in the break room with their studies. Their studies thus far had definitely not prepared them for this type of ministry. That left Nancy and me to handle the crowd, which we worked at all night.

The mats with the sleeping bodies on them were in tight rows, heads right next to feet. Throughout the night, in the darkened gym, people were occasionally stepped on by others who woke up disoriented, not knowing where they were, or got up to use the bathrooms, wandering out to the hallway. Some guests, once they lay down, never moved throughout the night until morning. Others never lay down at all but talked or played cards all night in a small room just off the main gym. We had never experienced anything remotely like this before. The whole scene was charged; it was like being in a room full of packaged explosives and waiting for the fuse to be lit. We both knew by morning that Nancy was not ever to come back—the entire setting was far too dangerous for a woman to be there. We had allowed our compassion to overrule our common sense.

As morning arrived, all of the guests were required to get up, wipe down their mats, and return them to the holding place on the stage. A fast sweep, mop, and wipe down and a meager food handout, and they were headed back onto the street. Following this regimen was absolutely essential in order for the church to be able to allow the facility to be used. For the elderly, very frail or unfit, sending them back out into that cold, and perhaps rain, seemed downright brutal. We couldn't even begin to understand what that had to be like. Unfortunately, it was the life they had and the life that most of them would always have. Working that shelter brought home the saying, "There, but for the grace of God, go I."

Years later, Nancy had more exposure to street ministry. The local food bank, Golden Harvest, planned to open a downtown soup kitchen, combining several smaller church soup kitchens into one. After our prayerful consideration, Nancy applied and was chosen to be the manager. This soup kitchen would be open every day for lunch and would serve approximately 175 people each day. The staff would include two assistants, and local churches would furnish the volunteers needed each day to do the work. Nancy was on duty five days a week, in rotation with her two assistants. On her Sunday (every third), I went and worked as a volunteer. This Sunday schedule was quite trying to us both in many ways. It was obvious that I didn't have the grace to do it as she did. She was called to the position and the grace rested upon her.

In the midst of this challenging and essential ministry, however, was an opportunity to watch Nancy's impressive, calm control in a high-tension setting. She would move easily among these fragile and frustrated outcasts, each made in the likeness and image of God. For some she was their brightest ray of hope. Sometimes their exasperation and anger would rise up and spill over. The grace that God had given her to take on the job was sufficient for each situation. There were times when she even had to require one of the guests to hand over his knife to her—and he would, usually with, "Yes, Miss Nancy." Maybe our house guests from the street back in Atlanta had helped prepare Nancy for this very hard but important new ministry. Her calm and confident manner was a far cry from the way she had walked into St. Luke's the first time.

On weekdays, Nancy and I usually arrived home for lunch from our different workplaces at about the same time. One day, I looked out the window as she came into view. She looked different, worn down and tired out from the work and the responsibility for all those people. I knew the grace for the job had left her. It had been five years since she had begun managing the soup kitchen (we had expected it to last three when she started). Those years included many, many grueling days and events. It was time for her to walk away from it—and so she did. It was time for others to take up this burden. We both knew that.

Jesus had told each of us, "The poor will always be with you." Even though this phase of our ministry concluded, Jesus' words have lived on in our hearts, and so have the weak, wounded and disenfranchised. They still hold their special place for both of us. We still have, and will continue to have, a ministry to them, probably on a one-on-one basis and more spontaneously. We also know that each time we're asked to help, our hearts are also being tested. We've come to know that with each call the Lord puts on someone for this very special ministry, He also gives abundant grace to carry it out.

We've gotten to work alongside so many of God's kingdom workers as they tirelessly serve in these ministries, many putting in incredible hours and/or personal finances. Many have done much more, and for far longer, and never expect anything in return. It's just what the Lord has called them to do. The service is so gratifying that most would tell you that the blessings they receive far surpass the effort they expend—they only wish that they had done more. And yes, not to be overlooked, these needy individuals have taught us so much about real life, and gratitude. Things we probably couldn't have learned any other way. The unspoken "thank you" said only by the eyes and hearts tells it all.

Whatever you do for the least of these, you do unto me. Matthew 25:40

Taking Them Home

As we mingle with God's people on His terms, we are nudged and tugged on to be willing to offer more. Our experiences in prayer group settings, and, especially, working at soup kitchens, caused us to establish relationships and develop empathy for special people who were disenfranchised, permanently or at least temporarily. Before long, the obvious "more" was to take or invite these individuals home with us, remove them from the problem situations, and give them a better chance at life. This was quite a switch from our attitude in the "previous life" when we could have found a dozen reasons not to consider the possibility.

However, Nancy and I did act upon the Spirit's leading with quite a few people, and tried to with others. Most turned us down on our offer. Over a period of time and because of these experiences, we learned a few things. Certainly, though, this ministry is not a science—it's always person by person, moment to moment. No two people are alike, and never should be treated as such. But we did learn three things. First, that taking them to our home didn't eliminate their problems. Second, that we were ill equipped to take some of them due to our own family's needs and our space limitations. And we learned that a support system was needed to really handle this type of ministry.

Even so, we came to realize that if the results weren't just what we had hoped for, the Lord wanted us to be happy that we had tried, and to know that our efforts had helped those individuals along and had given them fresh hope and a glimpse of His ways. He would use it for their good. We also were reminded of the times that we had been reached out to and helped when we needed it the most.

Do not forget or neglect or refuse to extend hospitality to strangers—being friendly, cordial and gracious, sharing the comfort of your home and doing your part generously—for through it some have entertained angels without knowing it. Hebrews 13:2

Crane Operator

Our building crew was well into the framing stages for a large house when we had a sizeable steel beam to set in the ridge of the 30 × 30-foot great room. Once the beam was set, the roof could be framed out and the house "dried in." This was an important milestone in any house under construction. The beam had been delivered and was lying in the yard, waiting, and the time had come to set it, but it had been raining for a couple of days and the red clay downhill yard was slick as glass. I was very careful about who worked on my houses and I almost always used only those workers whom I knew or had been referred to me. Not knowing any crane operators, I found one in the telephone book. I called to make an arrangement for the company to set the beam, but told them it would have to wait until the rain had stopped for awhile. It seemed too high a risk, trying to get the crane safely onto the property. They agreed, took the information, and wrote it down. I would call them when it was dry enough.

Sometime later in the day, my men noticed a crane out on the road. Sure enough, this company I didn't know had disregarded what I had said about the rainy conditions and sent the crane, expecting to do the job. So out into the rain I went to talk to the operator, to explain how the yard was too slick. With difficulty, I worked my way through the mud to the road and encountered Bill, the operator, eagerly waiting.

Bill was the kind of guy you would expect to see driving a truck or operating some kind of heavy equipment. He seemed the type who never met a stranger, almost overanxious to please, and was brimming with confidence. Normally, I would have just told him to go on back and that I would call his company again when the conditions were satisfactory. But Bill assured me that the lot did not present any problem, he did this kind of work in all sorts of conditions every day. He was absolutely sure that we should go ahead and set the beam, and that even though it was still raining, there was no reason to postpone or delay—all he needed was instructions on how it was to be set, and it would be a done deal!

With that, I walked with him to the side yard where the beam was and showed him a couple of young dogwood trees growing close by that absolutely were not to be touched by anything at all. This was a contract house, and the owners had already found and become attached to those trees. Bill replied, "No problem," and began to move the crane down into the muddy yard. Something about his confidence didn't add to mine, I wasn't sure why.

As I stood back, totally still, watching every move of the crane, it suddenly lurched forward and flattened the best dogwood tree—right to the ground. We lost both the tree and me simultaneously—I really lost it with Bill. I wasn't a Christian yet and had little tolerance for mistakes and slipups. I led mostly by authority. We would not get the dogwood back, and it took awhile to get me back—settled and calmed down. My temper really got loose. We almost lost Bill in the process; his look of confidence had instantly changed to that of a "deer in the headlights" as soon as the accident occurred. Like the little dogwood, he also had been flattened. I immediately had the rude awakening that he had probably run over and broken things before—lots of them—and he obviously knew what it felt like to be run over himself.

Now he wanted to make up for this mistake and do a good job setting the beam. To my own surprise, I found that I did not have the heart to send him away feeling defeated. That was definitely out of character for me. Subconsciously, I probably didn't want to risk his coming back on the property again. So we proceeded to set the beam and Bill handled the crane and the beam with all the care that he could muster. He did a faultless job. Now, I thought if we could just get Bill and his crane off the property and gone with no more calamities, we would have done as well as could be expected. We were able to do that, and I watched Bill drive off into the horizon with his crane. I gave a sigh of relief. Bill was a memory.

It was four years later before I would look into his eyes again, those childlike, wild eyes that had felt so much hurt. Bill showed up one night in our prayer meeting. I couldn't believe it, but I was coming to know that is often the way the Lord does things. He gives you a passing glimpse of someone or something, and then puts them right next to you. Bill remembered me immediately; he had good reason. He instantly recalled the experience of the crane and the dogwood and was once again reliving that mistake, feeling guilty and repenting. We met each other in a very different way this time, each as relatively new Christians. The slate was clean and we were starting over. I knew I would have to try harder with Bill than with most new friends.

Bill and his wife, Fay, would come into our lives over the next season in a pretty big way. Fay was a very domineering woman with a strong spirit of control, and treated Bill as a big child. She made life

107

fairly miserable for him. Even though their attendance became regular, the prayer meetings had little positive effect on Fay. She was convinced that it was just another of Bill's wild tangents that he would soon get over; she wasn't into all that Jesus stuff. But Bill took off like a rocket. Jesus and the Holy Spirit were the missing ingredients that he had been needing in his life. He just couldn't get enough. His enthusiasm was matched by his gratitude—he absolutely knew Jesus had saved him!

Before long Bill began to realize that his efforts to persevere and succeed in this marriage had failed. At our invitation, he moved in with us for a couple of weeks, mostly using it as a shelter and refuge while he broke free of Fay's control over him. She called our house a couple of times, pretty sure we knew where he was. We admitted that we did, but wouldn't tell her where; she was only interested in his pension checks and maintaining control over him. This was not the first marriage for Bill or Fay. To compound the problem, there were grown kids, both his and hers, and they all seemed to want to take advantage of Bill. Realizing that her reign had come to an end, Fay dropped out of Bill's life and moved on.

After working at various truck driving and similar jobs, Bill relocated to New York, his native state. Years later, the Lord brought just the right woman into Bill's life. Gail is loving, smart, thoughtful and diligent—just what Bill needed. They were married in a storybook wedding and have been married ever since. They have a really good marriage, a nice home, and he gets along very well with her grown kids. They both realize they are blessed and give the Lord all the credit.

Over the years, without even calling, Bill has just shown up at our door—1,000 miles from his—coming down for the day just to carry a cross on Good Friday. God has used Bill over and over to remind us that we don't do the picking and choosing, but that He, the Lord, does. Thirty years later, Bill still calls faithfully, at no particular time and for no particular reason. When we answer the phone, we are greeted with a booming, emphatic, "God love you!" and we know with all certainty that He does—and Bill does, too! Nancy holds a special place in his heart, much like a favorite aunt. He remembers her gracious treatment during his stay with us. He always thanks us, again, for our part in their great life, giving us far more credit than we deserve. And, again, we are humbled by it all. Nancy and I are very blessed that the Lord saw fit to give us a friend and encourager like Bill. The Lord helps me remember the way I treated him on our first encounter.

As the heavens are higher than the earth so are my ways higher than your ways and my thoughts than your thoughts. Isaiah 55:9

Marlene and Joey

St. Luke Episcopal Church in downtown Atlanta had the largest soup kitchen in the city. On any given day during the week, there might be 400 to 500 people, or more, for lunch. The guests were mostly home-less people who lived in vacant buildings, in the woods, under bridges, in boxes, anywhere that they could find shelter or hang out. The men outnumbered the women by fifteen or twenty to one. At the least, it was a challenging place for women.

When Marlene walked in with Joey, they were truly an eye-catching pair. Marlene was about six feet tall, with coal-black hair, big boned, but not overweight, stern faced, almost as if she was programmed to just go straight ahead. Upon first encountering her, she appeared to have no personality and no interest in any one. She was carrying Joey under her arm like a football. Immediately everyone knew that mothering wasn't her main thing, and we wondered if she was even capable of doing it. Joey was about six months old, strong and physically healthy, but unclean and neglected. Marlene seemed totally oblivious to his condition and surprised by anyone's notice or concern for him.

Babies were few at St. Luke's, but they always got special attention whenever they were brought in, their lives and future being at such high risk. When Marlene and Joey came in, some of the women volunteers would quickly take him and right away start to clean him up—and love up on him almost as if he was their own. He instantly brought out the mothering instincts in them. St. Luke's also had a clothes closet downstairs, and it seemed that any mother who came with a baby had lots of needs; they were given first choice of whatever was available at the time. The volunteers would look for the best for Joey.

We would later learn that Marlene's family was local; her parents were regular churchgoers, and she had a brother who was quite successful in his field. It was soon obvious that she was extremely intelligent, yet she was living on the street. She was around thirty years old and it seemed that many years of rebellion, bad choices and misunderstandings had brought her to this place in life. Apparently, her family had given up on trying to help her and had turned her out, hoping she would somehow realize she needed someone else's help, and be willing to accept it.

After seeing Marlene and Joey a few times at the soup kitchen, our hearts won out and Nancy and I made a really tough decision. We invited them to come home with us. They needed to live with someone, at least for Joey's sake; maybe it would work for Marlene, too. We didn't give a lot of thought as to whether it would work for our family. After all, Marlene and Joey were homeless—it was ministry, and our kids would come to understand. We hoped. Later, we would realize our kids should have at least been told ahead of time.

To her surprise, we think, and ours, Marlene reluctantly agreed that they would come, so we brought them straight from St. Luke's and got them set up in our home. Their presence certainly made a difference. Our kids felt uneasy and a little violated. We had not had a baby in the house for many years. Joey had all the needs of any baby, but he was a really good one. With the treatment, or lack of, that he had received in his young life, he had already learned not to expect much. He was easy to keep content. We soon learned that Marlene would be much more of a challenge than Joey.

Bringing them into our home brought a lot of stress with it; our sons took to Joey but never quite adjusted to Marlene. She would move about the house almost silently, sometimes coming up and standing right behind one of us without our knowledge. It was quite a shock to turn around and look right into her eyes, wondering what was going on in her mind. She had dark, troubled eyes with just a hint of hardness and vengefulness, as she silently stared straight ahead, as if to stare you down. Hurt just welled up in those eyes; we guessed that much of it was self-inflicted. We had a few ministry sessions with her, usually at inappropriate times (as is often the case). Most of these seemed to go nowhere, even though we knew they were needed. It was like pulling teeth for all three of us.

We did learn a little more about her, as time went on and she began to open up a little. She did reveal that Joey was the result of a rape she had suffered on the street. She didn't talk much about her street life. It was too painful. Over time, a dry sense of humor and a quirky personality down inside her would show through sporadi-cally—usually when least expected—coming out impulsively and then disappearing back inside, like a turtle's head. She seemed to take pleasure in startling us this way. When the battle in her mind would get to be too much, Marlene would sometimes just leave the house and walk for an hour or more without any explanation or forewarning. Joey would be left behind, somewhere in the house, but he never seemed to miss her. He was showing early signs of coping as a loner.

After a few months of living with us, in one of our ministry ses-sions, she confessed it just wasn't in her to be a mother. Even in a family setting, her instincts toward motherhood had shown no improvement. She knew she should be willing for Joey to be adopted by good Christian parents who could raise him and give him a chance in life. As we talked with her several times in the ensuing weeks, she would vacillate back and forth as to whether or not to release him and let him go. This decision was really tearing at her.

With a lot of real emotion and heartfelt pain, she finally settled the question and decided on giving him up. It seemed to her it was the right thing to do, but she also knew it was admitting another major failure in her life—she hadn't been and couldn't be a good mother. Possibly, this was the most she had ever felt her role of motherhood. It was hard even for us to witness and go through with her. She agonized over it as any mother would. We were both sur-prised by how much.

We helped to get Joey placed with a highly recommended Chris-tian couple who had no children. They were thoroughly convinced that he was the absolute answer to all their prayers for a child. They were ecstatic. For all we could tell, this certainly seemed like God's plan for everyone involved.

After the adoption was complete and Joey had been moved into his new home, Marlene stayed on with us for awhile. Her state of mind seemed about like it had been before, mostly troubled and muddled. She did seem to be more isolated. From time to time, she would complain that she just couldn't live like we did. To her, our home was too restrictive; she claimed she was suffocating. Nancy and I began to realize that we had little left to offer her that she was open to receive. The grace for her to be with us seemed to have left us all.

After several months' stay, one day, without a word to us, she disappeared. The next day one of our friends told us that they had seen her miles away, walking back towards Atlanta—an eighteen-mile walk. In all likelihood, she was returning to the street life. We didn't even want to think about all that that would mean. Nancy and I never saw her again, although later we heard from soup kitchen volunteers that she had turned up again at St. Luke's. Marlene was a truly troubled person, but she knew that Jesus loved her. She just had a whole lot of difficulty being able to receive that love and the people God had allowed into her life; it seemed as though her tormented mind considered almost everyone—and everything—a threat.

One thing we were sure of—Marlene was aware that God knew who she was, He hadn't given up on her, and He had sent her help. She also knew and accepted the fact that now Joey had a real chance in life, that she had done a very good thing in allowing him a family and a home. Perhaps giving Joey up was the best thing she had ever done. And, who knows, having done this good thing for Joey, possibly a day would come when she would treat herself as well.

Practice hospitality to one another—that is those of the household of faith. Be hospitable, a lover of strangers, with brotherly affection for the unknown guests, the foreigners, the poor and all others who come your way who are of Christ's body and do it ungrudgingly—cordially and graciously without complaining. I Peter 4:9

Toni

Toni showed up in the same time frame as Marlene and Joey. She was the nicest looking guest at the soup kitchen. In her early twenties, about 115 lbs, 5'5", she was rather frail. She dressed as attractively as one could, not having any money—she was even somewhat stylish. She had a boyfriend, a big, aggressive, rough type of character, with whom she had been living. When Tyrell and Toni came together to the soup kitchen, they would sit with the crowd, wherever he wanted to sit. He looked like someone capable of stirring up a group, or trouble, with ease. When she came alone, she tried to sit by herself, remaining close to the volunteer servers and away from most of the others. She was fairly easy to talk to, especially to Nancy. Their relationship took on something of a mother/daughter quality that Toni seemed to hunger for and likely had never experienced.

The more we were around her, the more we feared that something even worse might happen to her—like being badly taken advantage of and violated. She had that totally vulnerable look about her. Over the course of a couple of weeks of sharing and discussing, Toni agreed to take a chance and break from her boyfriend and come to our home. It would be tough—not only for her but also for our family. But it seemed the right thing to do. Nancy and I were somewhat surprised by her courage.

114

So, with Toni in the backseat of our car, we left St. Luke's, and, following her directions, went into the very dangerous neighborhood where she and her boyfriend were living. The neighborhood would have looked and felt ominous in the best of circumstances, but on this escape mission, with the clock running, we feared for all three of us. Tyrell was somewhere else at the time (we didn't know for how long), so we all rushed in to grab some of Toni's personal belongings and get out. We got that accomplished, unnoticed, and headed for our home, twenty miles away.

Since Marlene and Joey were already living with us, we added Toni to the mix. The three of them had seen each other at St. Luke's. Our own kids looked rather overwhelmed by it all. Our home was beginning to look like a cross between a home, a soup kitchen, and a night shelter, but we were sure we were doing it for Jesus and for His "little ones." On several occasions, our own kids voiced some doubt about our judgment, but we didn't pay a lot of attention. This was a new opportunity for them to learn to share and reach out to the less fortunate, to adjust to the "real world" we lived in. They sometimes had trouble appreciating this; other times, they surprised us all by how well they accepted it and stepped up.

After Toni had been with us about six days, she came into the kitchen just before supper and told us she had a confession to make. She was sure that after the confession, we would not accept her anymore. She said that what she had to confess was so terrible that we would not be able to deal with it, and she would have to leave our home.

With that, at the prompting of the Holy Spirit, Nancy asked her if what she had to confess was that she was really not female but male. That thought had not crossed either of our minds before, but that was it! A pure word of knowledge from the Holy Spirit and, of course, right on! That was the true confession. So Toni became Anthony! Forget supper and everything else. We entered into our first deliverance session without warning. It would last past midnight, with Anthony flat on the floor, feet up the wall, thrashing around, speaking in different, distressed voices—sometimes that of his mother, sometimes his aunt, sometimes demons. We used crucifixes, holy water, prayer language—everything we had. We called in a friend to help, and by the end of the session, we could at least see some tangible results. Anthony's wig, false fingernails, and jewelry came off, and he exchanged the women's clothes for some clothes belonging to our boys. He was being transformed right in front of our eyes.

The next morning, Anthony looked better, even peaceful, and Nancy and I took him to be prayed over by Fr. Al, a Spirit-led older priest that friends had told us knew how to deal with evil spirits. With the three of us in his office, Fr. Al began to read a simple rite of exorcism and called for the spirit to identify itself. Instantly we heard the voice of Anthony's mother—and then his aunt—speak right on command. We had heard them both the night before. They each gave their names, in different voices and in different speaking styles.

We were beginning to know that God is in control and has dominion over all evil spirits. They have to obey in the name of Jesus. Fr. Al prayed over Anthony, sprinkled him with holy water, encouraged the three of us, and sent us home.

Anthony told us that his mother had died during his first two weeks of life and he was raised by his aunt. As a child, he had been sexually taken advantage of and violated by older boys. Some of the adults in his family knew about this vile treatment but had not done anything to stop it, and so it had continued for years. Since he had been so small and frail as a boy growing up, and whipped up on so many times by bullies, he had decided his chances would be better as a female than as a homosexual male. His dominating, roughneck boyfriend, Tyrell, had Anthony taking female hormones to speed up the transformation process.

The day after Fr. Al's exorcism ministry, Anthony went out and applied for a job, for the first time in his life as a male—and got it. He was to start working the very next day. He surprised all of us, perhaps himself the most, and did well in his job as a waiter. He even worked overtime because he was doing so well. We were amazed by his daily progress.

During Anthony's second week with us, we were interrupted one night at our prayer meeting by a phone call from one of our kids. A taxi had just brought Tyrell to our home and he had taken Anthony away. As is true with many people who have had troubled backgrounds, one of the hardest things for them to do is to stay clear of their old friends. Often, when their old friends locate them, they come and talk them into going back, or take them back forcibly.

We didn't see Anthony for several weeks. Then one day he showed up at St. Luke's, looking just like Toni used to look, a chic, attractive female. Nancy talked to him, hoping to convince him to try again. Though embarrassed, he finally agreed and headed back to our house with her. As they pulled into the driveway, he began to take off the wig, fingernails, and jewelry, and came in ready to borrow our boys' clothes. When our kids came home to find him there, they were somewhat perplexed by it all (but also hopeful for him). Once again, with no problem, Toni got a job. The employer liked him, he did well with his new work, waiting tables, and he appeared to be adjusting to his new life and surroundings. It seemed a little easier for him this time to think of himself as a male. As he went about, handling his job and his schedule efficiently, even our kids were gradually coming to accept him more and think he could be a regular guy.

One Saturday morning, when he didn't come up for breakfast, I went downstairs to check on him. He wasn't there—gone again, the room vacated sometime during the night. We never saw Anthony/Toni again. It is hard to break from demonic strongholds—the past had gotten to him again with its powerful pull.

Undoubtedly, Anthony left in better shape than he came, so that's a positive. He had experienced two periods of time in a non-threatening family. For him, that was a first. He had gotten a glimpse of what it was to go out into the world as a man, and be accepted and treated like one. We also know that Anthony is in the Lord's hands—and our God is able. Our part is to do what He asks, and what we can, and not grieve over the results. We only see a small part of the picture, and it's not over yet.

For everyone who calls upon the name of the Lord (invoking Him as Lord) will be saved. Romans 10:15

New Back—New Direction

The fall of 1979 brought a sudden, severe challenge. On the morning of Friday, October 16, I awoke as usual, but that was the end of normalcy. While attempting to get out of bed, I realized that I could not stand up. My back was totally locked up.

I had experienced sporadic back problems for years. When a flare-up happened, it usually felt like there were two metal plates stacked vertically in my back, grating against each other. These occurrences had been happening more frequently in recent months, but on each previous occasion, I could, after taking care in loosening up, still manage to move about, carefully—and in awhile, my back pain would ease up. Not this morning, though. My back was completely frozen, leaving no option but to ease out of bed on my hands and knees, in excruciating pain, and crawl down the stairs backwards to the main level of our home.

With a lot of effort and sharp pain, I was able to crawl into the den and stretch out on the floor, face up, hoping my back would release and become functional. It didn't. For a self-employed builder with no medical insurance, this was a daunting way to start the day—definitely not what I had planned or expected. Suddenly my mind was filled with worry and apprehension. Nancy, of course, was very concerned, and as the day wore on, with my condition unchanged, she called for an appointment with a chiropractor in the area.

That afternoon, after a lot of time, effort, and more pain, and with much help from Nancy, who was straining to assist me, I arrived at the office of Dr. Lowell, the chiropractor. He took an x-ray of my back and reported that it showed an old fracture that had healed in a crooked, torqued manner. The muscles on one side of my back were doing all the work, trying to hold the back straight. He wondered if I had ever been in a bad accident, like a car wreck? After a few minutes of "therapy," which was more painful than anything I had yet experienced, Dr. Lowell ceased all his efforts and we left.

Saturday brought no improvement, so we made another appointment with Dr. Lowell. Nancy and I worked our way to his office, with difficulty similar to that of the day before. After a few minutes of working on me, he could see the futility of his efforts and gave up. He said the only thing he had left to suggest, which I probably wouldn't want, was to have him re-break and set my back properly. He was right, I declined—and we left feeling worse about everything than when we had come the first time. Later in the day, I realized that this was the tenth anniversary of the car wreck that had obviously fractured my back. There was no celebration, though. I was hurting and I was really worried—big time. I even had trouble reflecting on Jesus saving my life that night with the seat belt.

Now I knew my only hope was that the Lord would see fit to heal me. We had recently seen a number of people physically healed through prayer and the laying on of hands (I was coming to value this phenomenon and expect it more all the time). None of their ailments seemed as severe as my back problem, though. Also, I found it was easier to "believe for" others' healing through prayer than to believe for my own healing. But I knew God's promises. I needed to ask and believe, even for myself.

The following day, Sunday, brought very little change. I knew, though, that I had to be at church, even if I could only stand against the wall the entire time. Nancy got me there, very carefully, and that's all I could do, stand at the back of the church by the wall, very still and cautious. No hugs or quick movements at this service—I knew I could only stand before the Lord, presenting a need that only He could meet.

The church service concluded and the congregation began filing out. Most were people I didn't know—which was a good thing. Presently, along came Maryanna, a young girl from our prayer group. Maryanna was a pretty, vibrant seventeen-year-old who had been coming to the prayer meetings with her parents throughout the year. She had a strong, pure faith. If God said it, she believed it, and that settled it. She also had been baptized in the Spirit and was very charismatic; she prayed for everything.

Noticing my pained expression and rigid posture as I stood at the church door, she asked what was wrong. When I explained my situation to her, Maryanna said, "Well, let's just pray and ask Jesus to heal your back." With that, she bowed her head, put both hands up on my shoulders, and began praying away in the Spirit (the practice of tongues, or prayer language).

I'm sure this shocked a few of the parishioners as they were leaving church, seeing this vibrant young woman totally engaged in prayer, chattering away in an unfamiliar language as if her life depended on it. It crossed my mind as she was praying that some of the people, those who already suspected that Nancy and I were quite radical, would now believe this for certain. This could be the final straw. But that was okay, we believed in prayers for healing—and I needed healing much more than I needed their approval. After awhile, Maryanna concluded praying, and as we opened our eyes, we saw that the church and parking lot had both emptied. Wow!

What a prayer—"out of the mouths of babes," as they say—and what faith!

Over the next three days, my stiffness eased and the pain gradually subsided. On Wednesday, upon waking and sitting up in bed, something seemed noticeably different. For years, I had had to sit up slowly, brace my back with my arms and hands, and slowly rotate my upper body to get loosened up to stand and move around. Not today. My back felt totally free and loose. Upon moving more and testing it, I suddenly realized the Lord had done it. He had healed my back just as we had asked!

It was the last time I ever experienced a back problem—of any kind! Thirty years of strenuous physical activity and working out since have never again bothered my healed back. Jesus is the great physician—when He heals us, we are healed indeed. Hallelujah!

Epilogue

Three years before my healing, I had built a moderate-sized house in a nice suburban area for a doctor, Martin, and his wife, Gwen. They proved to be very agreeable to build for—altogether nice, considerate people. This house was to be their interim home until the bigger, final house was built. I was to design and build the final house for them in the coming year; we had already selected and procured a large, beautiful lot in a great location. During the three years, I had stopped in at Martin's medical practice a few times with minor ailments and needs. He had always taken care of me, more as a friend and as his builder than as a patient. A couple of years earlier, on one of those occasions, I had shared with him about my recent conversion to Jesus and Christianity. Martin was not a Christian, and had surprised me by his discomfort at my sharing about this major change in my life and my focus. He seemed to quickly distance himself from me. His response seemed very out of character; his manner completely unlike his always-personable demeanor. I was caught off guard.

Now, when the Lord healed my back, Martin was one of the first people who came to mind. I wanted to show him what Jesus had done—the practice of medicine and healing at its best and, I suppose, the wonderful blessing in my new life. So at the first opportunity, I stopped by his office. Upon hearing my exuberant report, his pleasant look instantly changed to a troubled one and he directed me right into his exam room.

To my surprise, this kind and considerate doctor and friend had now taken on a distressed countenance. Brusquely telling me to lie down on the exam table, Martin reached down, put his hand under my right heel and quickly raised my leg to full extension—straight up—then released it and let it free fall. He then repeated the same process with my left leg, raising and dropping it, each time looking right into my eyes. I felt and showed absolutely no pain as he did this, smiling through it all. With no other conversation, he tersely said, "You're healed," turned on a dime, and disappeared into his office. I would never see or talk with him again.

Two weeks later, I received a formal letter from Martin. He was withdrawing his verbal design and build agreement with me for the new house. They would be going a different route, using a different designer and builder. It took a couple of weeks for me to adjust to the loss of that big contract. I had looked forward to it and had financially counted on it. It would have been their dream house and a six- to eight-month, full-time project. As it turned out, I would never build another house.

When we pray and ask the Lord for healings, we shouldn't be surprised that He gives them. When we pray and ask for the Lord's will and direction in our lives, we shouldn't be surprised when He orchestrates change. Sometime even a major, unexpected one.

I can now look back and see the Lord changing my path, taking me out of home design and building and into commercial woodwork. He orchestrated this change easily, it was like walking through a doorway. I was involved with the same men and the same equipment, but for a different purpose. We were contracted and working on the first job almost before I realized it. I don't remember a single day of lost time. God can move mountains!

My prideful days as a "big-time Atlanta designer and homebuilder" had come to an end. I had known for awhile that designing and building these "bigger than life" houses had consumed far too much of my attention and focus, and had fed my pride excessively. The Lord probably saw them as an idol, a stumbling block to His being my "treasure." He was pruning me for the days to come. I couldn't see it then, but would later realize that losing the contract to build that nice house was probably not nearly so much an act on Martin's part as it was a movement of the Lord to change the course of our life. This time He had used Martin, an unbeliever, to accomplish this Kingdom work he was about.

I had needed my back healed, but I certainly couldn't afford to remain in idolatry, putting anything ahead of the Lord. I remembered the Scripture, *"Little children, guard yourself against idols."* As for the blessing that would follow this stepping-stone change, we had not the slightest clue. Nancy and I both knew, though, that we were in His hands and on a trip. He held the keys to our future and we were learning every day to be grateful, and to trust.

Do not seek what you shall eat and what you shall drink and do not keep worrying,

For all these things the nations of the world eagerly seek, but your Father knows that you need these things. But seek for His Kingdom and these things shall be added to you. For where your treasure is, there will your heart be also. Luke 12:29-31, 34

Kingdom-Minded Construction

Construction sites can easily be a breeding ground for rowdiness, rebellion, pride, profanity and ungodly conversation or commentary. Construction work, somehow, has the ability to bring out the worst in men, who quickly sink to the lowest level. But like many other occupations, it also has the potential to build up the individual and bring out the best in him, inspiring him to do his finest work, with the highest standards. On a construction site, the believer is called to set the tone. The Holy Spirit watches to see if we're willing to step up to the occasion.

Sometimes just bringing a Bible or cross and placing it in a conspicuous place while working will immediately change the spirit of the area. Bringing Jesus to work and staying tuned in to the Holy Spirit, and on duty, changes everything. A work environment can change 180 degrees in minutes. Consistency in faith is absolutely essential. Openly praying on construction sites does wonders; being ready and expecting to pray over the workers unlocks a storehouse of blessings. Paying close attention—watching and listening—for what's really going on is imperative.

Allowing space for Plan A (what the Holy Spirit wants to do) to override Plan B (our best plan), and then flowing right with it seems to be the key. I think of that as giving the Lord permission to "call an audible," or change the play at the last second, and our part is to embrace His plan with our whole heart. Living on this level brings an intensity and spontaneity to everyday life that's not attainable any other way. It's bringing "God's High Road" right through the guys' world.

I admit—I love work! And it's a great opportunity to evangelize. Men listen to those they respect; good work and courage usually gain their respect. There are many memorable construction and work-related stories, but the following are some of my favorites.

Man Down at Houlihan's

On our first commercial wood job, we were responsible for the wood interior of a new restaurant and bar named Houlihan's, a place a lot like TGI Friday's. It had an ornate bar area with stained glass ceilings and walls made of wood, with all types of wood detailing. Much of the woodwork was fabricated elsewhere and sent in for installation, although we did fabricate some on site. The owners of the restaurant supplied a substantial collection of architectural antiques and arti-facts to flavor the décor, many fine stained glass windows and other valuable pieces—mostly out of closed churches in Europe—that had been bought at auction and shipped over. Our group of six would work there for four months, helping to turn the owners' vision into an intriguing reality.

We had been there a couple of weeks and were just getting the feel of the place. I was trying to familiarize myself with operating in that type of environment, since I had been a residential general contractor for the previous seven years. This was new territory. I was used to being the authority figure on the site, regardless of which tradesmen were involved at a given moment. Adapting to being just one more trade among many would require time and effort. Asking subcontractors to work with my men, instead of just expecting them to, was definitely an adjustment for me. Even switching over to what was basically a concrete and steel setting was awkward and required a different approach and some additional equipment. This new work also had me spending more of my time as a woodworker and less time as a supervisor or designer.

In our short time there, I had tried to bring in the presence of the Lord and establish the best work space, attitude and outlook that I could. It was a challenge, as commercial work seemed a lot less personal than residential jobs; some workers hardly spoke in passing. Because of my Bible on site, some of them had already begun to suspect I might be a little strange, even an extremist. They kept their distance but also kept an eye on me.

One morning at around 10 am, our men were all in the bar area installing a large mahogany bar when suddenly one of the electricians came into our area, white as a sheet, and flattened himself against the wall. On earlier occasions we had all noticed this young guy, who was in his early twenties. He was usually playing his radio loud (I had already confronted him about the volume) and was rather boisterous and cocky, but now he seemed scared stiff. He could hardly talk. We asked him what was wrong, and he was barely able to tell us that one of the sheetrock men had just taken a bad fall onto the concrete slab floor in the next room.

We all rushed in there to see what had happened. The room was deathly quiet. The man down was named Donnie, and he was said to be a very good sheetrock finisher. He had made a big-time mistake— maybe he was too good, and overconfident. He had put a ladder on top of the scaffold (you just don't do that) and was trying to finish the interior of a skylight when something slipped and he came down from a considerable height. Falling all the way from the skylight, he landed over a one-step transition in the slab floor, flat on his back right over that break.

As construction guys are inclined to do at times, they all just stood there, thoroughly overwhelmed, not knowing what to do. Someone had called 911 and that was it for them. Donnie was lying on the floor, totally out of it, no one was anywhere near him. Because of the experiences I had been having at prayer groups and elsewhere, and probably because of my own wreck as well, the only natural thing to do was to quickly get beside Donnie, kneel down, lay hands on him, and start praying over him. So that's what I did. It definitely wasn't anything these guys had ever seen. They didn't have a clue as to what in the world was going on. Even my long-time employees had never seen a man down, badly hurt, being prayed over. They were motionless—all eyes and ears. I was aware of their intense watching, but was involved in something far more important. I continued to pray over Donnie until the EMTs arrived and began working on him. The EMTs' main concern seemed to be the possibility of a broken back or serious neck injury.

They brought the stretcher in and very slowly and carefully strapped Donnie in, loaded him up, and whisked him off to the hospital. From the time of Donnie's fall until the ambulance pulled away, the whole group of construction guys was dumbfounded and silent, pretty much in shock. They had all been working with Donnie for days. Although he was quiet and kept to himself, he was respected and well liked by the others. They all knew him as a real professional who did quality work and was good to work with. Now he was hurt and headed for the hospital. They were sure that he had a broken back or worse. It was hard to tell whether they were scared for Donnie or for themselves. Commercial construction can have its dangers and surprises.

Sometime after that, at lunchtime, my men and I left together to eat. When we came back, we were met at the door by a big surprise. All of the construction guys who had been present and watching were now waiting for us, lined up inside the big room. They looked like a group of miners waiting to hear the news about friends trapped in the mine. Watching me pray over Donnie was an unfamiliar and challenging experience for them, and now they wanted to know what had really happened, what I was doing while I was kneeling down with Donnie on the floor. It was a great chance to explain to those men the power of prayer, the power of laying on of hands, how Jesus heals, how He promises healing in Scripture, how He tells us we will experience the same as we walk in the Spirit and call upon Him. Since only the Holy Spirit could have stirred them to ask, and kept them still to listen, I was very thorough with my answer, trying not to rush or abbreviate it.

They were very somber and attentive to the whole dissertation, didn't show any doubts or skepticism whatsoever. Their unspoken respect for Jesus was noteworthy. They appeared to be held in time and space by something greater than themselves. They just took what I said as the absolute truth. They were very concerned about what had happened to Donnie as a result of that fall. Would he make it back, be able to walk, and be able to work again and support his wife and family? I told them only the Lord knew, but Donnie definitely needed our ongoing prayers—they were his hope.

I found out later from the project manager, Rolf, the name of the hospital where they had taken him. Rolf was very concerned about Donnie but declined when I invited him to come with me to the hospital to see Donnie at the end of the day. Rolf had been shaken by Donnie's fall and my praying over him, and wasn't ready for anything else—the experience had scared him.

When I arrived at the hospital I found Donnie's wife, Trish, sitting by his bed. Her routine that day had been instantly changed by a very scary phone call. She had been at the hospital for several hours, and was still processing what had happened. At first glance, it was obvious that Donnie was doing far better than anyone could have expected. He told Trish who I was. He didn't know my name (and probably not even my trade), but he somehow knew that I was the guy who had been down next to him praying over him after the fall. He looked healed and refreshed. The doctor's prognosis for him, even then, was great. Nothing was broken. Thank you, Jesus! The three of us joined in a prayer of thanksgiving for God's mercy on their young family and for Donnie's complete healing and recovery.

The next morning, I gave the men a report on my visit with Donnie and his wife, and his condition. As they quietly went back to work, they seemed reflective and grateful that Donnie seemed to have avoided significant injury. Only a few days later, Donnie walked back into Houlihan's to visit the guys. He told them it wouldn't be long before he would be back at work with them. No broken back, no broken bones, no broken anything. He was improving each day from the trauma of the impact.

This was my first experience of seeing the Lord heal someone right in the midst of a gripping construction accident. He did it among worldly construction workers who had never seen or heard anything about the healing power of Jesus and rarely spoke His name except in vain. Jesus was needed that day and was a welcome "walk-on" on the construction site; we were all glad to see Him show up. We were each touched by Him that day.

They will lay their hands on the sick, and they will be healed… And they went out and preached everywhere, while the Lord kept working with them and confirming the message by the attesting signs and miracles that closely accompanied. Mark 16:18 and 20

Jumping Red and the Tower

At Houlihan's, we were subcontractors for the first time to a commercial general contractor named Miko. Miko was headquartered on the 19th floor of Tower Place in Buckhead, an upscale suburb in north Atlanta. Tower Place stood 29 stories high, built of steel and blue glass, an imposing landmark even in a thriving area like Buckhead.

My working arrangement with Miko required me to go to the Tower each week to turn in our charges and expenses and to collect for the work of the week before. Since most of our contracts over the next couple of years would be with Miko, going to the Tower on Fridays became a regular thing. My trips were basically to meet with their comptroller, John D. In the coming months, my men would refer to John as the "money man."

My trips to the Tower became dual-purpose. One purpose was for business, and the other was for evangelical outreach. Certainly several of those at Miko needed evangelizing, as did many others in the Tower. I had already experienced several divine encounters there.

There were two elevators in the building. The first stopped at each of the first eighteen floors, and the second elevator was the express elevator that went straight to the nineteenth floor before stopping. That became "my elevator." The elevator trip took about forty-five seconds from the time the doors closed until the elevator stopped and the doors opened on the nineteenth floor. In some ways, elevator ministry is a lot like hitchhiker ministry; you have a limited window of opportunity. Many of these encounters over the weeks and months were almost as if the Lord had planted these people just to hear the Good News. Some of my favorites were the men in suits with briefcases scurrying to the next big appointment. Many of "the suits" seemed to need evangelizing (they had money on their minds), and my Jesus talk hit them like a sledge. Probably some of them thought the fast-track Tower was immune to the "God stuff."

One day, the Lord even sent a woman who was returning from a funeral, having just buried her best friend. Together, we experienced some wonderful moments of hope and consolation—God's perfect timing. The elevator trips up and down on Fridays were truly memorable, something I looked forward to, expecting the Holy Spirit to do something special, and allow me to participate.

Some months after completing the work for Houlihan's, Miko had a new restaurant to build named Sundance. It was located in Roswell, about a half hour north of Atlanta. The construction was held up by rainy weather. Atlanta had a very wet winter that had delayed the pouring of the foundation and slab. This made the entire project run well behind schedule. The owners of the restaurant had little empathy and still demanded that their restaurant be finished on time. When Miko was ready for us, we heard two basic things from them. They wanted us in—and they wanted us out. In other words, get in, get it done and get out.

Commercial woodwork wasn't always that gratifying from the customer appreciation standpoint. I upheld the same quality standards that we had lived by as luxury homebuilders, but sometimes we never heard the first good word. We learned to accept that as the way it was. Sundance would become our highest-stress commercial job yet. Miko was obviously getting tons of pressure from the restaurant chain to get finished. They had a project manager on Sundance who couldn't handle pressure. He believed in passing it on as quickly as possible with a little extra push of his own.

His name was Kyle, and he was in his late thirties, an average-seeming guy, except for being high strung. He had flaming red hair and a very short temper. Kyle was short on communication skills and quick to get into frustration and emotion. My men soon came to refer to him as "Jumping Red" because the slightest stress or provocation seemed to almost lift him off the floor; his body language gave the impression of someone jumping up and down inside, with steam coming out of his ears. I'm sure he couldn't see that, but it seemed obvious to everyone else. Even his fellow Miko workers agreed that "Jumping Red" was the only name for him.

As weeks turned into months, Miko and Jumping Red's patience shortened and tempers flared. Their attempt to deal with the situation meant applying more pressure on us, suggesting that I hire more men to get finished. I didn't even know where to start looking, so I just increased the hours of the men I had, and kept bearing down.

One morning, as we were getting started, we found Jumping Red had stationed himself right in our work area. He had the distinct look of someone who had just taken a lashing from someone "higher up," and had decided he was going to pass it on to us. After a few minutes of my trying to communicate with him in the hopes of resolving the situation, it was obvious that things were going from bad to worse fast. Red was way beyond reason. My men had all stopped working and were standing and watching to see where this was going. They weren't used to seeing me this hot, either. And then, I made a snap decision. I told Red I was going to the Tower to see John, the "money man," to get this thing straightened out. My men were to keep working while I was gone, and when I got back I would let them know if we would finish the job or load up and leave. We weren't going to work under these conditions and put up with this stuff!

With that, I left in a flurry, jumped in my El Camino, and headed for the Tower. Driving down the road, I could hardly believe what I had just said to my men. I had never walked off a job or left a contract unfulfilled. I knew, for sure, I must be really upset. I was hoping the drive to the Tower would settle me down so I could calmly meet with John, but that did not happen; instead, I got more upset. By the time I drove into the parking lot of the Tower, I felt as angry as Jumping Red must have felt. I even remembered the many good experiences on the elevator and told myself we definitely were not doing that today. I wanted to have all my anger intact and ready to use on Miko. No time or energy for witnessing this day! I was single minded and ready to unload.

Striding into the lobby area, I ran headlong into Rolf, the project manager from our earlier Houlihan's job. We had worked together for four months on Houlihan's, and I had found him to be a good project manager. He was a hard-nosed New Yorker, about my age, who had been out there for a long time. He didn't cut any slack, but he was a fair, efficient project manager. Rolf and I had developed a good rapport, mostly built on respect; we both knew what to expect from the other. I had tried various ways during those months to evangelize him. He would patiently listen, but was noncommittal. I knew the Lord was dealing with him, but he wasn't ripe to be picked yet. He definitely wasn't one to be pushed or rushed, either.

Rolf and I were both surprised to find ourselves waiting for the express elevator at the same time; this had never happened before. Rolf asked what I was doing at the Tower. He could tell that I was upset. I simply told him that Jumping Red was out of control and I was coming to see John, that we were going to get it worked out or else I was pulling my men off the job. Without saying a word, Rolf just nodded knowingly. He knew Jumping Red far better than I did, and showed no surprise.

Presently, the elevator door opened and we went into opposite corners—leaning against the elevator walls. The door began to close, and then out of nowhere, as the door was barely still open, a body hurtled through the gap and a man landed on his feet in the center of the elevator floor, almost like a paratrooper dropping from the sky. He landed, the door closed behind him and up the three of us went. He was a dominating sight. An athletic black man in his mid-twenties, in peak physical condition, muscular and poised, up on the balls of his feet as if to leap. He was looking right into my face, with an incredible smile. I had never seen such big, white, shining teeth. He looked as if he would literally explode with sheer joy.

This had definitely not been my best morning. I had reverted to my old way of acting—reacting to the circumstances. Definitely, I had not put on the "new man" this morning. Looking the overjoyed stranger in the eye, and with a displeased, impatient tone in my voice, I said, "What are you so happy about?" Without a pause, he enthusiastically said, "'Cause it's Friday and I don't have to work this weekend."

It's hard to explain my next action, since it was way out there, and even in an extreme moment, pretty suspect. For some reason, I reached out, and with the flat of my hand, briskly slapped him in the stomach—his good, solid, six-pack-ab stomach—much like a coach would do to an athlete. Then, like a drill sergeant, I said, "That's not what you're so happy about. What are you so happy about?" raising my voice and demanding the real, actual answer.

With that, he threw his head back, smiled even bigger, and sang out ecstatically, "I'm happy 'cause my name is written in the Lamb's Book of Life. You give your life to Jesus and yours will be, too!" Instantly, the doors opened and he rocketed through the opening, vanishing from sight. A quick breeze and silence replaced him. Rocked back into the corner of the elevator by the sheer energy of the experience, I turned toward Rolf, who was plastered in the other corner, looking overwhelmed. I said, "Rolf, you ever see that guy before?"

Very emphatically, he said, "No!"

I said, "You know who he was, don't you?" With total assurance, he nodded his head.

"He was an Angel," I replied.

"Yeah, I know," Rolf agreed, with no hesitation or doubt at all.

Wow! The Lord had sent an Angel to visit me—and Rolf, who needed power evangelizing—on "my" elevator. Suddenly, I realized that the elevator never had been "mine," but always the Lord's, and He had sent an Angel to speak correction straight into my heart.

We walked out of the elevator together quietly down the hall to Miko. There was not a trace of our Angel, who had disappeared as fast as he had come. I strode right into John's office. He was waiting for me, looking very apprehensive, girding for the worst. Sundance had been an ongoing pain for him, too, in many ways. With that, I sat down in a chair across from his desk and began to tell him the story of our Angel on the elevator, explaining it in great detail. He was hanging on every word. Then, surprising myself as much as John, I found myself leaning back in the chair, propping my feet up on his desk, and saying, "John, I'm going back to Sundance. We are going to finish the job the best we possibly can. It doesn't matter what you or Red or any of the rest of Miko does, we are going to finish it, the very best we can, just like we said we would. 'Cause, John, my name is written in the Lamb's Book of Life. You give your life to Jesus, and yours will be, too." John was stunned and speechless, riveted in his chair.

With that, I headed back to Sundance to tell my men about the Angel Visitor and his word, and our plans. We would finish, regardless, and it would be fine. My guys knew the Lord had sent an angel to speak to us. It was settled. We had new momentum, and it would be plenty.

About a year later, John gave his life to the Lord and his name would also be written in the Lamb's Book of Life.

The rest of the project at Sundance continued to be high pressure, but there was an abiding peace in doing it. Now, the demands weren't getting to us, we were just dealing with each day and situation as it came. As pressure mounted on Miko to get finished, they made another request for me to hire more people. When I didn't, they informed me that they were recruiting three woodworkers from another company to put on my payroll, under my direction, to help us get finished. We were saddled with these three men for a couple of weeks, and that caused far more distraction than production. Two of them were lackadaisical brothers in their forties. About all we ever saw them doing was talking to each other or leaning on a machine and smoking.

Adding them to our payroll cost me about $2,000, from which we could see no real results; we had to rework most of what little they did. We finished Sundance and I absorbed the monetary loss. A couple of times during the following months, I asked the Holy Spirit, "Lord, how come when I am trying to do the right thing, I get saddled with the loss? And the non-believers wind up making out like bandits?" I didn't hear anything back from the Lord, and I wasn't really surprised. I have since come to know better than to ask such questions.

Epilogue

About a year after completing Sundance, I got a surprising phone call. Jumping Red was on the phone—the most subdued, pleasant Red I had ever heard. He needed my help. Two of the projects that we had done at Sundance had been a long sit-up bar and another, smaller bar. They were to receive a finish later in thick, clear epoxy by another contractor. The paint contractors had taken that on, not knowing how to do it—and had messed it up. After a third effort they had totally ruined both tops, which now had to be replaced.

Miko wanted us to come back and replace the tops. Before I could say anything at all, Red assured me it was not my problem. Miko was ready to pick up all the costs. Trying to be as civil as possible, I assured Red that I knew it wasn't our problem, but I didn't know if I wanted any more of Sundance at any cost. With that, Red said they would pay me $1,500 to come and replace the tops. I suppose the ensuing silence was so loud to his ears that without me saying a word, he then said, "$2,000." Now the Holy Spirit just kept me quiet, with the phone held out from my ear. After a pause, he said, "$2,500." Since he had started talking money I had not yet said a word. After another moment of silence he said, "$3,000."

With that, I said, "We will come and do it. When do you want us there?" Three of us went to Sundance and replaced the tops. The materials and labor cost about $1,000 total. Then it dawned on me that the Lord had just restored the $2,000 loss of the year before—virtually to the penny. God is good, and He takes care of His people! I came again to learn, "Do the best you can, do the right thing, trust the Lord with the results. He will take care of all the rest!" And timing *always* belongs to Him.

I also came to understand the Angel's message more fully. "Give your life to Jesus" wasn't a salvation message for me, I had given my life to the Lord years earlier, but this time it was an "everything" message. That day, on the elevator, my life still included old sins like unchecked anger and pride that I had chosen to hang onto. Finally, by giving that anger (and some pride) to the Lord, I got His peace in return. Wow!

His peace brought completion and success to the job at Sundance—something that anger and pride could never do!

No temple could be seen in the city, for the Lord God Almighty and the Lamb are worshiped in it everywhere... Nothing evil will be permitted in it [the city], no one immoral or dishonest—but only those whose names are written in the Lamb's Book of Life. Revelations 21:22/27

And best of all, I truly believe that my name is written in the Lamb's Book of Life.

Go See Tommy

After about six years of juggling debts, accounts, receipts, and cash on hand, etc., and trying to keep our heads above the financial rapids, we came face to face with an immovable crisis. A sizable amount was due to a bank the next day, with no way to pay. The manager of the bank called me at home, the night before, to make sure I knew.

As I was driving up Northside Drive in Atlanta from a commercial woodwork job, straining my mind for some possible solution, the *Voice* gently said, "Go see Tommy, he is supposed to help."

There was no doubt in my mind what that meant or who it was, though I barely knew Tommy. At the time I was less than a block away from his business; it was just over the hill, the next turn to the right.

Tommy owned and ran an electronics business, the kind you used to see before Radio Shack. His father had started it decades earlier, probably in the same location. I knew the ramshackle old building, since I had renovated two offices there the previous year—a job I hadn't really wanted (I considered the building below my standards). I had spent a month working there alone, with only passing encounters with Tommy and his employees. Yet, I came to know Tommy as a spirit-filled Baptist brother, devoted in his faith, who had even brought his wife to one of our Catholic sharing groups. Aside from that, I hardly knew him. Going to see Tommy for help was not my style. Going to see anyone wasn't. I would rather have taken a beating than ask anyone for help, but in fact, I was already taking a horrific beating—and still needed help!

The Holy Spirit knows our weaknesses (and the things we avoid) and didn't allow me time to talk myself out of turning toward Tommy's parking lot. I then began a discussion with myself, reasoning that he probably wouldn't be there or would be too busy—and all those other disclaimers. As I entered the parking lot, it looked almost full. When I saw that, I was sure Tommy would be too busy. I just wanted to turn around and leave, but the Holy Spirit was really pushing me to be courageous and trust. He wouldn't let me choke. I got out and headed for the front door, wishing I was anywhere other than there. Pride, doubt and fear were all crouched, ready to take their best shots at me. I was hoping for the best, but fearful of the worst—really just following the *Voice's* directive.

Opening the door, looking in at a large group of customers sitting at the counter, my eyes immediately met Tommy's across the heads of everyone. With a rather surprised but exuberant greeting, he called out, "Hey, what are you doing here?" I had not seen or talked to him since finishing the project on his building the year before.

It was one of those head-snapping moments. With Tommy's enthusiastic greeting, all of the people at the counter turned in unison to see who might be standing there. I made my best effort to look and sound calm and said, "The Lord just told me to come by and see you for a minute, but I see you're really busy and I'll just wait over here."

Hearing the Lord's name used in public, in a business, seemed to jolt most of the customers, and they quickly turned back, looking down intently at their catalogs. As if the whole thing was staged, Tommy said, "Oh, it's fine, I'll be right out," and passing his customer on to one of his salespeople, quickly came out from behind the counter toward me.

Tommy was a tall, lanky, purposeful man about fifty, balding and very intense. We met in the center of the floor and he looked at me, totally focused, and quietly repeated, "The Lord told you to come by and see me?"

All I could manage was, "Yes."

With heightened interest, and great respect (for the Lord), Tommy asked, "Did He say what about?"

Trying my best to look him in the eye, I came out with the difficult and painful words, "He said you are supposed to help."

With real empathy, almost as if he was expecting me, Tommy put his arm around my shoulder, like a big brother, and in an encouraging and even enthusiastic sort of way, repeated, almost reverently,

"He said I was supposed to help, huh?" He seemed to be moving the process along more than I was.

"Yes, that was what He said." I nodded my head, hoping to add strength to the words. We were walking straight towards his office with our entire attention focused on this encounter. Respectfully, confidentially, Tommy lowered his voice and asked, "Did He say how much?"

Without breaking stride, I said, "$6,500," trying my hardest to sound normal.

With no more than a raised eyebrow he repeated, "$6,500, huh?" It seemed that he heard the amount not as a question or a suggestion—but as a directive.

By then we were in his office at his big old oak desk. Without another word he pulled open the top drawer and reached for his business checkbook, and still standing, began writing the check for $6,500, asking if he should make it out to me personally. I said, "That will be fine," trying hard to keep my voice from cracking. He didn't even ask for the spelling of my name, but got each letter correct. I likely couldn't have done that with his name.

He completed the check, tore it out of the book and held it in his right hand. Putting the checkbook back into the drawer with his left hand, he reached for a blank promissory note, one of a stack that he had in the drawer. Still looking down, he said, "I'll need you to sign one of these." Taking the note in his hand, Tommy straightened up halfway and then stopped abruptly in that bent over position as if he was held there. With great compassion and understanding, while still in that position, he looked up at me and said, "Oh, He didn't say it was a loan, did He?"

I responded, "That wasn't what He told me."

Looking relieved, Tommy then said, "He said it was a gift, didn't He?"

I said, "That was what He told me." The Holy Spirit had assured me this was to be a permanent help along the way—not just stopgap.

With assurance and great peace, like his own prayer had been answered, Tommy said, "We won't need this," and returned the promissory note to the drawer and closed it. Handing me the check, he put his arm around my shoulder and walked me back to the front door, thanking me graciously for coming, saying how good it was to see me again. It was as if I had made a pickup of a pre-arranged check from a bank, except a bank that demonstrated a whole lot more love and care, like none I had ever known. The entire experience from beginning to end was electric and otherworldly.

I was back driving on Northside Drive within twelve minutes of hearing the voice say, "Go see Tommy, he's supposed to help." The $6,500 check went straight to the bank the next morning and paid the debt in full.

This has been one of the great faith experiences of my life and also one of great learning. Wherever there is a need with God's people, there is also someone who is supposed to meet that need. As wonderful as it was to me to receive that check, no strings attached, and pay off that old debt, it appeared secondary to the joy on Tommy's face in being able to give it. Surely that must be what Scripture means in saying, "It is more blessed to give than to receive."

I have shared this story numerous times with individuals and in groups. It is an almost unbelievable story that came about and unfolded exactly as I recounted it. No words have been added and none left out.

The deposit of that check was a "gift from heaven" and meant so much to our wounded finances. The deposit of faith and trust that day was of far greater value. We have drawn off it for thirty years in all sorts of hard times—and it just increases. And oh, yes, what a new understanding of the Body of Christ we received that day. Due in part to that big help that day, we were able to satisfy the creditors, but it took six more years to do so.

Tommy's check to me that day was deposited right into my business checking account. I'm certain that a larger amount was deposited in his name in his heavenly account. Tommy understood that in God's economy, the only things you get to keep are those you give away. He had acted with godly principles even with someone he barely knew.

Back on the road again, I could barely sit still and drive. I wanted to get out and jump up and down and shout—that surely would have been just fine. My fears and dread had been replaced by jubilation—I was exuberant! Now I *knew* we would be able to stay the course and work through all those debts. I could hardly wait to get home and tell Nancy—and show her the check.

God's ways are higher than our ways and recalling this wonderful experience still makes me shake my head in awe. But really, it's just business as usual in His Great Kingdom. Our part is to really *live* in that Kingdom.

(Charge them) to do good, to be rich in good works, to be liberal and generous hearted, ready to share with others.

In this way laying up for themselves (the riches that endure forever) a good foundation for the future, so that they may grasp that which is life indeed. I Timothy 6:18-19

Winds of Change Begin to Blow

The summer of 1981 became an eventful season for Nancy and me. We had been "walking in the Spirit" for about four years and had witnessed and been involved in many life-shaking events—Holy Spirit encounters, major healings, outreach to broken lives, etc. Several of these events were extraordinary on their own, and they just kept coming. But something was missing. We knew there was more—but what? We both sensed an empty space in our spirits that called out. What was it?

A surprise visit to our prayer meeting by a couple named Bob and Sue Garrett and a single woman, Cathy McGee (later to marry and become Cathy Barbay), several months earlier had challenged us both deeply. The three had shared about many of their friends who had heard the Lord's call to life in covenant community and had given up jobs, homes, friends and even nearness to family to move to Augusta, Georgia. Bob, Sue and Cathy, who were all originally from Texas, had joined with others, through the Holy Spirit, to move from Texas and to live totally for Jesus as part of the Alleluia Covenant Community. They spoke of scores of others, from all over the country, who had done the same. The whole concept seemed totally impractical to us. We thought, "How could this work in our world today? Even if someone chose to do this, how could they actually bring it to pass? How could they even financially afford to make such a change?"

And everyone who has left houses or brothers or sisters or father or mother or children or lands, for my name's sake, will receive a hundredfold, and inherit eternal life. Matthew 19:29

Because it was in Scripture, we knew it was true, but it sounded idealistic; now we were confronted with the reality. Who were these people, and why and how had they come to do such a radical thing? And why were they at our prayer meeting, telling us?

In the late spring of 1981, we arranged a one-day "come and see" visit to this different and special place, Alleluia Christian Community. Augusta was only a three-hour drive away, but we found the Alleluia lifestyle was light years "away" from how we were living. Our twenty-four hour visit was a heady introduction to community life and filled us with questions about what it all meant. It would take two more years for us to "unpack" this information enough to come back for a second visit. (Two later chapters are devoted entirely to Alleluia.)

That summer we also considered going for the first time to an annual two-week Bible conference at Franciscan University of Steubenville in Ohio. Attending would be a stretch for us; we had not been sit-down students of anything for a long time. Also, Steubenville was a twelve hour drive from our home. But Franciscan University was special. Fr. Michael Scanlan had come there a few years earlier to rebuild the school from one that had slid deeply into the mire of secular lifestyle to one that was now a bulwark of holiness and deeply immersed in the charismatic movement of the Holy Spirit. Many spiritual leaders considered Steubenville to be the best college to train young people to live fully in the Holy Spirit.

Steubenville is a small town near the Ohio River, about forty miles west of Pittsburg, that sprang up because of the steel industry and related trades. The steel mills with their tall stacks still belched acrid smoke into the air. OSHA had brought about the cleanup of a lot of dangerous pollution, but much continued, along with the still offensive smell. Our one brief drive into town gave clear evidence of hard winters and rough roads. We wondered why God had chosen a setting like this for such a great work. We've since come to realize, more and more, that that's a paradox not uncommon for God. One of the most notable examples is Mother Teresa's pristine complex in the horrific slums of Calcutta, India.

The surroundings suddenly changed as we drove onto the campus. It was not fancy or overly impressive, but all was neat, clean and orderly. We immediately felt God's presence and sensed the ongoing work of the Holy Spirit. This was holy ground. We knew we were to be there.

The conference was to begin the last Monday of June and continue through the first week of July, two weeks in all. The big gatherings were to be held in a large tent on the grounds. A total of about 300 people were attending the conference. Without any foreknowledge, we had been dropped in among a very serious group of believers. For most of them, Jesus and the work of the Holy Spirit was the primary focus of their daily efforts. Most of the attendees were priests, nuns, missionaries or community leaders. No passive or part-time believers in this group. We couldn't identify with any particular group of the four, but we could relate to all of them. Mostly we related to their radical personal transformation. Nancy and I both knew we were moving up to a higher level.

The two weeks' time was laced with Holy Spirit moments and interventions. We were being affirmed and used in ways similar to what we had already been experiencing; plus, our eyes were being opened to a new awareness and revelation. Somehow, things looked different. It was not like we were arriving at a new destination, but more like we were crossing a mountain pass to a higher plain and higher altitude. We could feel the change as it was happening— perhaps the spiritual comparison to having our ears pop as we drove to upper elevations.

On the first night, everyone gathered in the big tent, filled to overflowing by the 300-plus participants, with at least a dozen priests for the opening session. The crowd in the tent was energized by faith. No sooner had everyone settled into place when a terrific thunderstorm broke out and engulfed the tent with a drenching downpour and earsplitting thunder, with lightning bolts flashing incessantly. Buckets were placed in various places on the ground to catch the water leaking through the tent. The storm lasted until the final minutes of the session—almost two hours. As the meeting ended, the rain just stopped, totally—not another drop. We later heard that all of the electrical power in the town had been knocked out, except for on the university campus, which was completely illuminated and unaffected by the outages.

The title of the main talk was "Holiness of God." Midway through the talk, the Holy Spirit inspired all of us to take off our shoes. As the talk ended, the speaker asked us to leave quietly and remain quiet throughout that night to give the Lord the opportunity to work with each of us. As we left the big tent, many went the few yards to the university chapel. Most prostrated themselves on the floor and remained nearly motionless for hours, some almost all night. Some tried to get up earlier and couldn't. The Holy Spirit just held them still and quiet. The conference had started! The Holy Spirit was definitely moving among us.

Reading the movement and actions of the Holy Spirit requires "eyes to see" or "Spirit eyes." Nancy and I witnessed a lot of those during the two weeks. Undoubtedly, scores of similar occurrences were happening on other parts of the campus. These people had come with high expectations of encountering the Holy Spirit during their stay. They were very open to His working.

We had the opportunity to pray over a number of people throughout the conference. Some prayers were for healing, others for the "baptism of the Holy Spirit." Believers often watch for the Holy Spirit "breaking out" through an individual, and those he or she prays for being slain in the spirit (resting in the Spirit). We noticed this happening—that the prayers of some individuals seemed especially effective—and saw even lifelong nuns in their seventies approaching some of the lay people they did not know, asking for prayers to be "baptized in the Holy Spirit." Most of those prayed over would be quickly slain by the Holy Spirit and laid on the ground; some for the first time in their life, and several were simultaneously being baptized in the Spirit.

A number of times during the two weeks, Nancy and I found ourselves in the same area with a Catholic priest from Ohio named Fr. Joe. We couldn't understand why we were so often together, in the same place. Years later, we recognized Fr. Joe when he came to visit the Alleluia Community. Then we learned that Fr. Joe was the family priest of our new daughter-in-law, Joyce—he was a very close friend from Joyce's hometown in Ohio. Small world? Yes, really small. Especially when the Lord is leading His people where He wants them to be. Distance means nothing.

Just by providence one day, we got to meet Fr. Michael Scanlan. We had seen and heard him at a few conferences, and had read some of his books. They were like textbooks or "how to" books on the release of the Holy Spirit and on casting out demonic spirits. He was also a highly respected prophetic voice among believers.

My exchange with Fr. Scanlan was very brief—it took just a minute. He was the main man at Steubenville and I was just one person in the big crowd. He was very gracious, though, treating me as an equal on a level playing field. I suspected he did that with everyone. After introducing ourselves to him, I asked him one question, "Are you seeing many physical healings through prayer?" Even as I asked him the question, I was convicted of spiritual pride and suspected Fr. Scanlan had probably discerned it.

His answer surprised me and adjusted my thinking. "Not so many, anymore," he said. "We used to, but not so many now. We're mostly seeing changed lives." Here was another insight to ponder. I didn't ask him anything else. Years later, his answer would have more meaning.

We learned it was prudent to avoid being overextended, over-committed, to admit to not having sufficient resources (for instance, to take people into our home to live). We even learned that at times, saying "No" was the most prudent thing to do. Common sense was gaining importance in our lives—that plus deepening spirituality made for a powerful combination.

With many community leaders there, we were also hearing a lot about the value of committed relationships, as in a community of believers, and the coverage and strength it provided for all the different ministries of the community. This was similar to what we had heard at Alleluia on our visit there in the spring. Any knowledge we had of covenant Christian communities was quite limited and sketchy, but we doubted it would be for long. We were running into "community" at every turn, and trying to take in what we could. There was much to learn. The word "call" had come up over and over throughout the two weeks. Most of the people we had met spoke of it, almost like "a call" was a passport for a mission—once it was received, it launched a journey into uncharted territory. The word had moved to front and center of our awareness.

During the closing days, we received much priceless counsel and wisdom, some of it direct, specific to us, some of it more general. Some words we received would prove to be prophetic for us, straight from the Holy Spirit, and pointed to events that would happen as soon as we got back home. Some would even be in process before we got there.

As the seminar ended and we loaded up and drove off the campus, we knew that we were definitely supposed to have been there. The Bible conference came and went, we retained very little of it, but the experiences with the people and the Holy Spirit would stay with us. The Holy Spirit had been with us each mile and step of the way. We sensed things were about to change, radically—and that the Holy Spirit was preparing us. That summer not only convinced us that there was "more" for us, but began to fill in some of the blanks as to what that "more" might look like. It would be a time to pay strict attention.

Driving back down through those beautiful, wooded mountains, we had lots of quiet time to ponder and reflect. We were both suspecting a radical pruning was coming for us, to be able to respond to the Holy Spirit's leading. Living at this new level, we had seen that materialism was neither required nor allowed. Willingness to "turn loose" or let go of what we did not absolutely need would now be called for. Daryl's prophetic word about the Suzy Wong painting,

"She's got to go," came to mind. What's next? Our seriousness and sincerity were about to be tested, but we also sensed fresh grace had been infused, to enable us to seek more for the Kingdom, and even to do the "harder" things.

Behold the former things have come to pass, and new things I now declare; before they spring forth, I tell you of them. Isaiah 42:9

Part III:
Your Will, Lord—Not Mine

In the Potter's Hand

After being in the Spirit for about four years, Nancy and I came to another plateau. The pursuit of God's grace and blessings to restore our position and get us "back to normal" wasn't what it was about; this was becoming very clear. We had started out hoping to return to "normal," but early in the prayer meetings, we sensed that we were heading to higher ground.

He was calling for more from us, a willingness to be put back on the potter's wheel and reshaped into whatever He chose. Life and our work as we knew it seemed likely to never be the same again. Surely, this must be the way he deals with so many of us and guides us toward His plan.

Wanting His will more than our own will (our plans and aspirations) became a doorway that we needed to pass through. Once we walked through, the grace was there to do anything He asked of us.

Looking back, I believe that was the key to the "more" for us. Had we balked at that important point, that might well have seriously limited our ongoing progress or even stopped us altogether.

It became obvious the Lord was using, or putting into place, circumstances to move us from one point to the next, closing a door here while opening a door somewhere else, along with providing the grace to recognize enough of His action to say yes to a life-changing call. We were being asked to make a willful choice to fall into the hands of the living God. We would later come to see this as the ultimate invitation. Learning to welcome closed doors as readily as open doors would require reprogramming of our minds and our desires. This transformation seemed to be moving us toward a very important place, known only by Him. Clearly each step was deeper into the unknown and would require more trust than any that we had taken before. We remembered the Scripture, "No one ever put their trust in the Lord and was disappointed." We had already learned this to be an absolute truth.

Then I went down to the potter's house, and behold, he was working at the wheel.

And the vessel he was making of clay was spoiled in the hand of the potter so He made it over, reworking it into another vessel, as it seemed good to the potter to make it.

Then the word of the Lord came to me; "O house of Israel, cannot I do with you as this potter?" says the Lord.

"Behold, as the clay is in the potter's hand, so are you in my hand, O house of Israel." Jeremiah 18:3-6

Down Is Up

I found that as I began to surrender more of my life to the Lord, the Holy Spirit began to show me what was out of order. Usually, it was first things first, but then it would start trickling on down, and other things would come under scrutiny. We were realizing that true transformation should touch every area of our lives.

By mid-1981, upon returning from the trip to Steubenville, Ohio, Nancy and I were convicted by the Holy Spirit that we were financially "out of order." In good conscience it wasn't right to have a large amount of debt, be unable to pay, and continue living in our upscale neighborhood with all of its perks. We had to sell, pay off what we could, and go "back down." This was, by far, our hardest decision yet. Selling wasn't our only option, but it was the right thing to do. This was not just a financial decision, but also an ethical one. After all, we were dealing with God, who sees everything. There would be no turning back.

We had put our house up for sale a year earlier (on the market for the whole year) with no nibbles or interest. Our hearts had not really been ready to sell. But now, with our hearts right, the Lord sent a buyer when our house wasn't even on the market! The Holy Spirit even told both the buyers and us, without any discussion, what the purchase price should be—to the penny! The buyer assumed our loan, bought our equity, and paid us in monthly installments. By carrying the second mortgage ourselves, so that the buyer could purchase our equity over a long term, we now earned the interest, instead of the bank collecting it. This allowed us to pay off many of our business debts. The high, going interest rate (up to 14%) that had been killing us for years was, in this case, working in our favor.

As the time approached for us to move, we began looking at apartments or houses to rent. It had been over eighteen years since we had been renters, and we found the experience very discouraging. Everything we saw was either too small or very dirty and old. After a few hours, we stopped looking—almost overwhelmed with a sense of heaviness. The new buyers of our home were planning to move in right after closing on the coming Friday, and we had no place to move into. The consequences of our decision to sell were now staring us right in the face.

A few weeks earlier, a single man, Jeff, had begun coming to the prayer meeting at our church. He was going through a divorce, and was pretty shaken up and trying to find himself. We had prayed with him several times and had developed a rapport with him. He had begun to develop a real trust in us. When Jeff heard of our housing plight, he immediately invited us to move into his house. He lived alone in a spacious house, similar to ours, that was about a mile and a half away, in the next subdivision. Jeff went on to tell us that he spent little time at home, since his job required him to travel extensively. He also had very sparse furnishings and wanted us to move all our family, furniture and even our dog into his house, to use it as our own for as long as needed. Jeff saw it as the least he could do after what Jesus had done for him. He would accept only a minimal rent—and that, very reluctantly.

We were humbled, but we recognized Jeff's sincerity and the Lord's provision, so as hard as it was to accept, that's just what we did. Again, Nancy and I were coming to know, as through so many things, that this was a "set-up deal." The Lord had this all planned and worked out. We stayed three months at Jeff's house, rarely seeing him but always aware of his generosity. We were approached several times by well-meaning friends, confused and perplexed by our move. Some voiced their doubts that we should have sold our home; they just didn't think it was fair to our kids. Our kids did fine and handled the change well. Some of our friends never did.

After we had been at Jeff's for several weeks, Nancy rushed in one day telling me that as she drove down a street a couple of miles away, she had seen a house that might just be for us. After giving me a brief description, she wanted to take me there and show me.

The street had mostly brick houses that seemed to be only about fifteen to twenty years old. All of the yards were very neat, except for one, that of the house she had noticed. The house was vacant. It looked abandoned, totally overgrown, with tall weeds and vines and low-hanging limbs. We could barely see the house. The yard was large and sprawling and went down a wooded slope with lots of fallen limbs and natural debris scattered here and there. It looked as if it had been vacant for a long time. Still, in the midst of it all, we had a feeling that we were on to something big. Our spirits were quickened.

Nancy and I walked around the house and yard awhile, becoming increasingly interested with each new discovery. But there were no signs, names or numbers posted anywhere, so we were about to leave. Just then, a door opened in the house next door, and a nice, middle-aged man came out, asking if we needed help. He told us his name was Carl, and that he and his wife were long-time friends of the owner of the abandoned house.

After a short exchange in which we expressed our interest in the house, Carl told us we just might be very fortunate. The woman who owned the house, Jean, now lived in Hawaii, and very rarely got back

to town, but she was going to be there that weekend. She was planning to come to Carl and his wife's house for a quick drop-in visit
and then check on the condition of her house. Carl said that if we
wanted, we could leave our number with him, and he would have
Jean call us when she got to his house.

We received a call from Jean on Saturday and arranged to meet her
at the house. Nancy and I went right over and met her in the carport.
Jean was a very gracious woman in her fifties, quite intelligent, well
spoken and perceptive. She would later tell us that she had lived in the
house with her family for several years. Her husband was in the
military and had been transferred to Hawaii. Not long after the family
had moved to Hawaii, Jean and her husband's marriage had broken
up. Jean stayed on in Hawaii with her growing children and would be
returning to the mainland when she retired from her job in a few
years. She planned to come back and live in the house at that time.

Jean had been renting the house through a rental agency, and she
had some fear and trepidation about the condition of the place when
she opened the door. As we all know, vacant houses can surprise or
jolt us, but none of the three of us—least of all, Jean—was prepared
for what we found. She could hardly bring herself to go inside.

The rancid smell of stale air and filthy carpets hit us immediately—there was no telling how long the house had been locked up. The
midday darkness inside required a little adjustment for our eyes, and
then we began to see movement—lots of movement. The house was
literally working alive with roaches, crawling on everything, everywhere we looked—even on the ceilings and out of the receptacles in
the walls. I don't remember if Jean went beyond the first room; she
just stopped, overwhelmed and virtually sick. It was a split-level
house and I remember walking across that long living room toward

the stairs, carefully dodging the roaches. Then, before I reached the stairs, I heard the Lord say, "This is it." The *Voice* had spoken again. I told Nancy what I'd heard and she nodded her head in agreement. She already knew.

Most of the rest of our brief time with Jean that day was spent in making our agreement, and in ministry. She was to be back in Hawaii in a couple of days. She was overcome by the magnitude of the problem and the lack of a practical solution, or the time to work on one. It seemed the Lord just told Nancy and me, right there, that we were to take the house, clean it up, get it livable, and handle it for Jean. She could pay for materials and trade us some rent for labor. We would do the rest. In exchange, she would give us a reasonable rental rate that would stay unchanged for the six remaining years until her return after she retired. We could stay any or all of that time—our choice. By now, we had told Jean that I had been a building contractor, and when we made the offer, she quickly agreed. This arrangement gave us a peace and sense of security we hadn't had since selling our home. Rough as it was, it was the next-best thing to having our own house again. The Lord knew we had "owner's hearts" and Jean immediately sensed that, too. Nancy and I didn't know if we would ever get to own our own home again, but we both were very thankful for this one.

All of us felt good about the agreement; the Lord had orchestrated it right on the spot. Nancy and I laid hands on Jean, praying for peace for her, grace over the house and the agreement, and His blessings for her as she left. She gave us the keys and headed out, believing the Lord had rescued her from a very bad dilemma. We all three knew God had blessed us that day. What a Lord we have!

The next few weeks were a whirlwind of activity. Friends from our prayer group and our three sons—now aged twenty, eighteen, and ten—joined us, diving into the filthy and the worthless, looking for the precious. It was somewhat humbling, subjecting our kids to such a step backwards, but the experience actually drew us closer together. The time at Jeff's house had been preparing the kids for this new experience.

The carpets were all ripped up, dragged out, and hauled to the dump first, and the worst of the smell went with them. The trail of greasy footprints on the carpets left by the last renters—four motor-cyclists—was a memory. As the carpets and pads were taken up, many roaches were even under them, next to the wood floors. Later, after lots of power scrubbing and polishing, the oak floors became beautiful again; they didn't even need refinishing.

Getting the roaches out was the hardest part. We went after them with all the conventional bug bombs and sprays, but with limited success. A professional exterminator suggested that we get a high-powered roach killer in powder form and put it into the heating and air system, running only the fan for several days to disperse it over every part of the house. That finally worked, and the house was roach free and stayed that way, even freer of such pests than most houses. It was rare to ever see a roach in that house again after that.

We were able to make many improvements during our first year there. Most of the materials that were used were left over from the contract homes that I had built: ceramic tile, wallpaper, paints, and more. They were usually just the right amount that was needed, no more, no less. We seldom had to buy any more materials to do the projects. The house became beautiful, with many nice touches, much like a contract house built just for us.

The family did a major ongoing cleanup and burning of a mountain of tree limbs and debris, and the property's natural beauty emerged. We even found old azaleas that had been buried under overgrown weeds. The big, two-acre overgrown lot became a park-like yard leading down to a fast-flowing creek. Down on the "back forty," as we called it, we later developed a large area for a garden which was Nancy's "farm." It provided many vegetables for food and much-needed therapy for our wounded pride. It's hard to go "down" after two decades of coming "up." We would soon come to understand that we were seeing this backwards. For us, that year's "down" became our real going "up."

An interesting situation happened one day as our family was cleaning up the large wooded lot. We were putting the debris into the back of my El Camino, and then hauling it to the area of the yard where our big brush pile was accumulating. I had backed the El Camino halfway down the long hill to unload the dead limbs, branches, and small saplings that we had collected. On this particular day, the daylight and our energy ran out before we could unload and drive the truck back up the hill. Over the next couple of days, there was a very heavy rain that soaked the ground. When the rain abated and we unloaded the truck, the slippery hillside was too slick for the truck to get any traction. After giving it a few tries, with tires spinning, I shut off the engine and left it parked, to move another day when conditions were drier.

More rain followed and the truck remained stranded on the hillside. Then a word came from the Lord, "Go out and back the truck all the way down to level ground, just before the creek, then put it in drive and just steadily drive all the way up the hill and out." That's just the way it worked, with ease and without a glitch. The

Lord went on to show me that sometimes in order to move forward, you first have to go backward to get firmly on solid ground. Then just begin—and continue—to move consistently forward until you get where you need to go. That invaluable lesson helped me to really stay the course, adjusting to this new awareness that for us, "down was up." We were going "down" to get on solid ground. "Up" would follow.

One of the little extras about Jean's place was a moderate-sized daylight basement. Inside it, Jean had all the yard tools necessary to maintain the grounds. Among them was a big old riding mower that had sat unused for years. With some prayer, patience and tinkering, it became workable again, and Nancy would drive it out and cut the grass—riding it like it was a prize thoroughbred on a ranch. It was great therapy for her—no keeping up with the Joneses here.

The basement also held the washer and dryer, and tightly packed up and pushed together was all my woodworking equipment from my furniture business of the fifties and sixties. The machines had been used regularly during the ten years of home building and my commercial woodwork era throughout the seventies. Now they stood dormant, almost forgotten. The three busy and fruitful years of commercial woodwork had come to an end, as quickly as it had started. All of my contacts had gone silent, almost as if I had dropped off the planet—in a way, similar to the time when my homebuilding business was shut down. I read this as a leading from the Lord. He must be calling for something new. As I worked at rebuilding Jean's house, using my building talents there, I engaged in a brief stint at real estate sales. My experience in building helped, but real estate didn't ever feel like it was "from the Lord," except as a stopgap measure.

Since my radical conversion five years prior, a growing desire to use my design and woodworking gifts, talents and life experience to serve the Lord was emerging. Like many people "laid hold of" by the Lord, I wanted my God-given gifts to be used to glorify Him. The time was up for using them for my own glory or to make individuals look great; I had learned the dangers of that pursuit. So, what was the Spirit saying?

After a good bit of talking and praying about it, Nancy and I thought we heard something. Just like my years of building custom furniture and then contract houses, we thought we recognized a need. Both of those businesses had gathered a following and clientele, mostly through referrals, because we could provide something that was in short supply but still in demand. Our businesses had been based on our recognition of a need for high quality, with the heart to meet that need.

So, what about crosses? Where were the high-quality wood crosses for believers who appreciated fine wood and workmanship? We didn't know of any on the market. Maybe that was to be our niche. Over a period of time, through prayer and listening, the Holy Spirit seemed to confirm this new venture. We could start it up in the basement, with no new equipment needed, using special woods that we still had from earlier businesses, and see where the Lord would take it. It was to be "Images of the Cross," crosses and woodworks to glorify God.

Some Christian friends wired the basement for my equipment and a woodworking shop was set up. I would do all the machining and woodwork inside and spray outside in the back yard. The handling of the wood dust was the tough challenge—Nancy had to share her clothes washing and drying space with the new business.

Knowing the importance of what we were attempting, she managed her part with virtually no complaint. Casual observers would likely have considered this a huge step backwards from where we had been years earlier. Fortunately, we were becoming more oblivious to the comments of casual observers.

Wood crosses, made from fine woods, began to emerge from the basement and were taken upstairs to our new showroom gallery, our dining room. Each wall was painted in a different shade of red, and this served as a worthy showcase for the new crosses. Word quickly got out, mostly through prayer groups in the area, and people began to come to our dining room/showroom and make their selections and purchases. Our clientele also became our marketing agents; the Lord was finding good homes for the crosses.

Two years after we first met Jean and saw the house, she wrote and told us that she was coming back to Marietta for another visit. She wanted to come by and see us, and the house. On this visit, like the first, she walked in the door and didn't get much further than that. She just stopped, stood there looking around and started crying—she was overcome and just had to sit down. None of the three of us were "criers," but we all just sat there awhile, each quietly crying in our own way. These were all tears of gratitude. No words were needed, none were spoken.

After awhile, when Jean had seen everything that the Lord had for her, she was ready to go. She told us she would be returning in four years and wanted us to continue to live in the house after she returned, but she also wanted me to seriously consider designing and building a house for her to live in on her adjoining lot.

Many wonderful and Spirit-filled happenings occurred while we lived in Jean's house. It was a meaningful time for our whole family and took us to levels of faith in God's leading and provision and trust where we had never been. It was a great stepping stone for things to come, and we were beginning to sense that even bigger things might be not so far in the future. Stepping "down" was taking on a whole new meaning for us. The realness, truth, and honesty of it all were so exhilarating. The light at the end of the tunnel was increasing, and the oppressive darkness decreasing. We were aware, more and more each day, that we were beginning to flow with God's will.

Therefore humble yourselves under the mighty hand of God, that in due time He may exalt you. I Peter 5:6

Your Pride or My Will

When we started the business, "Images of the Cross," we knew that it was to be "crosses and woodworks to Glorify God." I was to take no secular work. I had clearly heard the *Voice* say, "If you will consecrate all your work to Me, I will make sure you always have plenty of work." The Lord certainly knew that in my previous years of self-employment, running out of orders had been an ongoing concern in the back of my mind. Several people tried to convince me that this specialized work wouldn't suffice—that I would have to take on some secular work in order to be successful. That wasn't what the *Voice* had said.

So I embarked on building special crosses for special people. Right away, I was blessed with ebony and rosewood (which I had never used in all my furniture-building years). Other exotic woods from around the world were soon gathered in my makeshift little basement "factory," and the fine wood cross line began to develop.

Throughout my furniture-making years, I had done a fair amount of carving, so I began to wonder if I would get the opportunity to sculpt crucifixes (the three-dimensional sculpted likenesses of the crucified Jesus) for churches. That really would be a specialty item and I would be competing with multi-generational companies in Italy and Germany. It probably was a long shot, but it could happen through the Spirit's leading.

After nearly a year of building and selling crosses, I was approached by a Catholic Church in Atlanta about making a crucifix that would be almost life size. The assistant pastor had photos of one that he had grown up with in his home church in Michigan. The pastor asked if I would be willing to sculpt a prototype about twenty-four inches tall (about one third the size of a life-size crucifix) from the photos, with the possibility of getting the contract to sculpt the larger one.

I knew this was a gamble (I might not get the contract) and it would be a sizable undertaking. There would be no compensation for the prototype. Nancy and I took it to prayer, asking for the leading of the Holy Spirit. We got no definitive word, but the Lord seemed to approve, so I agreed to their proposal. I would step out and sculpt my first crucifix. For the next five weeks the crucifix became my work, full time. It was challenging, stimulating and spiritual, like nothing I had ever done before. The Holy Spirit gave abundant grace and the crucifix moved very smoothly to completion.

I called the pastor to set a time to bring the crucifix so that he and the committee members could see and consider it. Upon seeing the prototype, the pastor's spirits seemed lifted and he seemed some-what surprised, especially since I had never carved a crucifix before. He wanted to keep it for a couple of weeks so that all of the people on the committee could look at it and study it, to help them make their decision. Leaving it, I drove away feeling encouraged.

Two weeks later a letter arrived from the pastor. He started by telling me how much the committee had liked the prototype crucifix, and how appreciative they all were. Then he went on to tell me that they had decided to go with the Italian studio that had made the original crucifix in the photos. The assistant pastor had been the determining voice, the one most insistent about the choice. Suddenly I felt that I was reading a "Dear John" letter. Then, in the closing sentence, the pastor asked if I would be willing to build their altar furnishings, even though they were not choosing me to sculpt the crucifix.

Well, what about that? My first rejection in this Jesus business. I was stunned and disappointed, having pinned lots of hope and expectation on securing this contract. It wasn't so much the money as it was the prestige—as well as the door that would have been opened and where it might have led. I liked the sound of "sculptor of crucifixes." Starting over again to build furniture, fourteen years after I had left my last furniture business behind, didn't really appeal to me—especially in a small, cramped, almost packed basement shop. Rereading the letter two or three more times didn't seem to help. I had gone out on a limb, investing five weeks, and had now been rejected as a sculptor. My pride was hurt. Also, Nancy was out of town, so I couldn't talk it through with anyone who was really invested in this business venture.

The next morning, I prepared to go to the weekly men's Bible group that I attended. Our house was dark; no one else was up as I approached the stairs to the main level. Then, at the top of the stairs, the *Voice* stopped me and spoke rather sternly, "You can rationalize, you can justify—you can feel sorry for yourself, but I'm setting the question before you like these two walls..." (The walls on each side of the narrow stairway.) "Which had you rather have—your pride, or My will?"

There it was; it was over. At the top of the stairs, before I took the first step, the Holy Spirit ended the dilemma. By the first step down, I knew that it wasn't my role to orchestrate—but mine to follow. I would lay down my carving chisels (and "sculptor of crucifixes" dreams) and prepare to again build furniture—and I would be grateful for the opportunity. The Lord would multiply the space and the grace, because He was calling for this adjusted direction. The fact is, if I had gotten the contract for the crucifix, I would likely have greatly underpriced it and that would have put us in a tighter financial position.

The church gave us their furnishings contract—altar, pulpit, font, cross, chairs, tabernacle stand, etc. The Spirit must have given me a good referral. That contract was my major entry into the business. Building altar furnishings in that cramped basement alongside Nancy as she washed and dried our clothes was challenging for us both, but it worked out fine. Two more church contracts quickly followed and we were into the third, while still working out of the basement. Prior to the church's offer, I had not given a single thought to designing and building sanctuary furnishings. I had no knowledge of or training in liturgical design or symbolism.

I continued to make and sell the home crosses, and some went to distant places. Along the way, I've also gotten to sculpt a few cruci-fixes for churches, always in His timing—not mine. The original prototype has hung in our living room since being "rejected." The business would be a faith walk, maybe even like walking a high wire, but the Spirit was coaching us to step out and take each next step toward Him.

I've come to realize that God wants to see us use the gifts He's given us far more than we want to use them, and He wants us to use them to build His kingdom. He also understands full well the dangers of pride, ambition and our tendency to think we can operate independently, and He knows we especially need His help and restraint in those areas.

The question, "Which had you rather have—your pride, or my will?" still rings in my head from time to time. The One speaking those words set our course, and He has kept us on it. There are two trustworthy old sayings, "Grace precedes the call," and "God's will will never take you where His grace can't keep you." After many years of seeing those words proven true, I've come to consider them absolutes. And yes, the grace He gives us lines up with the desires He has for us. What a way to live!

Commit your works to the Lord and your plans will be established.
Proverbs 16:3

Visiting Alleluia

Alleluia Covenant Community was formed on February 11, 1973, in Augusta, Georgia, during a record-setting snowstorm.

It is impossible with words to give an adequate description of the Alleluia Community — one has to "come and see" it for himself. However, since Alleluia has been so life changing and life shaping for our family and so many hundreds of others, I must try to give you an overview. To be truly thorough would require an entire book. The community is every bit as unique as a fourteen-inch snow in the Deep South!

As I mentioned in a previous chapter, "Winds of Change Begin to Blow," Nancy and I made a one-day visit to Alleluia in the spring of 1981, after some members of Alleluia came to our prayer meeting in Marietta and invited us. We got an early reality check as our three-hour drive wound into its final two miles. The condition of the neighborhood and surroundings had suddenly taken on a very depressed look just as Nancy announced from our page of directions, "One more turn and we're at Faith Village." I immediately responded, "Oh, no!"

Thirty seconds later we were arriving at the "bell tower" located outside of the house where noon prayers were to momentarily begin. Without introduction, we were soon inside the house among a group of forty people, mostly young mothers and some not so young, with the largest number of small children we had ever seen in one room. The man leading the prayers was addressed as Dale — or as the kids called him, Uncle Dale.

As the songs rose up toward the ceiling, I became concerned with the floor, which was moving noticeably under our body weight. It kept shaking the entire half hour, but held. It seemed that Nancy and I were the only ones who noticed. Welcome to Alleluia.

While observing community life on our visit that day, we met twice with Dale, the man who had led noon prayers, who was also a community founder and elder. Dale was different from anyone we had ever been around; he was known to be very spiritually attuned and discerning and to intentionally say very little. He cut to the chase and didn't really encourage us to come to visit Alleluia again, unless we were "called." (There was that word again.) In their first eight years, the community had hosted many visitors, some who were emotionally or socially drawn, others who wanted a free ride. Over time, the Alleluia leadership had become more careful and was now much more discerning about why an individual was expressing interest in the community.

We tried to quiz Dale about the community mission. What was it? What was their work? He would only reply "To be a people." The community aspired to get everyone in their care baptized in the Holy Spirit and to work hard at "being a people," which to them meant living out Christian family together. And yes, they were ecumenical, that was even spelled out in their covenant. It was very important to us that any community we considered be ecumenical (multi-denominational), but I didn't yet understand this "be a people" part. To me, it didn't appear that the community's mission and purpose were anything like our own. I was used to spontaneously "going out" in the Spirit and working with strangers. Nancy, on the other hand, was tracking with Dale, and by the conclusion of our visit she thought she was ready (and I should be) to pack up and move to

Augusta and Alleluia. I just wanted to get back on I-20 to Atlanta—the sooner, the better! Our trip home was long and filled with tension and disagreement. I felt threatened and would have been quite happy to forget all about Alleluia and Augusta!

Nancy had, for a long time, been personally drawn to a Scripture in Acts: *They devoted themselves to the apostles' teaching and to the fellowship, to the breaking of bread and to prayer. Everyone was filled with awe, and many wonders and miraculous signs were done by the apostles. All the believers were together and had everything in common... They broke bread in their homes and ate together with glad and sincere hearts, praising God and enjoying the favor of all the people. And the Lord added to their numbers. Acts 2:42-44,46-48*

Nancy was convinced that Alleluia Community was that Scripture being lived out. I was really immersed in the workings of the Holy Spirit where we were in Marietta and wasn't looking forward to giving that up. To relocate to a place that didn't impress me that much, and start over among people I didn't know, in a town with uncertain business prospects, seemed questionable at best.

Our one visit in 1981 had been a shock to my system, from a physical and material standpoint. To me, the Alleluia Community was the most austere, bare-essentials place that I had ever spent time in—the extreme opposite of the well-appointed houses I had designed and built in upscale neighborhoods in Atlanta. Most of the community members lived in a partially renovated duplex neighborhood. It had been built in 1951, and by the time the community was founded and members began to move into the first renovated duplexes, the complex had suffered over two decades of abuse and neglect at the hands of renters. It also was located in an active red-light, crime-infested area with pimps and drug dealers cruising the streets. Even in 1981, gunshots were heard in the distance at various times of the day and night. The community's founders had sold their own nice homes on the west side of town to fund the purchase of this old, declining cluster of houses and had moved "down," praying against the surrounding evil and for the demons to be put to flight.

The first eight years that Alleluia owned the duplexes was a time of nonstop rebuilding and restoration. The efforts and commitment had been incredible, and the results were becoming obvious; even the crime was fleeing from God's new project. But it wasn't suburban Atlanta—not by a long shot. New church sanctuaries were being built all over greater Atlanta, and our business was taking off, with lots of referral contracts. There seemed to be no way Augusta could match that. I clearly remembered being on the brink of total disaster just a few years earlier, and I didn't want to risk that again. My old critical nature started to surface. I even had recurring dreams of being chained to the signpost at the Alleluia office, unable to ever leave. Any pursuit of the "finer things," ever again, could be in jeopardy. (I wasn't yet able to consistently recognize true worth.) Also, two words Dale had used continued to stay in my mind and haunt me, "headship" and "authority." Headship, I didn't understand at all, but I was leery of what it might mean. Authority was something I liked to have and to use, but I wasn't at all sure about being under it. In time, I would come to appreciate Dale and his directness, and his love for the community, and those two words as well.

It was two years before I could get over the jolt of the first visit and bring myself to make another visit. This time, I began to see past the duplex buildings in need of improvement, the abused property and the rough surroundings, and to try to appreciate the committed people and the working of the Holy Spirit among them. By our second visit, the area and many of its houses had been improved significantly (but not nearly so much as my tolerance and understanding had been). The Lord had been working on my attitude and my values, and helping me to look beyond material things. It would take every bit of what we had gained from our "going down" experience with Jean's house (all of which happened after our first visit to Alleluia in 1981) to prepare me to even consider moving to Alleluia. I had spent most of our married life trying to distance us from just this kind of housing and neighborhood.

On that second visit to Alleluia, Nancy and I were joined by Don and Karen, friends from our Marietta prayer group. They had heard the call to community a few years earlier, and were anxious to "come and see." That visit lasted two days, and we met with the head elder, Dennis, to hear him talk about community. Like Dale before him, he spoke of "being a people" and about the importance of the community's lifetime covenant, the value of headship, and the fruits of accountability and commitment. At least by now I had thought considerably about those words. Dennis told us that everyone in the community, including each elder, was under personal headship. I was surprised—but felt somewhat better.

During that visit, Don, Karen, Nancy and I agreed to start coming regularly that fall, every other weekend, which we did. We would travel in our two cars, driving together, leaving Marietta on Friday after work and returning home on Sunday around 9 pm. Each visit helped to release us from our attachment to Marietta. Many of our family and friends just couldn't understand why we would be making these visits, even though the community frequently hosts guests from all over the world.

Those weekends were chock full for us all. We were placed with different families to stay in their homes and experience community with them. We would be included in whatever they were doing. It was a great opportunity to learn to "fit in." Many times, Don and Karen's two adult daughters came with them, and Nancy's mother, Fran, usually came with us, along with one or more of our three sons. Don and Karen and their daughters would generally be hosted in one home, and Nancy and I and our sons in another, while Fran would usually be placed in a third home. On several occasions, we had not met our hosts before reaching their home. Sometimes, on our arrival, no one was home, and we would be greeted by a note of instruction on the front door. One such note read, "Welcome! You'll be staying in the room at the top of the stairs, the one with the sheetrock against the wall." These people were not out to impress, but were just very real and genuinely hospitable. They believed that the Holy Spirit selected those who visited. We sensed no attitude of exclusivity in any of the members, but rather a down-to-earth honesty and openness. On some of our visits, we would realize the next morning that we had been given the master bedroom, while the hosting couple slept somewhere else in the house, even on the floor. That's sacrificial giving! We were already witnessing a deeper level of "dying to self" than we had ever seen. We were always treated with great warmth and acceptance. Their kids always called us Aunt Nancy, Uncle Gary, and "Franma." Their love for Jesus showed in their care for us.

Alleluia had teachings for the newer people on Saturday mornings, a work party in the afternoon, and a Lord's Day meal Saturday night. Sundays were full: breakfast, then church services, brunch, and the general community gatherings (GCGs) on Sunday afternoon. At the end of the GCG, community members would "lay hands" on us, pray us up for the journey home, and tell us that they were sorry we couldn't stay and "live community."

We followed this schedule faithfully every other week. And came to know more individuals with each visit and appreciate their uniqueness and the ways that they had each been called to community. These people were genuine, they were in pursuit of God's will and the "more" for their lives, and we felt the call to join them. Nancy and I were both tired of being disappointed by believers who would eagerly go part of the way, and then no further. It was obvious from the costly moves that many community members had made to get to Alleluia—leaving homes, families, friendships, jobs, and even careers—that they were not counting the cost. They had found their *pearl of great price* and answered the call to this new life, not knowing what that entailed. Many of them were former leaders of prayer groups in their churches, but had been willing to forego that for this higher calling, starting over at the ground level in the community, in accordance with God's plan for their lives. Nancy and I wanted to live among believers with that level of commitment.

> *Then Jesus said to His disciples, "If anyone wishes to come after Me, he must deny himself, and take up his cross and follow Me. For whoever wishes to save his life will lose it; but whoever loses his life for My sake will find it. For what will it profit a man if he gains the whole world and forfeits his soul? Or what will a man give in exchange for his soul? For the Son of Man is going to come in the glory of His Father with His angels, and will then repay every man according to his deeds. Matthew 16:24-27*

Life in Alleluia

By the summer of 1984, our family had adjusted to the drastic move from our house and subdivision, and really enjoyed living in Jean's house on the two acres of set-aside nature. Our life had stabilized and we were living at a new level of peace. We had gotten quite comfortable. The Lord's provision had been a near-perfect fit for us, and none of us was excited about turning it loose—but God's leading for us to make "the move" was getting clearer by the day. The word "call" had moved to front and center.

We had made over two dozen weekend-long visits to Alleluia during the previous year and now it was time. We knew we were to be part of the community, either in Augusta or as part of a new branch in Marietta. Nothing seemed on the horizon for an Alleluia branch in Marietta, so that left Augusta. Our family and friends in Marietta distanced themselves from this radical decision; they considered it far too extreme. We would come to learn that many of the other community members had experienced the same with their own families and friends.

I made one final plea, like a defense attorney in a trial, reminding the Lord of all the great things He had accomplished in the house and on the property that He had provided for us (and the work that had been poured into it); maybe we shouldn't leave it. The *Voice* gently responded, "Unless you're willing to turn loose what I've given you, you won't be able to take hold of what I want to give you." The discussion was ended—and so was the questioning. We were moving to Augusta and Alleluia. This would be our most radical "stepping out in faith" yet and would require the most trust. There would be no turning back.

In the following days, the Holy Spirit even arranged for friends of ours from the prayer group to replace us as Jean's tenants. They moved in right after us and stayed there until Jean and her family moved back to Marietta. This was a great solution for everyone concerned. The Holy Spirit doesn't overlook anything. And no, I didn't get to consider designing and building Jean's house. We were in another life now, but her sincerity and trust in us were encouraging. She will always hold a special place in our hearts.

On a visit to Alleluia, the Lord provided the next home for our family. Because of all the community activity that revolved around Faith Village (a large group of houses that was home to hundreds of the members), we decided to look for a house to rent within a three-mile radius of the village. We actually got an Augusta map and, with a compass, drew a three-mile circle with the village at the center.

Again, by the Spirit's leading, we found ourselves looking at a vacant house that had a "For Rent" sign out front, a nice, seventy-five-year-old, rather quaint two-story house with a big front porch. The three-mile radius that we had drawn went right over the house. As Nancy and I arrived at the house, the owner, Ray, who lived in North Carolina, just "happened" to be there checking out the house, following the move out of the previous occupant. We discussed the rent and talked with Ray about improvements that were needed. Within minutes we reached an agreement similar to what we'd had with Jean. Ray gave us the key, headed back toward North Carolina, and we began planning our move. We have come to learn, over and over, that the Lord is number one in the relocation business.

Don and Karen, along with their two daughters, moved to Augusta in June of 1984. Nancy and I had two households to move, ours and Fran's, along with our business and shop equipment. It would be the end of August before we could move. Coming to Alleluia was, in and of itself, no great triumph, but it was obedience to the call. Now it was up to us to live out the call—we had all the resources necessary. We never looked back.

When an individual expresses an interest in joining Alleluia, and the community accepts that person's intention, the individual becomes an "underway" member. The "underway" period is a time of continued discernment of indefinite length, usually two to four years. Its main purpose is to determine whether underway members can begin to fit in with the people and routines, and live the life. When it has been clearly discerned that the underway members are ready to commit to a covenant relationship with the community, the individual or couple is invited to "sign covenant." A year and a half after moving to Alleluia, during a covenant signing weekend when Nancy and I had not been invited to sign (and were feeling sorry for ourselves), I heard a sobering word from the Holy Spirit that adjusted my focus. He bluntly said, "If you will quit worrying about what everybody else is doing or not doing, and just do what I ask you to do, I can really use you here." Wow! I felt like I had been punched, but I understood it instantly. A year later, we were invited to sign covenant—and we gratefully did.

The Holy Spirit-inspired covenant that we all sign is a major key to the long-term success of the community. It is a lifetime agreement, and, although the Alleluia covenant is secondary to our marriage vows, it is entered into with the same level of commitment. This total commitment does wonders for brother-sister relationships with people we don't yet fully know, from areas to which we've never traveled, who have backgrounds much different from ours. The Holy Spirit Himself selected us to share our lives together. Understanding this makes all the difference! It is a great opportunity to live out Jesus' two great commands: *love the Lord your God with your whole heart, soul and being,* and *love your neighbor as yourself,* and a chance to live alongside hundreds of believers attempting to do the same. We would learn that the second command is harder to live out than the first—but is of equal importance. We all need more shaping and molding by His hands and with the help of His people.

We soon realized that evil spirits such as pride, fear, anger, rejection, unworthiness, insecurity, resentment and others were at work here also. When we embarked on our visits to community, we assumed that almost everyone there had arrived in good shape. After our move, we began to learn that most had been healed and freed gradually, over time, from some of these stubborn spirits. We were learning that lasting freedom requires hard work and unconditional love from brothers and sisters in Christ. Through our covenant we agree to be held accountable to each other. Respect and loyalty bloom in such surroundings. There is also a deeply fulfilling sense of "belonging." Relationships are sometimes very hard, even painful, but the good fruit that comes from working at them is amazing, a fruit unattainable any other way. It is well worth the cost. In many ways, similar to a good marriage.

It is encouraging to look around the neighborhood—next door, across the yard, across the street, the next street over, and on and on (Faith Village is considered by many to be the best example of intentional Christian clustering in the world)—and realize that these families have relocated from all over the country just to answer the "call" and fully live the committed life. Part of this committed life is to stand for good and make a real impact against evil in this depraved culture, and to help others do the same. Being shoulder to shoulder with "stand-up" people puts a fire in your heart and increases the desire to do your best. We love that!

The Lord had provided hospitality and housing for our family through the brothers and sisters, and we also began to get opportunities to host guests. What a joy it is to welcome people who desire so much to be in His will. Offering hospitality to them and sharing in their discerning of God's call is a blessing of its own. The Lord even provided us with a home to rebuild and own right in the center of Faith Village—now our all-time favorite permanent home. Thank you, Lord!

Any early concerns or fears I had, and there were plenty, of being totally absorbed into the great numbers of Alleluia (stirred into the big pot of soup) and losing all personal identity and all opportunity to use my particular gifts, were certainly unfounded. On the contrary, I have found that community life actually develops and sharpens our individual gifts for better use by the entire body, a natural result of laying down personal claims and rights for the sake of the greater good. The community is blessed with an array of extraordinary gifts in operation. We also know that as more gifts are needed, the Holy Spirit will raise them up or call them forth.

All of the planned and spontaneous activities that go on in the community, virtually non-stop, keep everyone moving forward. It took a year for us to fully catch up to the community rhythm (sometimes our tongues were almost hanging out). We learned that that's normal. Of course, the many times when the Holy Spirit chooses to surprise and bless us, as only He can, add abundantly to the joy of this life with Him and with each other. During the large prayer and praise gatherings each week, or the big pro-life rallies, or the ultimate event—the Good Friday Way of the Cross, with 500 or more walking for Jesus—I am struck by the stark contrast with our former life, and think, how did we ever get here? I vividly remember where we came from—that world of empty promises.

One of the community buses frequently eases past our home, going or coming, taking our people, young and old, for sporting events, mission work, conferences or recreation. Going out on long-distance mission trips, often charismatic conferences, is a great opportunity. But invariably, the best part is returning home from those upbeat weekends and realizing that we are surrounded by this Spirit-energized life, every day! We wouldn't trade with anyone.

To say that Alleluia is the strongest assemblage of radically living Christian people I've ever seen is an understatement, but we could and should do better, given the support we have. The intensity, energy, fervor and faithfulness to live the calling and build His kingdom is incredible. On any given day, most of the over 700 men, women and children are "up"—far more than enough to lift the spirits of anyone who temporarily isn't. One of the agreements of community members is to be supportive, to help each member to do his or her best. This is especially noticeable in the Alleluia school, among our young people. Character, relationships, and academics all bloom in the fertile soil of the school. The Lord surely wanted it in place, so much so that He made sure we could acquire the property for it. Many personal sacrifices have gone into (and countless wonderful experiences have come out of) building and maintaining this extraordinary school, using minimal resources and maximum commitment. Each community member has some "ownership" of it.

Observing the kids as they grow up, and our older teens and young adults, one can't fail to see their love of Jesus and their pursuit of holiness. They richly enjoy the community life and its long-term, wholesome relationships. The stability and permanence is priceless. The great influence of godly parents and community "aunts," "uncles," and "grandparents," along with their own strong faith and the peer-pressure to excel, bear terrific fruit. Their mission/ministry trips to depressed areas to serve the less fortunate are life changing for them and a challenge to the rest of us. What a joy it is to share with them their special events: school activities, sporting events, graduations, engagements, marriages, the births of their children, their personal choice to go underway, covenant signings, ordinations, and the like. We're all so blessed to be part of that. (It keeps us younger, too!) Our four adult children and their families have been greatly blessed by being a part of the community—all live within minutes of our home. Our daughter and one of our sons and their families are also full-covenant members.

Sharing in the never-ending acts of service carried out with selfless attitude and surprising efficiency is one of the true joys of community. Serving feeds the spirit. Child care, providing meals (for as long as needed), construction help, help with moving, caring for the sick, hurting, and elderly, counsel for any situation, financial support in pressing times, and whatever else that's needed—that is really something. We sometimes refer to it as "womb-to-tomb" care. Due to the level of commitment firmly in place, the service often appears to be almost automatic. Everyone gets to serve, and we're all equal. The elders and pastoral leaders usually serve at the monthly work parties, working alongside the other men, under the headship of another designated leader for a particular project. I had never experienced anything like this before. Seeing such a radical contrast to the ways of the world lifts everyone's spirits and does wonders to level the playing field, given the broad range of positions and income among community members.

The services performed at the time of death are perhaps as meaningful as any. There are wakes, funerals and burials in our own cemetery. These are among the most spiritually moving events. They're often very painful—but it's a strengthening pain, deeply felt at this time of departure. Even individuals who have come to community with no "blood family" on earth receive the same regal sendoff when they go to Glory! Every time another brother or sister gets promoted, our hearts are strengthened as we reflect on the lives they laid down for Jesus (and for us) to build His kingdom here on earth. Guests often ask, "How can I have a burial like this?" Is there a better way to graduate?

And yes, we get to experience far more than our share of signs, wonders and miracles, but that is not the most miraculous part of Alleluia. Watching the Lord do extraordinary things with ordinary, Spirit-led people, rubbing against each other with care and love— that is truly something to behold. The Lord can do anything with those elements in place, and we've come to expect it. Community relationships often grow closer than many of our blood relationships because of the life that we hold in common, seeking first His kingdom and His righteousness.

Alleluia Community is certainly no great completed work, with everything in place and running smoothly—far from it. But it is a powerful work in progress, a place where we are being refined by the Holy Spirit and are allowed to enter into His work. We still make costly mistakes, poor choices, and questionable decisions, but God's mercies are new every morning. There seems to be an abiding grace over the community which enables the network of strength and support needed for so many of the experiences described in this book. It is probably fair to say that none of the members, including the founders, ever expected to get to live on such a level; they were just individually "called" for this particular work. Along with their "yes," His grace has been sufficient for living it out.

The Lord continues to call others and add to our number, but certainly covenant community is by no means the only way to live fully for Jesus. We don't believe that and I would never want to imply such. The Lord issues an unlimited number of different calls. Abandoning oneself, relinquishing one's own will and plans, and saying yes to His call, whatever it is, seem to unlock the grace for the wonderful life. Being wherever He wants us, doing what He has for us—that has to be the highest level of living, for anyone!

I hope the description of my "turned off" first impression of Alleluia, in contrast with the present reflection (after twenty-seven years of living here) helps the reader to discover, to some extent, the unique and wonderful work of this Jesus happening and some of the transformation He brings about. I am one of those who had a doubtful first impression of Alleluia, mostly due to my own pride and independent spirit, and to seeing it through the eyes of the "old man." I later came to appreciate and to love it. It far surpassed my hopes years ago. Many more people loved it from their first visit and never looked back. Probably none would say coming to community was easy, but all would say it was worth far more than any cost. My description doesn't do it justice, but anyone can "come and see."

In reality, this account of Alleluia might compare with a colorful postcard of a setting in Rome; impressive, but only a fleeting glimpse of the real grandeur of Rome. So it is with Alleluia, there is so much more—and still so much more to come.

Translated, Alleluia means "God's inexpressible joy."

Come, Holy Spirit!

Therefore, since we are surrounded by such a great cloud of witnesses, let us throw off everything that hinders and the sin that so easily entangles, and let us run with perseverance the race marked out for us. Let us fix our eyes on Jesus, the author and perfecter of our faith, who for the joy set before him endured the cross, scorning its shame, and sat down at the right hand of the throne of God. Hebrews 12:1-2

Augusta/Broad Street

As we planned our move to Augusta, Nancy and I knew that a commercial building for our growing business was an absolute requirement. We needed both space and visibility. On one of our prior visits, Mike F., the founder of the local food bank, had told me about their recently vacated building. The food bank had outgrown its old building, which now stood empty. Mike said that I could rent the building very reasonably from the food bank and move right in when we relocated to Augusta. Mike showed us the old warehouse-like structure; it was plenty big and sitting right on Broad Street in downtown Augusta. How about that? The Lord had met both needs — we were set.

Loading and moving two households of furnishings and a shop full of equipment and materials, plus the altar furnishings I had in process, required two trips using the largest rental truck available. My fully loaded El Camino and two cars, plus the big truck, gave us a ragtag, caravan-style appearance on arrival. But we were in Augusta and Alleluia, answering the call.

All three of our sons plus Nancy's mother, Fran, who had also heard the "call," would be living in our new home with us. It would be our first time sharing living space with Fran. She was an independent woman who had lived alone since becoming a widow, and would now be squeezing in with us and adapting to a larger household. This would challenge all of us, but was all right. Since the floor space of this house was smaller than our last, most of Fran's furnishings and lots of ours could not be used. Fortunately, there was a sizable shed in the backyard where most of the unusable furniture could be stored until it could be passed on to others.

We made a number of improvements on the house, and it served us very well. The style of the old house, plus the quiet street, relaxed us all and lessened the stresses of this major change in all of our lives. The full-length front porch was a godsend that drew our family together. The location was good for us, just close enough—and far enough—from the Faith Village for our adjustment period. This style of living was totally new for us; we had been concerned that the communal aspect might crowd our space, especially that of our sons. It didn't, but rather, it gradually pulled us toward the village.

The new shop location was definitely uncharted territory for me. Nancy and I had driven through downtown Augusta only a couple of times. Augusta had acquired many undesirable hangouts, night spots and businesses, due in part to the long-time presence of the nearby army base, Fort Gordon. I quickly became aware of the challenging surroundings in the 500 block of Broad Street, where my new shop was located. There were several strip joints, an x-rated movie house, tattoo parlors, pawn shops, and bars. Next door was a low life bar named Mom's Place where occasionally large groups of people, all ages, young and old, male and female, just circled up in the back lot, smoking joints and passing them around until the vice squad rolled in, instantly dispersing them like a flock of birds scattering. Fortunately, even the building would soon be gone; hardly a trace remaining.

Even my new shop building had once been a bar called Daddy's Money. There were still traces of its décor, a black ceiling and black and white art deco bathrooms. This was the world I was to be in— and not of—and it would be home to my business building crosses and woodworks to glorify God. I felt as if I had been placed on Evil's doorstep. It was completely different from my very sheltered basement shop in Marietta. I considered it an evangelistic promotion from the Lord.

Whatever hardships the building presented were balanced by the abundance of floor space, probably ten times more than what I had before. That was really appreciated. This would be my shop environment for the next three and half years until the Lord opened up the next place. It proved to be a good shop and location for me. I had a full work schedule—plus, the increased Kingdom work, the work of evangelization, now all around me.

Broad Street had two distinct, different groups frequenting the streets: the street people and homeless of the daytime, and the night crawlers of the evening. The shifts changed by the light. With darkness, the daytime people faded from view and the night people appeared. It was eerie to watch in the winter when it began to happen around 5:30 pm, almost as if on a timer. A street that had been nearly vacant minutes earlier would now be dotted by figures moving about in the semi-darkness; some strippers arriving for the evening work. I grieved for those caught up in this evil culture, especially for the young ones who didn't yet know the cost.

In decades past, Augusta, the second largest city in Georgia, had had a thriving downtown area, with a retail district over a mile long on Broad Street. Now, with the growing popularity of suburban shopping centers, most businesses had closed or moved out of downtown. While the signs remained on the buildings, most were vacant or underoccupied. Some scattered businesses remained fully operating, but much of downtown spoke of the past, not the present, and certainly not the future. It seemed to be gasping for survival, flailing away in an effort to not go under. Downtown Augusta would make a considerable turnaround, but it would be slow, taking decades to accomplish. I didn't yet know why I had been put in this exact place, but I suspected there was a reason. Evil spirits abounded and I would need to be alert.

The Lord kept me totally clear of the night people and downtown after dark, but quickened me to the midday people on the street; they would soon become my lunch-hour concern.

Going out on Broad Street at midday, with my shop locked behind me and Bible in hand, became quite a ministry. The panhandlers soon spotted me. I took no money with me so as not to give away everything. I came out to them with hope, prayer, and encouragement—not money. As in the book of Acts, Peter said, *"Silver and gold have I none, but such as I have I give to you—in the name of Jesus, walk!"* Broad Street had many who were crippled in various ways, physically, mentally, spiritually. The Bible was like a magnet, and frequently someone whom I had never met would come and sit on a park bench with me just to read it.

My front door was usually kept open during hot weather; street people often walked in, hoping for something. There were regulars who would come from time to time, others who came only once. For the regulars, it was mostly a place where they could come for a few minutes and just stand and not be run off. Before opening the shop on Broad Street, I had little exposure to panhandlers, aside from those in soup kitchens and night shelters. It would be a long time before I would see them as viable people. When they presented themselves, I began to realize the Lord was watching to see how I would treat them. Sometimes I was impatient or insensitive, not wanting to be bothered, and didn't do very well.

After a year, my primary attention began to shift from the wounded and needy individuals walking the street to the defiled culture swirling around us, and those who were driving it. I felt led to trade the results of the problem for the causes of the problems, and work on them. The strip joints in my block, which was the worst block on Broad Street, were the most obvious. The Holy Spirit clearly told me to stay away from those places—they were too high a risk for me.

Soon I was drawn to a music store, The Pinnacle, located in the center of town. I didn't know why, but it was a clear leading. As I walked in its door, I was surrounded by a jungle of large hanging posters, displaying in full color and make-up the heavy-metal "artists" of the time—AC/DC, Motley Crue, KISS, and others. The showcases and counter were stocked with products of the culture, tapes, albums, etc. I hoped no one had seen me go in.

Behind the counter was a man in his late forties, pleasant and gregarious. When I introduced myself as a fellow business owner from down the street, he said his name was Roland. Noticing my Bible in my hand, he wasn't surprised that I was there to check out his store and pray. He invited me to come anytime—he said that he also was a Christian.

I began stopping in a couple of times a week to pray against this evil culture that Roland was marketing, and his mixed witness of being in both worlds. After a few visits and quiet prayers, I would stand in his store, not bothering anyone. I was shocked one day when I walked in. Roland was actually broadcasting Christian music on a live radio show, while manning the cash register, racking up big bucks selling the pagan products. I was appalled and told him so, but he saw nothing wrong with marketing both cultures, good and evil—even simultaneously.

On my next visit, Roland's wife, Shalika, was there. After meeting me, she soon disappeared, returned with a large can of Lysol, and promptly began to spray it in a circular motion around my head. She laughed mockingly while spraying, telling the amused customers nearby, "You can't be too careful, these days—especially with AIDS and everything that's going around." Then they all just smirked and turned their backs on me, ignoring me.

A few days later when I walked into The Pinnacle, Shalika was there again. Immediately she disappeared, and within a couple of minutes, a very large black policeman walked in the front door. He almost filled the door opening. He gave one glance to the side, then kept walking straight toward me. He knew, and I did too. He looked me in the eye and in a firm but pleasant manner said, "You have to leave, they don't want you in here."

In all of my visits with Roland he had never complained or asked me to leave, but Shalika wasn't as tolerant. As I walked out without a word, I felt the eyes of a dozen customers on my back. I had never been expelled from anyplace—and this was with a police escort. The evil voice, seizing the moment, made sure that I knew I was the only one of a dozen people in the store that had been ordered to leave. The others all stayed, somewhat surprised, but savoring the moment. Quickly the *Voice* explained to me that I was the only one who got out! Praise God, the outside was great!

Now, walking out onto the sidewalk, a milestone event unfolded. This big nice policeman reminded me not to go back inside or disrupt their business, then carefully explained that I had every right to spend any amount of time on the sidewalk where we were now standing. He made it clear that it was public property and belonged as much to me as to Roland and Shalika.

It was almost as if the Holy Spirit had sent this considerate policeman to fully instruct me of my rights, so that no one could deceive me or take those rights away, ever! Anywhere!

The policeman again encouraged me and told me he had to keep moving, but I could stay as long as I liked, and come whenever I wanted. He turned and walked away, leaving me standing there, Bible in hand. I never saw him again.

The Holy Spirit right away brought to my remembrance: *Whenever you go into a town and they do not receive and welcome you, go out into its streets and say, even the dust of your town that clings to our feet we are wiping off against you; yet know and understand this, that the Kingdom of God has come near you. Luke 10:10 and 11*

I wiped the dust off my feet and never returned to The Pinnacle. The mission there had been accomplished. The Holy Spirit gave me a new commission and sent me directly from there to the Planned Parenthood building further down the street. I was standing there almost before I realized I was going.

And it was then I knew that I had a responsibility to the unborn and their deceived parents, plus every right to be there. The Holy Spirit had defined the mission and given me authority. He had been preparing me to enter the battle against the culture of death, the killing of the innocents for huge money—and now it was time to go stand up. And I have, ever since, with many of the faithful, regularly, for well over twenty years.

So you, son of man, I have made you a watchman for the house of Israel; therefore hear the word of my mouth and give them warning from me. Ezekiel 33:7

Epilogue

There was a touch of sadness and regret when it was time to move from Broad Street. During the years there many projects had been built and installed in various places. As a shop it had been challenging—but quite sufficient. The next shop would be a nice improvement and six miles closer to our home, but I would miss the downtown location. The Lord had used the bawdy Broad Street surroundings to hammer my steel—to get me focused and alert and set against evil. It had in fact defined much of my evangelical call and had prepared me for the unknown that lay ahead.

I had spent all of my lunch hours for a year in front of the murder clinic. Now, working at the new shop, that time would be reduced. But even to this day, I am still in front of the clinic several times every month, hoping to help others do the same.

Perhaps the biggest lesson I learned from Broad Street was that I was to be an impact player, with my career work, woodworks to glorify God, and my career call, evangelizing anyone to a closer walk with Jesus. It has been very exhilarating—I'm always looking to see which I will be led by the Holy Spirit to work on in the next moment. Like moving from picking up hitchhikers to evangelizing elevator passengers, so was moving from downtown to the suburbs; each had its place and time because the Holy Spirit orchestrated it all.

Whatever you do, do your work heartily, as for the Lord rather than for men, knowing that from the Lord you will receive the reward of the inheritance. It is the Lord Christ whom you serve. Colossians 3:23-24

Standing Up for Life

During a visit to Alleluia in January of 1984, on the anniversary of Roe vs. Wade, Nancy and I joined a large group, quiet with apprehension, to watch "The Silent Scream," a video of an abortion in progress, filmed from inside the mother's womb. The camera was positioned behind the back of the baby (fetus), who was approximately three to four months old. In the film, a horrifying event was transpiring. This clearly well-formed baby was sensing the impending brutality and violence that would end his life. The body language of that baby was chilling. Fear and terror were captured in this tiny soul caught between two states: new life and imminent death. Watching this child was like watching an adult, overcome with fear, chained in a dark room, sensing the coming of an executioner—with no possibility of escape and no one to lend help.

That film shook Nancy and me to the core. For eleven years, we had been deceived by the "tissue myth" and had allowed apathy to keep us from learning the truth. We had not yet come to really *know* that life begins at conception. We had paid little attention to the issue, since abortion was not something we would ever consider doing ourselves. Now, having seen this desperate child with our own eyes, we both knew we were culpable and had to respond. We didn't know what, but something was expected and required of us, some action on behalf of these most defenseless.

A year and a half later, when I walked onto the sidewalk in front of Planned Parenthood, the memory of that video again put a chill through me. I had been silently commissioned by the Holy Spirit to get involved in this battle. There was no doubt. I was a total novice—but I had been sent. I had never stood up publicly for any cause, but now I must. I could no longer buy into the false ideas that I had accepted before: that it "wasn't my job," or that "we would never have an abortion but we couldn't tell others what to do." I could no longer condone such statements by others either. I was to be a watchman on the wall to help alert others to the truth about this abominable deception. Nancy would soon join me. I would come to see why my business had been located on Broad Street—just a few blocks away from Planned Parenthood..

Standing for the unborn and their parents and the culture of life was something I would have much preferred not needing to do. But my personal preference wasn't a consideration. I knew that I was to fully embrace the Holy Spirit's call and give this my best. I would have to learn from the street up. My only training was walking in the Spirit into other "unplanned" encounters.

My early years in that ministry were a learning experience, for sure. I first had to deal with myself and how I felt about public opinion. I still considered the approval of other people to be important. The evil spirits tried to persuade me what a fool I was, standing with a cross and a signboard painted in red letters with the message, "Babies Deserve Life—Not a Dumpster," right in front of an internationally known organization. At that time, there were a number of women and some men coming regularly during the lunch hour to counsel individuals coming to Planned Parenthood for abortions, and to protest. The counseling frequently bore great fruit; the protesting did not. Gradually, the number of counselors and protestors would dwindle. Even very good people can struggle with long-term patience and commitment.

My main gifts in those days were zeal and boldness, and the demons countered with their version of the same. Cars would rush past with voices screaming out, "Get a job!" or "Go home!" or "Get a life!" It would be several months before I could take in those shouts and react rightly, developing a deep inner peace about it all. When I could begin to recognize the voices as those of demons who were using people, I did much better. It was only after I stopped worrying about what other people thought of me out there that I could begin to be effective at all.

One day in the late eighties, as I stood in front of Planned Parenthood, something happened that shocked me. A car pulled up, and out jumped two frivolous teenagers about seventeen years old. They were in high spirits, as if they were out on a date. Arm in arm, they headed for the front door. Without delay, I asked them, "Do you know they kill babies in there?" (Many people still claim not to know.) With no shame, the boy replied, "Yeah, we gotta get rid of this young'un 'fore she sees it—if she sees it, she'll wanta keep it!" They both laughed and brushed past me into the abortuary, much like they were walking into a fast food place.

The truth in that flippantly delivered statement has haunted me for two decades. The boy's street smart reply clearly proves the value of sonograms in overcoming the denial that a pregnancy is truly a life. When expectant mothers see a sonogram of their babies, most no longer consider an abortion. It opens their eyes to the truth about the pregnancy and the life developing within them.

The old myths that a fetus is "only tissue," "not a real baby," and "not yet a fully human life," and other such false ideas, misled many in the early days of legalized abortion. Also, because it was legal, the law of the land, many thought that made it acceptable (unfortunately, many still do).Thankfully, over time, more men have come into the battle, possibly due to their certainty that there is a life in jeopardy, and their inner call to be defenders of the defenseless. Men standing for the preborn are not taken in by "women's rights" myths or the "reproductive health care" catchphrase that tries to disguise the over fifty million recorded abortion-caused deaths in America.

The pro-life movement across the country was primarily confrontational during the earlier years, due to the passion surrounding the issue. Most of us were there to stand for what we "knew" to be right. I don't know which side had more fervor or anger. Medical students were regularly stationed outside the abortion clinic to escort girls and women inside for an abortion, past the pro-lifers standing on the sidewalk. I frequently returned to work feeling bad about what had happened—and my part in it. Kevin, a community elder, who is also a psychiatrist, had been in front of the clinic many times and had witnessed the results of my unbridled zeal. He prayed over me that I would speak differently (with less abrasiveness and more gentleness) and listen more.

One day in the mid-nineties, something major happened that redirected us. I heard the *Voice* clearly say, "I want you to be invitational, not confrontational. You are not to focus on the evil—but to invite them to Me and My ways." That simple word would completely change the direction of our pro-life ministry. It called us to lay down our arguments for life and truth and opened us up to love the sinners and meet them where they were. (*"Father, forgive them, they don't know what they're doing."*) We began to understand that they couldn't truly grasp the magnitude of an abortion and still go through with it. This was a major breakthrough, moving us toward the disposition we were called to have: loving the sinner but hating the sin. We later learned that a shift in this direction had happened in many parts of the country, almost simultaneously, apparently called for by the Holy Spirit. Since that time, throughout America, many abortion clinics have been closed, simply by agape love. I now know that anyone who can't come to the street trying to love the sinner isn't yet ready to come and stand at an abortion clinic. Loving the sinner, even the clinic staff, is probably Jesus' work through the pro-life movement that has borne the most fruit.

Going to the street with the intent of bringing the love of Jesus to anyone and everyone definitely broadens the scope of the ministry, but it in no way diminishes the pro-life work. The knowledge of being on holy ground, ground ordained by God for your presence as a witness, is a wonderful advantage over any evil sent in your direction. Street people are frequently drawn in and are recipients of the Lord's blessings. They feel His love through the people He calls to be there.

When we have a group with crosses and banners standing outside of a clinic, the most favorable response we usually get from passing motorists is a light tap of the horn and a thumbs up. For this we are grateful. The vast majority of passersby go to great effort to appear oblivious or ignore our presence and deny any responsibility. (Lord, open their hearts.) Through it all, we work at maintaining an "outdoor church" spirit and atmosphere, giving the Holy Spirit the opportunity to use us as He will.

The depraved state of our culture is so clearly evident at an abortion clinic, and the numbing deception of the general public is downright appalling. Abortion kills much more than the baby. It has severely wounded the conscience of our nation. A few encounters through the years have stayed in my mind as though they just happened, I suppose because each one jolted me to some degree.

One morning a young woman parked her car and approached us, noticeably shaken, saying that she saw us there each Wednesday morning with the crosses. She went on to tell us that each time, it made her relive her own abortion, which had been forced on her by her mother after she was raped at twelve years of age. We assured her that we were not there to increase her pain or to heap guilt on anyone, but were there to warn and to help spare others the same suffering. We offered to pray with her, but she declined, and went away sad. Her unwanted abortion and false guilt continued to torment her.

Another day, a cocky and confident father and his pretty, college-age daughter came around the corner, arm in arm, laughing and enjoying each other on the way to abort her child and his grandchild. On their way in the door, they slowed down just enough for the father to mock me and hurl insults at me for being there. As intelligent and gifted as he appeared, the father was pitiable for failing his family that day—and in that way.

A number of couples drove three hours or more so that the wives could be sterilized, only to come upon us standing in front of the clinic, holding our large crosses. They had been sent by their local health department, which had not informed them that Planned Parenthood was an abortuary. When they were made aware of this, they looked violated and embarrassed by just being on the property. Some received prayers, got in their cars and went right back home, not wanting to be involved in any way with abortion providers.

On another occasion, a nice-looking, well-dressed family, a father, mother, and three vibrant children, arrived to have the fourth child aborted. They were escorted right in, and the three children were given toys from Planned Parenthood's toy chest. They played on the floor right inside the front door as their sibling's life was about to be terminated. By now, the father was distraught, wanting this child as much as the first three, but the mother didn't want the inconvenience of another pregnancy and child. The father, in tears, came outside several times to talk with us and receive prayers, but the mother resisted each of his attempts to beg her to reconsider. She remained adamant. Their fourth child was summarily put to death, a victim of the law of the land — abortion on demand, for any or no reason. Even after many years, I can't get this scene out of my mind.

It's hard to forget the many patrons at the abortion clinics wearing Christian shirts, or with evangelistic license plates on their cars. Today's "churchianity" paints with a broad brush, and situational ethics blur the lines. Right and wrong get lost in Satan's divisive rabbit trails. Many of the leaders who should know truth don't have the courage to stand up and lead their flocks in this most important area.

Sad and disturbing is the zoned out, oblivious mentality prevalent on Saturday mornings at the Women's Preferred Health Clinic in west Augusta. The parking lot is jammed with cars, mostly late model, with young women and girls rushing inside. Outside are a group of men, individually killing time, some milling around, some smoking, some with cell phones to their ears, some dozing in their cars, others giving in to impatience. Inside, their "loved one" is being inflicted with a wound that may never heal, and their child's life is being snuffed out. After the death is accomplished, and as the couple drives away, it's not uncommon that their relationship is already over — even then. Abortion is a multi-tasking destroyer, and can wield a lifetime's worth of accusations and torment.

But there have been situations that make it all seem worthwhile. In the midst of all this suffering, death and demonic activity, we stand on holy ground. This very "prayed up" terrain is host to some of the best people and happenings. *Where sin abounds, grace abounds all the mo*re. Few things sharpen faith and character like street ministry for life.

One morning, high school and college students from our Alleluia school unexpectedly joined us in front of the clinic. Young people kept arriving and climbing out of cars until about twenty were there. Regardless of the weather, this pattern repeated itself each Wednesday morning throughout the school year, for about three years. Sometimes it was so cold and dark in the morning as they arrived that they were hard to recognize, all bundled in their coats, hoods and multiple layers. They were there for the hour on behalf of the babies and mothers. Because they had good formation, they already knew how to come in love. Several of them went on to become leaders in college, gathering pro-life groups around them. We've observed that just by their presence at the clinics, young people of any age, but especially infants, high school age, and college age, have a powerful impact on the abortion providers. There is probably much to be learned in that.

Many faithful of all ages have for years come in the cold or the heat or the pouring rain to stand up for the babies and their parents. There have been many times when their schedules were tight, their energy low, their bodies sick or their joints aching, but they've come—and kept coming. They've endured the jeers and the silence equally well. They don't have to see the outcome to know their efforts will bring results. As Mother Teresa said, "We're not called to be successful; we're called to be faithful."

Along the way there have been countless babies saved, and parents spared. Most of those we never heard about. Abortion is a shameful and embarrassing option, and most who reconsider and turn away will stay far away. For some women, just getting out of the car to go into an abortion clinic is a traumatizing ordeal; for others, it looks like a walk in the park—their mental anguish is deferred for a later time.

In Augusta, many women have been redirected to the Care Pregnancy Center located near the abortuaries. The care given there is the extreme opposite of the "care" offered by Planned Parenthood. At the pregnancy center, women can get all they will need through the time of the child's birth and beyond. Other women have received loving counsel right outside the clinic doors and made a good choice to turn away from any thoughts of abortion, to trust the Lord and bring their children into the world. Over the years, many women already in the abortion clinic turned away at the last minute, after seeing or hearing people standing outside praying and singing. Or maybe they finally heard and heeded the desperate warnings from their own consciences. However it happened, they fled the abortuary, terrified by the near brush with a mistake they would regret all their lives. We've even known clinic workers and an abortionist who had radical awakenings and came to actively stand for life. Some of the most staunch and active pro-life workers were once personally wounded by abortion. Jesus' redemptive work has no limits.

Many times pro-life people get accused of opposing abortion with no concern for what happens later to an "unwanted" child. We should all be very clear: there are no unwanted children. If the Lord has given them life, they are wanted. *He* wants them and will make a way for them.

Right now, as I'm writing, Bob and Alice, who live on the next street, have cared for over sixty foster children. The babies come to their home when they are just days old, and usually stay for two or more weeks, sometimes even several months, as they wait for their new adoptive parents. The babies get a wonderful start in life with a caring, praying foster family. This is Bob and Alice's primary way of standing up for life—and what a selfless work of mercy it is.

Several families in the Alleluia Community have adopted from one to seven children. These great acts of caring and giving happen across the country. Pro-life people are serious about the sanctity of life, from conception to natural death.

Who would have ever thought that America's values would sink to such depths that we wouldn't protect our most defenseless, but rather would choose to get rid of them. Our apathy, complacency and acquiescence toward such horrific abuse must grieve the Lord just as much as the abortions. As a nation, we have surely condoned this holocaust by looking the other way and failing to stand up against it.

Cases of rape and incest that lead to pregnancy and abortions are very rare, numbering under 2% of abortions in total. Despite the terrible sin involved, these babies are also special. God has given them life and, as much as any of us, they deserve the right to live it.

With every situation and pregnancy, there is help available. The Lord has His people on duty. Abortion is never an answer or solution; it violates everything about God's plan. We must all be crystal clear in our own thinking to help others see this issue correctly. The Lord is watching. I believe He is also waiting for the church to wake up and take responsibility; when a sufficient number do, the Lord will bring this horror to an end. We want to see that firsthand! I can't imagine walking away from this battle before our land is rid of this evil.

> *O Lord, thou hast searched me and known me! For thou didst form my inward parts, thou didst knit me together in my mother's womb. I praise thee, for thou art fearful and wonderful. Wonderful are thy works! Thou knowest me right well; my frame was not hidden from thee, when I was being made in secret, intricately wrought in the depths of the earth. Thy eyes beheld my unformed substance; in thy book were written, every one of them, the days that were formed for me, when as yet here was none of them. How precious to me are thy thoughts, O God! How vast is the sum of them. Psalm 139: 1, 13-17*

Faith on the Street

I received a call one day from Bill C., who told me of an interesting proposal that he thought I might like. Bill had received an invitation from Jerry, a faithful, committed Christian friend of his whom I had not yet met, to meet regularly to pray. Jerry thought of Bill since they were long-standing spiritual brothers who both expected Jesus to make lots of good things happen, especially when He was asked. Jerry left it to Bill to find someone suitable to fill out a threesome.

Bill called me, believing that my kind of faith would fit the agenda. "By the way," Bill added, "Jerry is a firebrand and he suggested holding the gathering behind Shoney's, outside where we won't disturb anyone." This was out of respect for Shoney's customers—outdoors, we could be as vocal or animated as seemed appropriate. The time would be 6:30 am on Wednesday morning, every other week, and we would meet for about a half hour. All right, this could be interesting, I thought. Let's give it a shot and see where it goes.

A couple of times, I pondered the line, "outside where we won't disturb anyone." When in Atlanta, I had joined up with two friends on occasion for a similar outdoor prayer session. We had met just off the edge of a small airport, really out in the open. Anyway, I would definitely be there with Bill and Jerry.

As I arrived on that first Wednesday morning, ready to pray, I got my first look at our setting. Shoney's restaurant backed up to a very large asphalt parking lot, probably eight to ten acres, that cornered on two major highways, both heavily traveled in the early mornings. Bill had just arrived and Jerry rolled up right on time.

Bill was a good Alleluia friend whom I had known since our earliest visits to Augusta. Nancy and I had stayed with or eaten with Bill and his wife, Dian, a number of times and had grown close after moving to Alleluia. Bill was a tall Texan (Texans are always Texans no matter where they live), late forties in age, chock full of the Holy Spirit, a devout Catholic, loaded with ministry gifts and very hands on. Bill did everything full tilt.

My first impression of Jerry was that of a "man's man," full of joy, high spirited, gregarious, a disciplined body builder, just oozing with strength and energy—a former Ranger in Vietnam. He was very well known in his Baptist church, had experienced a radical conversion from a former life as a hell-raiser, and now frequently preached at many different churches, mostly Baptist. Jerry didn't come to socialize, but to pray. He was ready, so pray we did. I soon learned a new phrase from Jerry, "Take us to the throne room." That meant Jerry was asking one of us to unleash a bodacious prayer for the group.

The half hour flew by and as we were leaving, my eye caught sight of two establishments at the upper end of the parking lot. They both appeared to be all-night bars and still had lots of cars parked outside, even at 7 am. I hadn't expected that.

Two weeks later, when we returned, I brought a 5-foot-tall cross to hold, to give us some credibility. I didn't want us to be mistaken by people driving past as leftovers from the all-night bar trade. Bill, Jerry and I prayed about various things. We again noticed the cars parked outside the bars and the myriad of beer bottles and cans scattered in the area. Both men and women were slowly coming out to their cars.

We continued our gatherings every other Wednesday, but soon lengthened our time to an hour. Before long, we all three felt that every other week wasn't often enough, so we adjusted our schedule to every week. By now, we had started to add guests to our group, mostly Jerry's friends. Several of them were already spiritual leaders in their church. He was such a personality and leader in his church that he was like a magnet to men (I'm sure he had formerly been to women as well).

These Baptist friends were not yet accustomed to taking their faith to the street, nor to joining together with Catholics who loved Jesus as much as they did. From the beginning, these gatherings were Spirit-led and very ecumenical.

Our group steadily grew in numbers and intensity, and we found ourselves including prayers for the closing of the two bars. The bars were adjacent to each other at the opposite end of the parking lot from where we were stationed, probably a hundred yards from us. One bar was named "Bubba and Bud's" and the other, "The Last Word." Even from a long distance, the fruit of these all-night drinking emporiums looked very bad.

Soon afterwards, we arrived one Wednesday morning and noticed that something looked different. As we looked more closely, we could see that the large letters "Bubba and Bud's" had been removed from the building; only the unfaded paint behind those letters gave any indication that they had ever been there. Wow! The bar was closed—gone. We had asked and the Lord had delivered. We tried hard not to look too shocked.

That success so filled our minds that it dominated our time together that morning. We all went across the parking lot and looked into that huge building—it was virtually empty. When God delivers,

He delivers! It didn't take long for us to realize, too, that God had given us a new gathering place. All those weeks, we had been out in the open parking lot. Now the Lord had given us a nice metal over-hanging roof to protect us from rain, and a storefront to block the wind. We were still outside and winter was coming, but our accom-modations had improved substantially. Bubba and Bud's was gone and we had replaced it. What an upgrade! We suddenly realized that being in this parking lot had never been about being near Shoney's, but rather about taking our faith out into the world.

Our new location put us right next to The Last Word, where we could now gain momentum for its closing. It was a thriving place, with lots of people that seemed to be heading down a bad path. Morality seemed to be really put to the test there. Our focused prayer gatherings at the beginning had now developed into prayers and ministry—both individual ministry and ministry against the evils of the culture. We never knew what was coming next, but we knew that the Holy Spirit was in charge and that we better stay alert.

Not everyone at The Last Word was really happy about our pres-ence—we now had an arsenal of crosses—some 7 feet, 8 feet, and 9 feet tall. Demons hate the cross, and sometimes act up, but the cross shuts the demons down. We had a number of occasions when we got to pray over the bar patrons, and even over some of the employees. Some showed real remorse and repentance over their behavior.

One day we arrived and The Last Word was closed. The Holy Spirit had closed it down. Again we were greatly encouraged, looking at that vacant building and the Lord's response to prayers. Obviously, He wanted those places closed even more than we did and had been waiting for someone to ask Him.

After the bar had been vacant for several months, we arrived one morning to discover new construction in progress, renovation for a new bar. The work progressed over a number of weeks and the new bar emerged and opened. We began praying for its closing right away. The bar's stay in business was brief, probably no longer than it took for them to renovate. The Holy Spirit closed it, also, and the building became empty again. Amen! Wow—three in a row!

While these renovations and closings were happening, the Kingdom was breaking forth also. There were only two businesses still open along that end of the vast parking lot, and they opened later in the morning. Sometimes, drivers passing by would go out of their way to pull slowly alongside our group and ask for personal prayers (some for very serious needs). Somehow, they just seemed to know to come, and when. Several of these drivers were police. They treated us as if we belonged and were the owners of that space. This area that Satan had once claimed for evil, God was now claiming for good.

Bill C. was the head of youth development for the community, and by this time, fifteen or more high school students from the Alleluia School came regularly. The experience was a wonderful opportunity for developing their faith. During Lent, we would walk "the way of the cross" several times around that huge parking lot, switching the bearers of the big crosses with each lap so more could feel the weight of Calvary. It would bring tears to our eyes, watching all of the crosses against the dark sky, many reverently carried by teenagers. Frequently, drivers who were leaving Shoney's, seeing the cross procession passing in front of them, would wait quietly with only their parking lights on, savoring the moment themselves—and experiencing Lent in a more profound way. Those times were priceless.

By now, the gathering had grown in size to twenty-five people, and sometimes more. Nearly a dozen came at one time or another from Jerry's church. Several of them were baptized in the Spirit while there and were laid out (slain in the Spirit or resting in the Spirit) on the asphalt, both very different experiences from what they may have been accustomed to even after years of churchgoing.

One particular Wednesday morning, a sizable group of young people came—high school and college age—along with more than the average number of adults. We were praying over a couple of the young people, and then it happened. The Holy Spirit broke out, and people were going down all over the place, slain in the Spirit. For several, this was a first-time experience. Soon, our area on the concrete under the storefront overhang looked like a temporary morgue. Bodies were laid side by side like cordwood—we were having to step over people to catch the next one going down. I believe that everyone there was slain before it was over, about twenty-five or more people in all. What a power display by the Holy Spirit that morning, out in plain view. I have devoted a later chapter to what it means to be "slain in the Spirit" to better explain this phenomenon and to recount some memorable occurrences.

Soon renovations began again, for a third bar. The story was similar to that of the second bar. The renovations seemed expensive, and the bar's open time brief. The Lord closed it, also. By now it was obvious He didn't want any bar in that building.

After awhile, construction workers converted the building into a video poker establishment. Soon video poker places sprang up all over that corner of North Augusta, South Carolina. Now, instead of beer bottles in the parking lot in the mornings, we had the gambling addicts still inside who couldn't quit 'til they had squandered all their money. Their threadbare old cars were scattered in the lot as a tribute to this evil, life-wrecking addiction. Our group regularly walked around and into these places with the crosses and prayed for their closing while their operating managers stood by with guns on their hips. We sometimes wondered if the first evil that we prayed against had been replaced with an even worse evil.

As a real credit to the state of South Carolina, political leaders soon recognized the destruction video poker was creating with individuals and families and outlawed the practice altogether. Not only were the poker places closed, and their licenses revoked, but their machines were confiscated and sold by the state. Hallelujah! The parking lot was cleared again. Evil had been evicted.

We later came to see that this parking lot had been a wonderful spiritual stepping-stone for those of all ages, a great opportunity for sharpening our gifts to go out and stand against the evil culture and culture of death. Considering such a simple beginning, the Lord surely brought forth a bountiful crop in that prayed-up parking lot. It had been like a huge and holy greenhouse for us to grow in.

The kingdom of heaven is like a grain of mustard seed which a man took and sowed in his field; it is the smallest of all seeds, but when it has grown it is the greatest of all shrubs and becomes a tree... so that the birds of the air come and make nests in its branches. Matthew 13:31-32

For over six years we had gathered each Wednesday morning, in all kinds of weather. Even though the parking lot was privately owned, we were never asked to leave or change any of our activities. It was as though we had been there by virtue of a six-year lease, written by the Holy Spirit, hand delivered to us. But now, our time there was up. At the Holy Spirit's leadings, we prepared to move our Wednesday prayer times from the parking lot to another location a few blocks away. An adult "bookstore," a vile pornography shop that had already been open around the clock for decades, was calling for our attention. Our challenge was to point their patrons toward Jesus, the only way of escape from this corrosive addiction. Although they may have wanted to think of pornography as entertainment or recreation, they were already under assault by the evil one—their very souls in jeopardy. Also, the murder clinic (the abortion clinic just across the river) needed more of our presence. It was time to step out and be about the Lord's work. We had all been groomed for the challenge that lay ahead. We were stepping up to the cutting edge of good and evil.

Our Wednesday morning group now congregated along a very busy highway with loud, fast-moving cars, trucks and tractor trailers, with the traffic noise punctuated with a few jeers and blowing horns. Our procession of men with crosses along the roadway and near the shop's driveway had an immediate impact on those trying to drive in "unnoticed." The store's management responded straightaway by summoning both city and county police. Three cars arrived within minutes. A quick visit to city hall verified our right to be there. Since the store was such a repugnant blight on the area, with their business license "grandfathered in," the city highly encouraged our efforts, and even agreed to have the police keep an eye out for us. We would have to stay on the right-of-way, off the store's property, but we were duly "permitted." I remembered the big policeman on Broad Street who had explained how it worked and what my rights were. Even so, the sounds and smells and wind from the rush-hour traffic roaring past on the highway and the crunching sounds of gravel from the patrons' cars slinking up kept us quite alert. Unpleasant as it seemed at first, we continued to have many diligent Kingdom workers present. We soon came to realize that the patrons were affected much more by our presence than we were by theirs. Evil operates under the crushing burden of guilt, a guilt so heavy there that it seemed to blanket the entire property.

That guilt and shame would manifest in two vastly different ways with the patrons. Most would keep as much distance as possible between themselves and our crosses, some almost running off of the property to avoid us. A few would pull alongside us in a state of repentance, asking for prayers. In both cases, they had come under the conviction of the Holy Spirit. We experienced some extraordinary results.

The Lord soon added a 5 pm assemblage each Friday due to a heavy influx of customers rushing in after the work week with their pay in hand. Our gathering would alternate back and forth each week for the next few years between the porno shop (men only at that location) and the abortuary. At first we felt filthy just being outside those noxious establishments, but the infectious evil being pushed on a deceived public has to be confronted by those who know better and are called to stand for the good of all. Certainly, no part of this activity looked or felt like the pristine image of Christianity that is usually visualized, but it must have resembled Jesus' ministry while walking the earth and undoubtedly was the fleshing out of our group's commission from Him.

The famous quote by Edmund Burke, "The only thing necessary for evil to triumph is for good men to do nothing," took on greater meaning for us. I could never disregard it again.

Go to the River

About a year after moving to Augusta, we were building all of the altar furnishings for a large Methodist church in Dunwoody, an upscale neighborhood in North Atlanta. This project was to be our second one in the same area. The year before we had done an Episcopal church, just around the corner.

This church project consisted of building the altar, lectern, altar rails, baptismal font, large hanging cross and several smaller items. All of the pieces were done in cherry and swirl mahogany; they were large, very elegant, and were going into a spectacular new sanctuary, by far the largest church project that we had received. We had completed the woodwork on these pieces, and it was time for the finish. Our son, Craig, was working with me, and we were ready to apply the stain and lacquer. Even unfinished, they were an impressive collection of pieces lined up in that old building.

It was a beautiful warm spring Saturday, ideal conditions for finishing. We had started right into the project with the expectation that, by the end of the day, all of the pieces would be stained and sprayed. This was essential to stay on our completion schedule.

Life experience is a wonderful thing; other than grace, nothing else quite compares. If any of us has worked in an area for many years with the same type of materials and equipment, we develop certain expectations. When things don't go quite right, we make adjustments and move on. We try to anticipate and read the results we're getting, paying close attention. With some adapting and adjusting, we can usually accomplish our aims.

This particular morning, we opened with prayer and got started. Right away, materials and techniques that had worked for over twenty-five years weren't working—not at all. This was the day for these pieces to get sprayed, and nothing was going right. When the compressor and spraygun were working right, the chemicals weren't. The stain and lacquer were not working together—none were flowing and taking well, none were "sitting down" and drying as they should. It was becoming more exasperating by the minute. After about an hour and a half, with only lost time, lost materials, and frustration to show for it, there came a silent word from the *Voice*, "Go to the river." Like a coach calling, "time out," the game was stopped—abruptly.

I knew the *Voice* and I knew the river. The Savannah River flows through Augusta just north of Broad Street where my shop was located. It was an eighth of a mile away, just beyond the next street. I had occasionally gone to the river at lunch time just to be quiet and clear my head. The Riverwalk, a beautiful brick-paved, landscaped riverfront that now stretches along downtown Augusta, had not yet been built, and the area was still very natural and undeveloped, with hardly anyone around most of the time. I told Craig what the *Voice* had said and to stay and get things in order. I was going to the river and would be right back.

My trip to the river was very much like some people's experience of going to a church when things are just going from bad to worse and they're losing ground. Somehow, at those times, we each need to find a way to get quiet and collect ourselves—and, hopefully, take the opportunity to call upon the Lord for clarity and direction.

As I walked to the top of the long bank going down to the river, the Lord's peace began to settle over me. I barely had time to still myself, standing there, looking down at the river current flowing along, when the *Voice* spoke again, sternly this time, "I have a wood ministry and I've allowed you to work in it."

And there it was. Nothing else was needed. No more words, definitely no discussion—back to the shop. In the three or four minutes it took to walk back to the shop, it became crystal clear. The Holy Spirit had brought clarity.

When I arrived at the shop, I told Craig what the Holy Spirit had said, and that we were to get on our knees before Him and repent. I led us through a prayer of repentance. We soon felt renewed and encouraged. Our confidence was being restored; we could move forward.

We started back to our finishing process, with the same equipment, same materials and the same techniques—but a different outlook. This time, it all worked beautifully, beyond textbook, far better than we had expected as we had driven in earlier that morning. The day became a wonderful experience, both with the work and in the Spirit. We walked away that evening with all of the pieces sprayed and a real sense of gratitude—and relief.

What the Lord showed me that day was that I had become proud and ungrateful, that I had begun to take His grace for granted. The business had been going well, we had done several large church jobs back to back, with more on the horizon, and I had probably come to believe it was due to my skill, or hard work, or diligence, or even, that maybe it was just time for good things to happen. None of which was true.

I suddenly realized it had never been my business, but His. I was being allowed to manage it for Him, but He was the owner and I was the steward. He also showed me that I was to be a good steward, not just of workmanship, but also of good attitude and a grateful heart (they were the most important).

That encounter transformed the business and me, bringing incredible peace and assurance. I try to do my best, working in it and representing Him. He does the hard part: marketing, finances and making everything work (providing always-sufficient grace and much unseen help). Also, He bears the rigors of ownership.

There would be a lot less stress, and fewer heart attacks, broken lives and failed businesses, if we would take more time to "go to the river," and then listen to what He tells us. And, of course, keep in mind that we own nothing. We are just stewards of what He's entrusted to us—the best of all arrangements!

That brief time required to go to the river was one of my best investments. I've reflected on it for years and come to know it was not just a one-time correction, but rather a lifetime word of warning. It has been like a divine GPS keeping me on the straight path.

Abide in me, and I in you. As the branch cannot bear fruit by itself, unless it abides in the vine, neither can you, unless you abide in me. I am the vine, you are the branches, he who abides in me, and I in him, he it is that bears much fruit, for apart from me you can do nothing.

If you abide in me, and my words abide in you, ask whatever you will, and it shall be done for you. John 15:4-5,7

Wilma's Birthday Present

Al and Wilma were not your ordinary couple. I hardly knew them and had never spoken to her. Al was a sizable man, a rather gregarious type, probably about fifty in age. Wilma was a slender little gray-haired, demure lady about ten years his senior. I don't know how long they had been married, but they seemed deeply in love.

A few weeks earlier, they had asked the Alleluia Community elders if they could become members of the community. Al and Wilma were accepted as underway (in process) members and began merging their lives and schedule into the rhythm of the community.

On the day of the Alleluia School's first Christmas Festival, Al and Wilma came by my booth and bought a small piece of woodwork from me, and happily walked away. Some time later that day, they returned, both quite excited. They wanted to know if I would be willing to make Wilma's birthday present—her casket. She would be needing it before too long—she was dying. They both acted as though this was a special purchase they'd dreamed of for a long time.

Needless to say, I wasn't prepared for such a dire health report, nor such a question. For me, it was the first of its type. I had built lots of furniture, a number of houses, but had never considered building caskets. The combination of the jolting question and their beaming, almost exuberant faces caught me totally off guard, flat-footed. I came out with the best response I could. "I'm honored to be asked," I told them. "But I'll have to pray about it and get back to you." Al and

Wilma were fine with that and walked away hand in hand, mission accomplished.

When Nancy and I had felt led to start our business, Images of the Cross, a few years earlier, we knew it was to be "crosses and woodworks to glorify God." We knew that meant no secular work and only woodwork that pointed directly to Him. Until now, it had been just crosses and church furnishings.

At the first opportunity, I took to prayer the question of whether to build Wilma's casket. Would this glorify Him? The Lord immediately answered, "Absolutely!"

Well, all right then! That was settled. As with most of my communication with the Lord, it was quick, concise, and required no discussion. He doesn't need my input.

A few days later, I saw Al and informed him that the Lord had given me an "absolutely" about their casket question. He lit up, saying that was good, that we still had some time yet—Wilma was doing pretty well. We parted with no more discussion. Subconsciously, I probably hoped the illness would just go away and Wilma would get well, and that they wouldn't need the casket.

One Friday in early February, I came back to my shop after lunch, and as I reached to unlock the door, I noticed a quickly scrawled note taped there. The note read, "It looks like Wilma is going quicker than expected, we better hurry," and was signed "Al." Wow! Reality check. I didn't know anything about sizes, details, burial requirements, nothing. I realized I had better get on it.

Leaving the door locked, I turned right around and walked the block and a half to a large downtown funeral home owned by the second generation of the Poteet family. Surely they knew the answers to my questions. But I didn't know if they would give out information to a private casket builder.

I walked into their starkly silent entrance. It was so quiet, I even felt self-conscious of my footsteps, and there, straight ahead, sat Tommy Poteet. He looked like someone in a movie, cast as an undertaker, even looking above his glasses—first to the top of my head and then to my feet, seemingly measuring me for a casket. Wasting no time.

As I began stumbling around with my explanation for being there, Tommy seemed to rather savor the moment. He was used to people being uncomfortable in his office; perhaps it gave some relief from an often morbid business. But he readily shifted into a gracious, helpful host. We were about the same age and had some similarity in life experiences—both husbands, fathers, Christians, and businessmen. Tommy was not at all threatened by my casket building, and over the course of the next half hour, he gave me a tour through his whole establishment.

We walked among the caskets, most new and ready for selection, others occupied by clean-scrubbed, well dressed bodies, quietly lying there waiting for the final send off. This was a totally new experience for me, but for Tommy, it seemed to be comfortable and even fulfilling; he also seemed to sense this was the beginning of something important. I will always be grateful for that time with Tommy. I came away knowing all I needed to about caskets, vaults, sizes, burial plots, state requirements, etc. God had met my needs again. Tommy enabled me to get knowledgeable enough to move forward with the birthday gift.

That night, during a large prayer and praise gathering, Al was called to the phone used there for emergencies. It was urgent. He was told that Wilma was gone; the Lord had taken her home. In a loud, excited voice, Al burst into rejoicing, saying, "Praise God—she's gone—she's gone—praise God!" He was almost jumping with joy.

Al's exuberant pronouncement of Wilma's passing momentarily shocked the big group. The suddenness seemed to stun a lot of us, but Al's immediate, sheer joy really caught us off guard. The meeting ended and Al, without wavering, made his way through the well-wishing brothers and sisters, walking straight toward me. As I looked into Al's rather wild-looking eyes, he reached out, firmly gripped my hands in his, and said, "Brother, it's in your hands." With that, he turned and left.

So, there we have it. It was 10 pm Friday night and Wilma's body was to be placed in my very first casket early Monday morning. I had no plans drawn, no sufficient amount of wood on hand for a casket. Lumber wholesalers were closed on Saturdays, a weekend-long community celebration was planned that weekend, and I had no help lined up. "Brother, it's in your hands!" resounded in my head a few times. "Okay, it's yours to do," I told myself. "Now start doing it."

Fortunately, on Saturday, a long-time local retail supplier was open and had sufficient 8/4 cypress in stock—so that quickly became "the wood." Our sons and some of the community brothers came by the shop off and on to help as needed. The building of Wilma's casket became an almost continuous Saturday/Sunday project (the ox was definitely in the ditch), with the exception of one church service we attended, and very limited "crash time." Throughout the machining, gluing and sanding, the clock kept speeding along and Satan kept telling me, "You're not going to make it—it won't be ready."

Well, at 4 am Monday morning, the casket seemed ready, and the Lord said, "It's finished." Lloyd, a friend of mine and of Al and Wilma, would arrive at 6 am to load it into his van to take it to the funeral home for Wilma's body. God is good! I began to feel the cold; my shop had no ceiling or insulation, it was just an old masonry warehouse. I went over and lay down on the concrete floor right in front of the gas heater to wait for Lloyd. Wow! Everything felt good. God had carried us—again. "In Jesus' name, get out of here, Satan!" I said. "We're not listening to you." With the casket completed, God had again trumped Satan's lies.

Wilma's going to Glory was not only my first casket but also the first burial in the Alleluia Community Cemetery. For several years, the community leaders had talked of a cemetery, and had even set aside land for it. Wilma's death brought it to life.

On the day of the funeral, the winter weather was unpleasant and threatening to get worse. It had been raining most of the weekend and the temperature was in the low forties. The clouds were so black and heavy, it seemed that at any moment they would open up and drench everyone. The casket arrived with Wilma's body. Some of the men had dug the grave on Sunday. The water table had been so high, and the ground so saturated, they had to pump out the hole in order to finish.

The Spirit-filled minister, Fr. Lou, preached a great going-home message of hope, reminding us of who Wilma was and about her great reward. It seemed his powerful words might puncture the clouds and set off a downpour. Al stepped forward and shared gracious words about Wilma and their brief but wonderful life together. Just as Al sat down, a large volley of guns—just like a twenty-one gun salute—went off. We had heard that earlier in her life, Wilma had been a career Naval woman. We later came to realize the guns had been a practice round of very large guns at Fort Gordon, the large Army base a few miles away. The Holy Spirit likely set the timing of their firing.

As Wilma's casket was lowered rather precariously with ropes into the grave, we heard a clear "splunk." The water in the grave had come back up again, and on impact, the casket spewed red muddy water up into the air. Al later told us that because of Wilma's naval background, she would have loved it—she would have thought of it as being "buried at sea."

As the casket settled in place, we all became aware of the large pile of red clay by the grave and the shovels leaning against it. What happened over the next fifteen or twenty minutes was truly gripping and heart rending. All of the people there had a chance to shovel dirt, beginning with Al, the closest to Wilma, then other family members and close friends, and then those who barely knew Wilma came up and shoveled, including little children, with help from their parents. That heavy wet dirt hitting the casket lid sounded like large drums being played. It had a melodic finality about it.

After everyone had an opportunity, then "the brothers" finished filling the grave and leveling it out. This was really closure. To this day, with every burial, we close this way—shovel by shovel, always done by those who've come to celebrate this life.

As we headed for our cars, a steady rain began. By the time we got into our cars, it was pouring. God's timing, again.

Hopefully, this was Wilma's favorite birthday present. The entire event meant a lot to the rest of us as well. It was definitely a milestone. We've improved our methods and techniques over time, but Al couldn't have been happier about how it all went. We had celebrated

Wilma's birthday and her going home in style. Just the way she wanted it.

Our casket making has continued. And yes, we now build a few ahead and keep them ready, because God still does not announce graduation day ahead of time—some things He keeps to Himself.

Watch therefore, for you do not know on what day your Lord is coming... therefore you must also be ready; for the Son of Man is coming at an hour you do not expect. Matthew 24:42 and 44

Epilogue

It's amazing how the most unlikely event can expand or develop into so much more. Responding to Al and Wilma's request was an adjustment for me, but I considered that job a solitary work that just needed to be completed. Within months, however, I had built caskets for a woman and then a young girl, both of whom had died unexpectedly.

Before I realized it a tradition was developing in the community and I had become the unofficial casket builder. That has continued throughout the past twenty-five years; we've built and provided the caskets for approximately two thirds of community members who have gone to Glory during this time—and also for a few non-community people as well.

Building and stocking caskets has been both business and ministry and, added to crosses and church furnishings, fills out my "life and death" ministry. I would never have expected caskets, but when you're in Kingdom building, it takes you where it will.

Whether unlocking my shop in the morning, building or installing church furnishings, standing at the murder clinic, maintaining our line of crosses, entering church for mass, delivering a casket or praying over a stranger on the street—all of these are Kingdom building and are all life giving. They are our call and the life we have to fulfill. I need to always be mindful of the treasures I've been entrusted with—no part of this even faintly resembles the former life I had planned on. Praise God!

> *Come now, you who say, "Today or tomorrow we will go to such and such a city, and spend a year there and engage in business and make a profit." Yet you do not know what your life will be like tomorrow. You are just a vapor that appears for a little while and then vanishes away. Instead, you ought to say, "If the Lord wills, we will live and also do this or that." James 4:13-15*

Part IV:
Grace Abounding

Holy Spirit Provision

As formerly stated, the primary business through the years as Images of the Cross has been to design and build custom altar furnishings by contract. Basically, this means providing a product that is designed and drawn to scale, all original, and built to specifications. All of the projects require creativity and many are very involved. Much trust on both sides—on our part and the part of our customer—is required. The customer is contracting for and making the first payment on a sizable product and service, not yet in existence. In today's world, such a business is a real rarity, but the Lord has always made a way.

Through the years, I've thought of this "making a way" as "Holy Spirit marketing," but I now realize it's actually Holy Spirit provision. The customers and timing are His doing, especially since many of the projects take over six months to complete, and the church schedule and ours have to coincide. These major projects have numbered well over thirty, and have been located as far as 500 miles away. Many moderate size and smaller jobs have been interspersed at just the right time. Over the years, our crosses have made their way to virtually every continent on earth—and even into the Vatican in Rome, Italy.

A few examples of His provision for the business follow; there are many others also.

I was working toward completion of our third church contract, an Episcopal church in Dunwoody, Georgia. Around the corner in the next block a very large Methodist sanctuary was being built; it was well along in its construction. A sign was out front and I wrote down the name.

Over the years, I had netted almost no results from cold calls or letters, but for some reason, I felt a strong inclination to send a letter of inquiry to the church., even while knowing that it might already be too late. Within days a call came from Joe J., a man who had become a good friend while I built his large house nine years prior. He didn't know that we had relocated to Augusta or that I was now in this new line of work. He said that he was on the building committee at the Methodist church and had been given my letter to follow up. Joe asked how soon I could come and meet with them about designing and building the new furnishings. This would become one of the largest church jobs we were ever given, and was ongoing, lasting three or four phases. I felt it was almost settled before I met with the committee. This church job led to another one in North Carolina twenty years later through a retired former church member who had also been on that building committee.

Business contracts didn't always fall into place so neatly and smoothly. A couple of years after moving to Augusta, we reached a challenging impasse. I was approaching the completion of my last church contract with no active calls or inquiries for future jobs. Every bid or proposal that we had submitted was at least two years old and dormant. I remembered the friends who had told me that our business was too specialized and that we would have to take secular work to survive. But that was not what the *Voice* had said when He called the business forth.

As Nancy and I sat together on a Saturday night during that period, our spirits weighted down, she anxiously reminded me that we were very low on funds and would soon be into our meager savings.

I remembered Elijah and the widow in Scripture. The widow had only a handful of flour and a few drops of oil. Elijah told her to make little cakes for him, her son and herself, and her supply would not fail, and then she needed to trust the Lord. She did, and she never ran out of ingredients for making the food she needed (*I Kings 17:12-16*). We were really concerned, but we prayed and asked for the Lord's help and provision. That's all we had going.

The following week, three unexpected calls came in, each from an old proposal. All three calls led to contracts during that week. Those contracts came to represent over a year's worth of work. The Lord chose to come through at what seemed to us like 11:59 (maybe it was a little earlier). The jobs were clearly a godsend, and the timing greatly helped us to develop trust. Similar experiences have been shared by seasoned "faith-walkers," notably Mother Teresa, Mother Angelica, and many, many others. We were reminded of the scripture, *"Nobody ever put their faith in the Lord and was disappointed"* (*Sirach 2:10*).

Some time later a surprise visitor walked into my Broad Street shop. It was Fr. Walt, looking very upbeat. He had just ridden his motorcycle in from North Georgia. Due to his different assignments and changing locations, we had been out of touch for some time. He was now the new pastor of the Catholic Church in Dalton, Georgia, and wanted to know if I would be willing to design and build new altar furnishings for them. I said, "Sure. When?" He said, "We're ready as soon as you are." I went to Dalton the following week and the contract was settled. It was like picking apples off of a tree.

While working with an Episcopalian priest named Fr. David on the sanctuary furnishings for his church, I met Pastor Ray. Ray and David were longtime minister friends. Ray asked me to meet with his

Lutheran church committee to discuss the proposed renovations of their sanctuary. The planning went well, and just as we were about to finalize the contract, Ray was hired to pastor a larger church in upper South Carolina and he quickly relocated. Since my dealings had begun with Ray, I was a little concerned about how we might be affected, but the contract went through to completion and all went well.

A year later, Ray called me from his new church. They wanted me to handle a major project: designing, renovating and building new pieces for their sanctuary. Ray's change of location became a blessing for us, and another good lesson in the scripture, *"Be anxious for nothing."*

All of these large projects were placed in my hands through the Holy Spirit's leading. Most of my other projects have come about as a result of simple referrals. I have never had to take secular work, and He has always kept His end of the bargain: that if I consecrated my work to him, I would never be without work. I've never been without orders to fill. They've always just come in, often when—and from where—I least expected. I am usually booked four to six months ahead, sometimes even a year, and that happens with virtually no advertisements—just referrals! I believe the Lord stirs the hearts and minds of others to look with favor upon us, and prompts them to action.

I've spent most of my working life as a small business owner, and having this part of the business (the next jobs) taken care of by the Lord Himself is huge. Fear of failure—and the stress that goes with it—have hounded many a small business owner into a bottomless pit. That was the very fear that had driven me, years before, to listen to the imposter voice.

Because of the nature of the business I can't overlook mentioning the designing. The vast majority of what we build, I also design—over 95%. The provision for design has been as strong and prevalent as the providing of contracts and sales. The Holy Spirit sharpens the gift for the occasion. Many design concepts or individual designs are given to me in my mind's eye like a detailed color photograph, just as needed. These might come at anytime or anyplace whether I am quiet or busy, awake or asleep. Most of these move on to full development and tangible products, from houses to furnishings to art pieces.

Certainly, when we're working the Lord's field, His grace is sufficient. We're just blessed to get to work in it.

I've learned that life on this level that we now live means that my professional work and His Kingdom work are all rolled into one. If I make His Kingdom work my top priority— Plan A—I don't have to worry about my professional work. If we represent Him, He most assuredly will represent us.

I am mindful of how far we've come since that fledging start. It could only have happened with the Lord's blessing each step of the way. By the grace of the Holy Spirit, larger, better shops and showrooms followed the original shop in our basement and we are now celebrating our thirty-year anniversary since starting the business. I never forgot the word I received at that very first prayer meeting:

Unless the Lord builds a house, the builder builds in vain.

Trust in the Lord with all your heart, lean not on your own understanding. In all your ways acknowledge Him... Do not be wise in your own eyes; Honor the Lord with your wealth, and from the first of all your produce... so your barns will be filled with plenty and your vats will overflow with new wine. Proverbs 3:5-7, 9-10

Harold and the 12/4 Walnut

Woodworking has been a passion and a large part of my life work since my teenage years, covering lots of work and lots of woods. It all started with maple, cherry and mahogany, and sometimes, walnut, considered by many to be the best of all. Over the years, the list of woods I've come to know has grown and grown; I now work with ten species of rosewood alone. Walnut, though, remains my first love.

Holy Family Catholic Church in Marietta was planning to upgrade and replace the sanctuary furnishings. They contracted with us to design and build all the new altar furnishings. It became a multiphase project, stretching over a few years.

Walnut seemed the ideal wood to use, with touches of ebony and bird's-eye maple as accents. The difficult part was getting the 12/4 (three-inch thick) walnut that was needed for the rails and posts. Walnut this size is very hard to find; few mills cut it anymore. It has to be dried very slowly to prevent honeycombing (splitting open) inside. Because of that, most mills don't cut and dry walnut over 10/4 thick, since the drying process slows down the recovery of their investment.

Knowing that the Lord always provides, I wasn't worried about finding the 12/4, just curious as to where it would be found. I had been buying from two different sources in Atlanta for decades. Because this was a specialty item, I first went to Carlton's Rare Woods, an exotic wood dealer. This supplier had such a variety of lumber and veneer that he didn't know about everything he had in stock, but he did not have any 12/4 walnut. Richard, the manager, thought he might be able to locate some and order it for me, probably at $7 per foot. This was the cost I had projected in pricing the contract, so that price would have been all right. I wouldn't have been able to hand pick the boards, though, so I would have had to order extra, because of my specific width and length requirements. Silently, the *Voice* said, "Call Harold, he is supposed to have it."

Harold was an old friend from Sweetwater Lumber, which was located about fifteen miles away. This company had been supplying the bulk of my lumber for over twenty years. Harold knew that I was very selective and that I only bought the highest grade of lumber (hardwood lumber grading).

When I called Harold about the 12/4 walnut, he said they really didn't have any, beginning to again explain why it wasn't available. I told him I understood, but it seemed unlikely that he wouldn't have it, since the Holy Spirit had just told me to call him, saying, "Harold is supposed to have it."

Harold is not your ordinary lumber man. He is a spirit-filled Baptist brother with a strong faith. Years earlier, when I had just started the business, I had come to him looking for 8/4 bird's-eye maple, which he was sure he didn't have. That time, I stood in their small warehouse, perplexed because the Holy Spirit had told me that they had the wood I needed, and I had driven over only to have Harold say he was sure they didn't have any. Suddenly, I found myself staring at two pieces of wood standing in the corner. For all the world, it looked like 8/4 bird's-eye. "What wood are those two boards?" I asked.

With a shocked look on his face, Harold said, "They sure look like bird's-eye." He did not remember ever seeing them before. It turned out they were bird's-eye. I quickly grabbed and bought them.

This had been burned into Harold's memory because he "knew every board" in that building. So now, when I asked him again about the 12/4 walnut, and why the Holy Spirit would say to call him if he didn't have it, he made a surprising disclosure. Almost like he was confessing a secret, he said, "Well, there is one little pile of 12/4 sitting out on a pallet in the middle of the floor. It's #1 common..." (This is very low grade.) "I don't know if it's good enough that you can use it, but you're welcome to come look at it." I told him I was on my way, and headed out.

Sweetwater Lumber is an imposing place to behold, with tractor trailers waiting and lumber stacked in the warehouse twenty-five feet high or more, just about every kind of American hardwood you could ever need, with lots of large forklifts to move it around. When I arrived, the pungent aroma, like no other, of hardwood lumber filled my senses, and my adrenalin began to rise. You almost have to see it and smell it to really appreciate it. I'm sure I'm addicted.

I found Harold, and he took me right to the pallet. This little pallet looked pretty pathetic, surrounded by huge stacks of lumber, like a rundown old shack in a city of skyscrapers. It was stacked just two boards deep, and that alone made it look out of place; it also had a layer of dust on it as if it had been there for years. The ends of the boards were sealed with stark white paint. The little stack of dusty wood stood out and looked very suspect in this state-of-the-art lumber warehouse—almost like an embarrassment to the company. Harold began to apologize for how bad the boards looked, as if he could only see what was on the surface.

The Holy Spirit began to show me what was inside those boards, beyond the rough edges and split ends. This was really good walnut with an ugly exterior that had been rejected, neglected and abused by rough handling. Carelessly used forklifts can be hard on lumber, especially on boards considered rejects. I quickly thought of people I had met through the years that had encountered rough treatment and fallen into similar conditions. I began turning the boards over, one by one, and inspecting them; I could feel myself being drawn to them.

Harold began to explain that if I could use them, he would really like for me to take the whole stack. He went on to confess that he had sold them and shipped them twice already, and each time they had been rejected by the buyer as substandard. On both occasions, Sweetwater Lumber had to pay the returned freight charges. He said, "If you can find a way to use them, I will certainly make you a good deal on them." The term "good deal," not one usually associated with walnut, sounded interesting. Buying that quantity of 12/4 walnut had not been on my agenda—not even close.

I could only say, "What does that mean?"

Harold said, "I don't know yet, but I really would like you to take it all. I'm almost afraid to send it out again. Let's see how much board footage there is."

We both measured it, and came up with 222 board feet. Harold said, "Let me go back to the office and do a little figuring. You stay here and pray about it." I sure did; I wanted the Lord's price on this wood.

Seven dollars per board foot had been my projected figure before starting the trip, and I thought Harold might possibly offer this wood at five dollars per foot. Then the question would be whether I could buy it all, since I only needed half of what he had. I had planned to come and buy just over one hundred board feet and spend between $700 or $800. Maybe I could stretch to $1,100 to get twice as much walnut.

Harold returned looking excited and happy. Almost exuberant, he said, "Could you go $1 a foot and take it all?"

I said, "You gotta be kidding."

"No," he assured me.

"You would sell me all of this for $222—and you can do that?" I knew that he was only part owner of the company.

"Yes, and I want you to take it." Harold announced, as though it were a victory for both of us (with a gift from the Lord mixed in). Without any more talk, Harold and I started stacking the wood into my old van, dust and all. We worked fast; neither of us wanted this one to slip away. The Lord gives and the Lord takes away—blessed be the name of the Lord!

As we were loading it, I told Harold that the walnut was looking better by the minute. He nodded and agreed. Looking him right in the eye, I said, "I'll be surprised, by the time it gets to Augusta, if it's not one face and better." (One face and better is the highest grade of walnut.)

He said, "Yes, I bet you're right." His eyes were twinkling, as if now he saw a great work of the Lord unfolding. By now, we both knew we were in the middle of a "God happening." Just let it roll!

"Harold," I said. "You know why those people couldn't keep this wood and had to send it back?"

He said, "I'm just starting to see it."

Making sure, I said, "You know, this wood was too good for what they wanted to use it for, and they couldn't keep it. This wood was meant to go into the Lord's house—to bring Him glory."

Harold stood there, nodding his head with certainty. "I can see that now." I could tell he was totally convinced—no doubt. We were both grateful.

The walnut almost completely filled my van. I drove back to Augusta in my rolling warehouse, singing praise songs down I-20. Even with that heavy load it felt like we might just get airborne. I realized that the Lord had saved me about $1,000 that day—by His direction through the *Voice.*

We not only made the pieces for Holy Family from this walnut, but also other key pieces in several sanctuaries since then. Years later, I was still working with some of the boards. That was some great walnut and an extraordinary gift. The Lord's provision!

My interactions with Harold through the years have blessed us both. I've been blessed with wood I needed and have been an encouragement to him and his faith in some of the tougher times. We always "talk Jesus" and he always remembers the details of the wood experiences when the Holy Spirit took charge and overrode what we "knew."

A few years later, Harold's wife, Joanne, was in a car wreck that left her in a coma. After a few weeks, the doctors, having done all they could to save her, totally gave up on her, and told Harold to prepare for her death—there was no hope. They tried to convince him to go on home and let her go. Harold would not accept that, but stood on faith, and the promises in Scripture that he had internalized, just claiming them and believing for her healing. Joanne was miraculously healed by the Lord and restored with no lasting damage. The medical doctors and staff were completely amazed, even acknowledging it as miraculous.

Soon afterwards, Harold retired from the lumber business, and he and Joanne travel around visiting lots of churches, giving testimony about Joanne's miracle, God's great love and healing power, and His intervention in our daily lives. I wouldn't be surprised if Harold's experience with the 12/4 walnut helped to build his faith to such a level as to be able to believe for Joanne's healing. God's never doing just one thing with us. We have to be able to see through "faith eyes" — and step out in that faith.

And if the *Voice* speaks, even silently — pay attention! And do what He says!

Now faith is the assurance of things hoped for, the conviction of things not seen.

And without faith it is impossible to please Him. For whoever would draw near to God must believe that He exists and that He rewards those who seek Him. Hebrews 11:1 & 6

Slain in the Spirit

Since the movement or the power of the Holy Spirit is manifest, subtly or more strikingly, in all of these stories, we should not overlook being "slain" or "resting" in the Spirit.

In the Pentecostal and charismatic movements there are countless occurrences of people slain in the Spirit. Extraordinary as these may seem, these are very normal results of a touch of the Holy Spirit, when God chooses to operate this way. The experience will usually draw the person closer to God, build his or her trust, take away fear, provide healing or revelation knowledge, and sometimes take the person to a new level of spirituality, deliverance or freedom. Placing ourselves in God's hands spiritually, without resistance, helps to enable such a touch, but God can lay anyone out, anywhere, anytime, ready or not. Some people are "slain in the Spirit" and receive the "baptism in the Spirit" simultaneously, but this is far more rare than it is the norm.

This gift from the Lord has been denied by scoffers, primarily because of heavy-handed tactics by aggressive televangelists and their forehead thumping, pushing style. This is in no way what I am going to describe. Also, Satan surely must hate this work of the Spirit and tries to discredit it. It is perhaps the most maligned of all manifestations of the Holy Spirit, and likely gave rise to the old derogatory term "holy rollers" (I have never witnessed this rolling phenomenon).

Typically, most occurrences of being "slain" happen in a group setting such as a prayer meeting. Individuals will come up to a prayer minister asking for prayers. Prayer is usually administered by

247

a laying on of hands, and the prayer minister can be anyone filled with the Spirit, ordained or not. When feasible, someone will stand behind individuals being prayed over to act as a "catcher" in case they do go down (not all do). Most frequently, the person who is slain falls backwards, much like a tree falling when cut down, his feet staying in place until his body approaches the floor. The catcher watches carefully and at the first sign of the person falling, catches him under the arms and lets him come down to the floor in the gentlest way. Obviously, the larger the person coming down, the more challenging the catching and lowering. Sometimes, to the catcher's surprise, the person will fall back quickly as if being hit in the forehead, even though there is at most only a gentle physical touch, and sometimes not even that. Some go down as soon as they step forward. The Spirit moves as He will.

Most people who have been slain describe their experience as very peaceful. Their eyes are usually closed, and while on the floor, they can sometimes hear what is being said by those standing around them. Many tell of feeling a deeper sense of God's love through the experience. During the time down, they either have no ability, or desire, to get right up. To many, it's a strange but very peaceful feeling of being in two places, on the floor and "somewhere else." Some don't know that they went down until they "wake up" on the floor. They can be down for any amount of time, but most stay down for just a few minutes. Assisting members of the prayer group allow the person to lie peacefully and watch carefully for his or her eyes to open and for any signs of readiness to stand up. This person or persons will help the one who has been "out" to get back to his or her feet. After being slain and getting back up, the person may or may not be somewhat dazed or lightheaded for a few minutes. There are many accounts of individuals being "out" for a long block of time—a whole night or day—but I'm only telling about what I've personally witnessed.

I've never seen anyone go down in any fashion that results in their getting hurt, even those who went down hard on concrete floors, asphalt parking lots or streets. I've never heard anyone who was slain say that they felt embarrassed or wished that it had not happened. I've never seen this occur at an inappropriate time or place, either. The Holy Spirit is always a gentleman and gives good things. Those who are fortunate enough to experience such events treat them with respect for what they are—a touch by the Holy Spirit. Certainly, my brief overview is in no way an exhaustive report, but is only intended to provide a glimpse of this phenomenon. It has been more than thirty years since I first witnessed someone slain in the Spirit, and having since seen numbers of people slain, in all kinds of settings, and the varied fruits of this phenomenon, my spirit is still lifted each time the Spirit moves among us in this manner.

Having given this short introduction, I want to recount a few instances worthy of singling out. Remember, these occurrences are normal "walking in the Spirit" happenings that the Holy Spirit brings about. We can't make them happen, and shouldn't ever try.

For a couple of years after being baptized in the Spirit, Nancy had resisted believing this phenomenon was "real" and not somehow self-induced. One day, we scheduled ministry for her (related to other issues) with an Episcopal pastor's wife, Jennie. As Jennie laid hands on and prayed over her, Nancy went right down and I caught and laid her on the floor. She was down for over ten minutes, with her arms extended straight up in the air over her head, toward the Lord, the whole time. When she got up, we told her about her arms high in the air—she had had no idea, and she felt no tiredness or discomfort in her arms or shoulders. She never doubted again.

A young woman named Kara, in her late twenties, had brain tumors. But she loved Jesus. She came to many gatherings, even though her condition made it difficult for her. A world-renowned Pentecostal leader was leading a weekend conference for the community. Dr. V. S. asked anyone wanting more of Jesus to come up for prayers. Many of us jumped to our feet and rushed forward, but Kara was seated up front and got to him first. Dr. V. S. touched her head and she was knocked backwards about six to eight feet, airborne. Many people were slain that night, but none were airborne like Kara. She went past too fast for us to catch her, but was not injured in the least.

A couple of times at Franciscan University of Steubenville and also in Atlanta, the Spirit moved among the congregation and it looked like various individuals were being hit on the top of the head with a hammer blow. Their knees buckled and they dropped straight down like sacks of potatoes. Some had no one praying over them or touching them, but were just standing there, then crumpled and went straight down. Many were big, solid looking men. If they had doubted before, they never did after that.

Francis MacNutt was conducting a healing seminar in an Atlanta church when he invited those attending to come up for healing prayers. The group began lining up and working their way up the center aisle. At a certain point in the aisle, about halfway, men and women began dropping to the floor with no one touching them. They went down at the exact same spot. We referred to it as "a grace line" where God's grace touched each person as they got to it. Many of them went on to receive physical healings a little later.

One night during an Alleluia Community gathering, married couples began coming up to be prayed over, standing side by side. They were soon being slain at the same time and began falling back like trees, requiring two catchers per couple. Both members of the couple went down simultaneously. Apparently it was a special "togetherness" thing the Spirit was doing. I never saw that anywhere else, before or since.

One night, on a trip to Florida, Nancy and I went to a prayer meeting and became very moved by what was happening. A ministry session was in progress with groups praying over anyone who came up. Everyone was standing, and we soon noticed that one particular group stood out: each individual who was prayed over by them was slain. The group consisted of two young men and two young women, very clean cut. One of the women was the lead prayer minister, and she would hold her hand about a foot in front of the person's forehead as they all prayed. The person being prayed over stood with eyes closed. At the appropriate time, never rushed, the prayer minister would gently move her hand toward the person and he or she would begin to slowly fall back. Her hand remained that same distance from the person's head, never seeming to touch or get any closer. Those slain seemed to get up with a new peace. It was a beautiful display of God's gentleness.

Fr. Ed M. from Boston came to Atlanta to conduct a healing conference. He was widely known for his exceptional gift, and people were often slain in the Spirit without his directly touching them. His manner was totally different from that of others that we had seen. His "hands" came in the form of holy water. After a quite unexciting talk and brief time of singing, Fr. Ed began walking through the gathering, sprinkling the people with holy water (blessed water) which he would cast out over the crowd. As the holy water touched them, they would go down, fast, as though they had been hit with a thrown baseball. (Again, no one was harmed.) Some entire rows of people would go down like dominoes against each other. Several of the designated "catchers," poised and ready, went down rather than those they were set to catch. Nancy and I were in the balcony looking down. The bodies laid out looked like a forest after a tornado had come through. After many people went down, Fr. Ed returned to the platform where he had started. The music ministry of four young people, two men and two women, who had been softly playing continuously, were set up on his right. With a final flick of the holy water in their direction, all four were knocked off their feet, backwards to the floor, their guitars flying.

One of our more extraordinary slain in the Spirit experiences is described in "Faith on the Streets" in a previous chapter. Again, the Spirit can do this anytime, anywhere.

Fr. Peter H., an internationally known Catholic priest and author from Belgium, came to visit the community and give an evening of reflection. The service was held at St. Joseph's, one of our local Catholic churches. Fr. H. was billed as a teacher and theologian who was quite knowledgeable on ecumenism; he was not known as a dynamic speaker. Upon completing his prepared talk, Fr. H. decided to close the session by asking if there were any young people in the congregation that had ever had any interest in considering a vocation to the Catholic Church. If so, he would like them to come up to the altar to be prayed over.

Very quickly, about forty people, male and female, stood up and with urgency, moved toward the front of the church. Fr. H. looked surprised by the eager, sizeable group, and started to pray for them.

Right away, various young people, scattered throughout the bunch, began falling backwards, slain. Fr. H. looked quite shocked; this was definitely not what he had expected. That began the largest "slain in the Spirit" assemblage that I have ever witnessed. The congregation was momentarily caught off guard, but some soon realized that the Holy Spirit was "breaking out" and that many more would likely be slain. Additional people began moving forward. Probably 200 or more were in attendance. It was a rare person who wasn't slain that night. This went on for probably an hour and a half. Some people were slain twice or more at the hands of different prayer ministers.

Finally, Fr. H. encouraged even the children to begin to pray over the adults. Without a pause, the Spirit continued to lay people out. My favorite memory of that extraordinary event was seeing Fr. H. laid out, flat on his back with his face to the ceiling, alone on the top step of the altar platform. A few feet away from Fr. H. was a young girl, around six years old, the fifth daughter of a community family, sitting on the floor with her hand stretched out in prayer toward Fr. H, patiently watching him. You could almost guess what was going through her mind: "We got you, Father." It may well have been the first time Fr. H. had witnessed or been part of such a spectacular slain in the Spirit happening. Fr. H. has visited the community several times since but nothing extraordinary has happened like that night.

Countless people have undoubtedly received wonderful touches from the Holy Spirit through this "otherworldly" gift. Most never have, and many remain shackled by skepticism. As great as it is to witness or participate in, we must always remember the Holy Spirit does the orchestrating and supplies the power. He does what He will. We are blessed just to be allowed to experience our senses being engaged by the Holy Spirit and today's Pentecost breaking out among us!

> *The wind blows where it wishes and you hear the sound of it, but do not know where it comes from and where it is going; so is everyone who is born of the Spirit. John 3:8*

Out of the Blue–
Holy Spirit Surprises

The following stories are just a sampling of the many times when the Holy Spirit set the stage, called the shots, and made extraordinary things happen. They are included in this book only because they represent an integral part of my life over the last thirty-five years. They reflect just a glimpse of the evangelical call and workings of the Spirit. That may occur anytime with anyone "living in the Spirit." Following His gentle nudges, listening for His voice and direction, without doubting, and trusting Him to carry us where He's going seem to be our parts to play. Also, the response time is very limited; we must be vigilant and on duty, with expectant faith.

I believe these experiences demonstrate some of His agape love and provision for each of His people, regardless of their needs or their conditions at the moment.

These are some of my favorite "riding the wind" stories. *"The wind blows where it will, and you hear the sound of it, but you do not know where it comes from and where it is going; so is every one who is born of the Spirit"* (*John 3:8*). Like the glide of the hawks or eagles on the high currents, so that their flying appears almost effortless, so too can be our movement with the Spirit if we are fully "going with it." In a sense, it's like riding the divine escalator. Each time I think about these stories or share them with others, they lift me to new heights and raise my sights as well.

And it shall be in the last days, God says, that I will pour forth my
Spirit upon all mankind; and your sons and your daughters shall
prophesy, and your young men shall see visions, and your old men
shall dream dreams; even upon my bond slaves, both men and
women, I will in those days pour forth of my Spirit and they shall
prophesy.

And I will grant wonders in the sky above, and signs on the earth
beneath. Acts 2: 17-19

Four Ladies in Hats

It seems that the Lord has interesting things for us when we go out on
the road, and gives us opportunities for some surprising encounters.

About the third year of our walking with the Lord, while we were
still living in Marietta, Nancy and I were looking forward with great
expectancy to the arrival of our first grandchild, Jordan.

Our daughter, Sherre, and her husband, Dave, were living in
Waycross, five hours away from Marietta, and Jordan was due.
Nancy had already gone down a couple of days earlier to assist
Sherre, so Franma (Nancy's mother, soon to be a great-grandmother)
and I were to drive down on Saturday and visit with them, and bring
Nancy back after the weekend. If you have ever driven to Waycross,
you know you can go for miles and miles string straight, with a
railroad track alongside and tens of thousands of pine trees on both
sides.

Late in the afternoon, on the last leg of our long journey, Fran and
I were riding along, enjoying each other's company, when we became aware of another car. Neither of us had particularly noticed it,
but the car had been in front of us for a long while, moving at the

same speed we were, and we had been staying the same distance behind. It had been out in front of us so long that it had become part of the landscape, like the trees around us. It was as if our two vehicles were caravanning on some journey together. The car appeared to have four ladies in it, two in front and two in the back. The two in the back had to be really small; we could only see their hats.

We had been driving about seventy-five feet behind them when we realized that they had slowed down a bit, which caused us to slow down, also. Then a little puff of smoke went up from their car, and they slowed down even more. Then a big puff of smoke, apparently from the engine, curled up, and the car seemed to die. The woman driving steered it off the road onto the shoulder and it rolled to a stop. The car seemed to have died a natural death.

We slowed way down, and as we eased past them, we could see two middle-aged black women in front and two very elderly black ladies, probably in their eighties, in the back. They were all well dressed with fancy hats, as if they were going to church. We had driven a few yards past them when I told Fran we had to see what we could do to help them. She fully agreed. We had been behind them for such a long time that we somehow felt responsible—at least to do something. I pulled our car onto the shoulder and parked. I told Fran that she would need to go back there with me; we didn't want to scare them, they were already having enough problems with their car. They didn't need to see a white man, a stranger, coming back there toward them. She nodded in agreement. (Fran was also a people person and wouldn't have missed this for the world.) She didn't have any solution for their car but she wanted to make them feel safe. We got out of our car and started to walk in their direction. They were watching us like eagles, fixed in the car, not moving a hair. From the time we got in clear sight of them, we could see that the driver had a death grip on the steering wheel—and the other three looked just as gripped.

It is always challenging, putting someone at ease to be able to try to help them. So you pray that the Holy Spirit will give you some sort of a lead into these situations. Somehow, it's just there. As we approached, I gently motioned to the driver to roll her window down, which she did. I said, "Looks like you're having trouble with the car." She nodded—the other three nodded also, in unison. Given their dilemma, I don't think the driver really was able to say anything. I continued, "Looks like the engine went," and all four heads again nodded in agreement that that was what seemed to have happened. I said, "Well, you couldn't have possibly picked a person to come along that knows less about cars than I do."

They all looked rather wild eyed and very disappointed. I said, "I don't know anything about cars except how to turn them on, how to steer and get them in gear. As far as what makes them run, I don't have a clue. It wouldn't do any good for me to raise the hood and look inside, 'cause I wouldn't even know what I was looking at."

Now they appeared totally perplexed and lost about the whole situation; they seemed to even feel sorry for me. I seemed to be making their very bad situation worse by the minute.

"But," I said, "I have a friend who knows everything about cars, and I bet He's your friend, too—Jesus!"

Boy, they just lit up like torches, all of them. They all nodded their heads enthusiastically, high expectations on all four faces. Now we're talking. We're getting somewhere!

This next part is so outlandish it's hard to believe (I could barely believe it as I heard it), but I just said, "Ok, here is what we're going to do. We are just going to pray a bodacious prayer, and ask the Lord to heal this engine or give you a new one, whatever He wants to do. When we get through praying, I want you to just turn the key and make a run for it!" They nodded a quick yes.

Looking back, it seems preposterous to have said that, but, anyway, that is exactly what I told them (I believe it was under the Spirit's direction).

We started to pray. Fran and I laid our hands on the car, and we all prayed our hearts out with expectant faith. The four women had their eyes closed tight, praying and beseeching the Lord. He was our only hope for their situation.

We finished praying, and I said, "Ok, now just turn the key and make a run for it."

Immediately, the driver turned the key, put the car into gear and rocketed away from us—almost running over our feet. They began going thirty-five or forty miles per hour right away and almost went out of sight as Fran and I stood there with the wind blowing our clothes. We rushed back to our car and took off after them. By the time we got going, we were probably well over a half mile behind them and could barely keep them in sight.

The road split after awhile, with us going left and the four ladies in the car going right. Our last glimpse of them was a fast-moving car—the front end slightly up and the back end slightly down, as if the car was "hunting the road." Four black arms were out of the windows waving wildly at us—they were almost leaping, like four young girls! It looked like they had gone ahead and started the church celebration early, right there in the car.

God is good! All the time! All the time, God is good!

Nothing is too big for God. Sometimes our faith at the moment isn't big enough to ask Him. Let us all pray to use our faith more. Our God is able!

> ♫ *"What a friend we have in Jesus,*
> *All our sins and grief to bear.*
> *What a privilege to carry*
> *everything to God in prayer." ♫*

A Colorful Encounter

A couple of years after coming to Augusta, we had established a presence at Planned Parenthood; we were there frequently, standing against abortion. One day a young man walked by and offered us a word of encouragement, and we invited him to join us. He said he couldn't at that time, but invited us to meet up with him and his group the coming Saturday night. They were planning to be at a little park in the center of Broad Street, a few blocks away, playing Christian music and evangelizing. He gave us the time, and encouraged us to come.

The next Saturday morning at our men's prayer breakfast, I mentioned his invitation to the group, and about a half-dozen men showed some interest in going. We guessed there would be praise music, with "walk-ons" coming up and a chance to witness to them—and hopefully, pray over them. Sounded like our kind of outreach.

Six of us did go that night, a real mix of backgrounds and ages, from late twenties to sixties. Only a couple of their guys showed up, but since it was their program and we were just invited to join, we went with their agenda, which turned out to be very different from what we had expected. They were interested in playing some Christian music, as entertainment, with no outreach to the people on the street. This quickly proved to be unfruitful and they soon lost interest, packed up and left. We began to look at each other, wondering if we had misheard? Had we wasted our time? Had we really come at the Spirit's leading?

About that time we became aware of a group of young people (late high school and college age), numbering about fifteen or so, wearing really strange "mod" clothes, with hair in iridescent colors— pink and green! They passed by and walked to the next block in a procession, made a loop, and went out of sight, back in the direction from which they had come. As they passed by us they looked intently in our direction. Talking among ourselves, we began to wonder if these strangely decorated young folks were the reason we were down there that night. Maybe we should stay around a little longer to see what might happen.

In just a short while, we saw them coming back up the street, but this time their numbers had swelled, maybe even doubled. It now appeared they were coming primarily because we were there. As they reached us, we tried making conversation to draw them in, asking how many of them there were altogether. They answered that there were about fifty, gathered in an abandoned old law office that was left open in the next block. They were having a party—music, food and all.

We suggested they go back, get the rest of their group, and come join us in the park. We were hoping to put this game in our field, not theirs. They said they would really like to do that, but were sure the party's hosts wouldn't go for it. Even so, they would really love to have us come join them. It's amazing, when you walk in the Spirit, how quickly things can turn. All of a sudden the hunters had become the hunted and we had a decision to make. We asked for clear directions to where the party was and told them we would see what the Lord told us to do—no promises.

With that they went off into the distance, around the corner, with all their bright-colored spiked hair and weird outfits; they were truly challenging to the visual senses. Strangely though, they seemed to express a respect and almost reverence while they were there, as if the Lord had sent them to us. After a short conference among our six, feeling that we had bombed so badly with our original plan, we decided to take courage and believe that this was probably why we were there—and step out in faith. Filled with uncertainty, Bibles in hand, we started down the street, heading toward their party. We wondered if our invitation would be really valid once we got there.

The abandoned office was on the upper floor of an old building with a narrow stairway, two dozen steps nearly straight up, three feet wide—a typical old downtown office. Some of the pink- and green-haired teens were milling around on the sidewalk at the base of the stairs; they paid us little notice. Looking up to the second floor, more were sitting on open window ledges and one, not quite out of sight, was standing urinating into mid-air from the second floor. Surely, this must be our group. Welcome to the party!

Dan, whom I considered to be the most careful and prudent (he is now an elder in our community), was behind me, and I believed if he joined me, we were to go up. He did, and the others followed. I guess we all pushed each other up the stairs with a big nudge from the Holy Spirit.

Approaching the top of the stairs, the place was alive with people. Three hardened rock musicians, not young like the kids (maybe a hungry semi-professional group), were set up with all sorts of equipment and amps. People were sitting on the floor, standing, propped against the wall, slowly getting positioned. Some girls were going through the group with little plates filled with cheese or something. They offered us some but we declined, suspecting it was laced with drugs. It appeared to be a gathering without real purpose or direction—like they were waiting for something to happen, but deep down fearing what that might be. There was a sense of foreboding, like these young people had been taken somewhere they shouldn't be.

One of the most notable things in the room, which apparently had been vacant for a long time, was a whole wall decorated in big, bold graffiti, many different styles and colors—most quite profane. To our great surprise, at the very top was a line capping this mountain of obscene graffiti. In small, plain letters was the phrase, "Jesus is Lord." Wow! Surely we were in the right place. God always leaves His little signs and calling cards. It was small, but it was the last word, and was our confirmation.

We took our places, scattering in the room wherever we could find a place to stand. The lead musician tore into a super loud rendition of something; it was almost earsplitting. Even though this building had been there a very long time, you wondered if it could handle this noise and vibration. The crowded condition of the room left me only one place to stand, right next to the band leader, almost close enough to look like I was about to join him in a duet. What a set-up.

As I stood there, enduring the noise, wondering what was coming next, trying to listen, the Holy Spirit told me again what I had heard Him say on the way up the steps. I was to speak to the crowd—and if I would step out in faith and ask, the leader would give me the microphone.

Mustering up what boldness I could, as the musicians brought the first excruciatingly loud song to a close and welcome silence returned, I just leaned over and spoke right into the leader's ear, "I think I have something to say to your people." With that, he looked at me as if I was insane, and tore right into the next song, equally earsplitting, deafening.

Their amps and speakers were pouring out the aggressive, harsh music that could have been heard blocks away. By this time, I knew the Holy Spirit was going to give me the microphone and I would have forty-five seconds to speak (when necessary, the Holy Spirit will be very specific). In several previous encounters I had experienced the reality of the Scripture, *"Do not be anxious about how or what you are to speak; for what you are to say will be given you in that very hour and moment. For it is not you who are speaking, but it is the Spirit of your Father speaking through you. Matthew 10:19-20."* So I just quieted myself and listened, trusting the Holy Spirit. The second song finally came to a close. Blessed silence came again and the leader looked at the group and, with some disdain and almost as though he had no choice, said, "This guy thinks he has something to say to us," and handed me the microphone. We had to use the time to the max—there was none to spare and none to waste.

It was almost like a Holy Spirit script, being played out, line by line, with all the people doing their part. One of our men, a 230 pound brother who was 6'6' tall, had come up the stairs carrying a 5-foot cross. Smelling the drugs, he went back down on the sidewalk. Because of his prior addiction to the same stuff, he couldn't stay up there. So now "our church" not only had a microphone and five men with Bibles upstairs, but a cross and cross-bearer on the sidewalk. It was quite a scene, especially with all the iridescent-haired, strangely clothed young people—almost like the Scripture, *sheep without a shepherd.*

The word the Lord had for the group was very encouraging. It was about His love for each of them, the plan He had for their lives, and the hopes He had for them. They weren't to squander them; they were not to continue on this path that they were on. He had some-thing far better for each of them. This was definitely not it. They were in a dangerous spot that moment. The message flowed out clear and easy, down the street with great clarity, washing against the bricks and concrete of a hard city. It was as if a CD was being played and, along with this colorful group, we were all being instructed on life by the Holy Spirit Himself.

The forty-five seconds went quickly, the message (which I heard at the same time they did) got delivered, and time was up—we all knew it. The bandleader took back the microphone and his leader-ship, looked me right in the eye, and harshly told us, "This next song we dedicate to you. The name of the song is 'Be Gone.'"

We all looked at each other, and simultaneously started toward the stairs to go back down. Then an amazing event followed. It was much like the angel opening the prison doors and leading Peter out. Several of the young people followed us down to the sidewalk, a few clearly shaken, some in tears, some asking for prayers. We brought the healing balm of Jesus to them. Our prayers for them were mostly an assurance of God's love and for His protection and direction. It was very moving and spiritually uplifting. The whole encounter didn't take long but was quite an experience. The Holy Spirit had asked us to "get out of ourselves" that night and let Him work through us. We tried and He sure did!

Our group was well aware of the magnitude of the moment. Each of these unsuspecting young people was already targeted by Satan, and the next bad choice could lead to long-term misery or disaster. That night the Lord extended an open hand and a fresh chance to them—also to those musicians who probably had already experienced the fruits of lots of bad choices.

We hope it moved that confused and misguided group of people, made in God's likeness and image, as much as it did our uncomfortable and surprised little group. We all grew a lot that night as first-hand witnesses of the Holy Spirit's power over Satan's' evil attempts to steal, kill and destroy. We walked away almost as dazed as our colorful young friends.

> *When He saw the throngs, He was moved with pity and sympathy for them, because they were bewildered—harassed and distressed and dejected and helpless—like sheep without a shepherd. Matthew 9:36*

Easter and the Blessing Cart

For many years, we have had a Good Friday "Way of the Cross" in our area. We gather at midmorning on Good Friday, at a nearby Methodist church, beginning with praise and worship, and then embark on a mile-and-a-half walk through an urban, somewhat depressed, residential/commercial area. We make two stops along the route, first at a Lutheran church, then at a Baptist church. At each stop we have Scripture reading, praise and worship, and music. The walk takes an hour and a half to complete, and then many participants stay for "stations of the cross" at the Catholic Church where the march ends. This event has come to involve 500 or more adults and children, and half a dozen or more different denominations. It has been an ecumenical blessing for all involved. One of the most meaningful aspects of it is carrying crosses in honor of the Lord. These crosses range from small sizes for kids, to seven- and nine-foot-tall crosses carried by adults and teens—and a whole lot of them. Anytime you are on the street with a cross, it seems to affect other people, but when you have a large procession carrying crosses, it really makes an impact.

This particular Good Friday had been one of our best yet. The Spirit was strong, the people more reverent. It was our largest group, and there were many first-timers. Even the drivers, in the cars that would stop and wait as we crossed the streets, seemed more patient and respectful. After the march, I delivered Mike, a good friend and the Lutheran pastor, back to his church. Sitting on a stack of crosses that virtually filled the back of my van, he decided he would like to borrow a large cross and a stand to use that night at his church's Good Friday program. The cross was with us, so we took it out and placed it in the church, but the stand was back at my shop. I would bring it later that day. Since his church's service was at 6:30 pm, Mike and I agreed it would be good to bring the stand at 6:15 pm. With that, we parted ways for the rest of the afternoon.

Late in the day, I took the crosses back to my shop and picked up the base for the cross that Mike was going to use that night. As evening approached, I was still "into" Good Friday, one of my most favorite days of the year, and was regretting that it was winding to a close.

I arrived a little early at the church, before Mike. Not wanting to sit in the van and waste time, I was trying to decide on the best use of the few minutes I had to wait. I suddenly realized I still had two five-foot crosses in the van that were later going to another man. One last little walk with a cross on Good Friday seemed fitting. My first thought was to walk down Lyman Street, which was across from the church (a very depressed area with lots of drug addicts and prostitution, etc.), but I felt the Lord waving me off of that, probably because I would most likely get involved praying with people and be late getting back in time to meet Mike. It seemed the best solution was to just walk down the street that Mike would be driving up, so I wouldn't miss him—simple but foolproof.

I began walking with one of the little 5-foot crosses, but I was feeling pretty insignificant, giving the Lord little to work with. It seemed like a letdown after the big walk earlier with all the people and all the crosses. Would this really make any difference? Was I really doing this for the Lord, or myself? Before I had gone past two houses the silence was shattered by a voice calling out in a scornful and mocking way, "Where are your followers?" The words pierced the evening air like a thunder clap.

Looking across the street to my right, I saw a woman, rather vexed, intently watching me. I had heard exactly what she said, but cupped my hand behind my ear to get her to repeat it, to allow me time to close the distance between us. As I walked toward her, again she hollered out, with disdain, "Where are your followers?" The tone of her voice was taunting.

Sometimes when you are walking in the Spirit, the voices themselves—or the phrases—put you on alert that you are dealing either with the Holy Spirit's prompting or with demons trying to intimidate you. In this case, it sounded like a demon's voice and challenging, but the Holy Spirit also seemed to be quietly calling me into action in an effort to dispel the demons.

The woman and I converged at the edge of her front yard. Probably in her late forties, she was going on mid-sixties in appearance, and seemed like someone who had encountered every hard lick that a person could expect in a lifetime. Her voice was rough and she seemed like someone who would normally be rash and impulsive, intentionally abrasive and repelling. She was an imposing figure standing in front of me, a child of God very much "in the rough." Now, with the cross right in front of her, the challenging demons went quiet. She began to talk about the cross walk the year before, when she had seen hundreds of us come by her house. She said she was hoping to see us again this year, but didn't, and had decided that we hadn't had the cross walk this time. She was apparently disappointed that we hadn't continued to have it. I explained to her that she had missed the cross walk by a few hours; that we had, in fact, come right past her house again this year with hundreds of people and lots of crosses. We would have loved to have had her join us. Even to me, my explanation seemed totally inadequate. She obviously wasn't impressed—she was still being left empty handed and dissatisfied, like one who had come to a soup kitchen only to find the food all gone and only empty bowls left, and hearing, "Sorry, we had lots of really good food earlier."

Sensing that God wanted to do something for her, I told her we could still pray for a blessing for her—right then. She nodded approval. I asked her name. "Linda," she responded readily. I asked if I could "lay hands" on her while praying for her. She said that was fine, and quickly put her hands together and bowed her head, waiting, with seemingly strong anticipation. Her demeanor and body language were taking on peace right in front of me. The Holy Spirit was claiming the moment.

Then, just like a bolt of lightning had hit her, Linda remembered something. She turned like a shot and hollered in a loud voice, "Jessica, get down here!" With that, a little girl about five years old, apparently Linda's granddaughter, leapt out the front door. She was on the way but wasn't fast enough, and Linda hollered again, louder, "Jessica, get down here right now!" This was tough love. Everything in Linda's life was probably tough, and so was her way of showing her love for Jessica, but she didn't want Jessica to miss the blessing. Jessica got herself down there quick. She didn't know what for, but she knew she better do it quick.

Watching Jessica running toward us, I had noticed a young woman standing inside the screen door. The Spirit revealed that she was Jessica's mother (Linda's daughter). I sensed she had experienced lots more disappointments than Jessica and didn't want to risk another; she stayed put in the house. Now, as Linda and Jessica stood there at the edge of the street with heads bowed, waiting for a blessing, I began to do the best I could to deliver what I had promised, what I thought they really needed, and especially what the Lord wanted to give them—a blessing, a touch from Him. This prayer was intense but didn't take long. I was suddenly struck with the magnitude of what was happening with the three of us. It was a very holy and profound time. If they had been Catholic, standing before the Pope to receive a blessing that day, I don't think it would have been any more important to them than this seemed at this moment. When the blessing was completed, they turned back toward the house with an appearance of such fulfillment that I would never have imagined could result from that brief prayer.

As I left Linda and Jessica to head back to the church, I was almost overwhelmed by what had happened and the "right now" quickness of it on this "insignificant" little walk. The Spirit revealed that we had just celebrated their Easter together. That had been it. No church, and it wasn't Sunday—but it was their Easter service and blessing! I had almost missed it completely.

It would be some time before the Lord would provide me with an analogy that would help me understand the fullness of what had happened. He reminded me of when I was a young boy, growing up, and the ice cream cart or truck would come down the street. You probably had one, too. The truck with hunkies, Eskimo pies, fudgesicles, etc. We would hear it coming from way down the street with the little bell, "ding, ding, ding." There would almost instantly be this flurry of activity, kids running to their homes asking for money for ice cream. Some just stayed in place—they knew not to even go ask. Their best hope might be to beg a bite from a treat a friend got, or, maybe, to get to share the whole thing. They just stood there with rather downcast, wistful looks on their faces. The ice cream cart coming down the street brought forth lots of emotions, mixed, for sure. A lot of those emotions were tied to money—even a little bit of money—and whether you had it or didn't. For some of the kids, it was the happiest moment of the day, but a few parents—and even some kids—would have preferred to just avoid it altogether.

The Lord showed me that as believers we have a "Blessing Cart" from which to dispense all kinds of blessings—whatever is needed. Wherever we go, we can push our cart fully loaded with every kind of good blessing. (If we will push it, the Lord will surely load it.) Our smile, our gracious countenance, our gentle body language, our outstretched hands and arms, or even a cross provide the "ding, ding, ding" that draws people to our carts. Down deep, the people hunger for a touch from the Lord, whether they "know" it or not.

People will come right up to receive the blessing. Packaged and waiting, with their own name on it. "Jessica, Linda, what would you like? Oh, I see them right here, honey, with your names on them—from Jesus!" Probably most of the blessings from the cart go to people who rarely get to the "Blessing House." For lots of reasons, they don't get there; they may think they won't be accepted, don't have money, don't look good enough or dress well enough, or haven't acted worthy to go through the door of the Blessing House. No telling how long it had been since Linda had been to the Blessing House, and it's likely that Jessica had never been.

If we don't keep our carts full and push them along where they can be seen, how are the blessings going to get where they are needed? Generation after generation are starving for the Blessing.

That day, I probably got blessed even more than Linda or Jessica. I also learned that there are no insignificant people, times or efforts in the Lord's eyes. Our God wants to bless everybody—and frequently will even use us to help—maybe when we least expect it.

You are the light of the world—a city set on a hill cannot be hid. Let your light so shine before men that they may see your good works and glorify your father in heaven. Matthew 5:14 & 16

Dan and the Man at BP

It was about 8:15 on a Monday morning. This Monday looked like lots of others; I had met with our men's group for an hour, and I felt prayed up and ready for the week. I was thinking: "TGIM—Thank God It's Monday!" We had all week to use our gifts, and I didn't want to waste any of it.

I was on my way to work, just a few hundred yards from my business, when I noticed that the gas gauge in my van was reading almost empty. I could have waited until later to refill, but if I did it now, that would be one thing off my list for a couple of weeks. It seemed like the thing to do. Pulling the van into the large gas station just ahead, I drove to the last pump at the far end. This should be an "in and out," I thought, and I'll be on my way to work.

Hose in hand, meter running and gas flowing, I heard a voice. Dan, the principal of our community high school, had pulled his car alongside the gas pump and was trying to get my attention. I was engrossed in the moment and in my plans for the day and hadn't noticed him drive up. Our community school is directly across the street from the gas station, and upon noticing Dan, my first thought was, "Why isn't Dan at school?" It was almost time for classes to start. No way that Dan would be late.

As I directed my attention toward Dan, it became obvious to me that he was very concerned about something. With some urgency, he said, "That man needs prayers." Since no one was in sight, I asked, "What man?"

Dan replied, "The one the police have over there," motioning toward the center of the big lot. With that, I turned loose the gas hose to walk toward the front of my van to be better able to see. I saw a tall, lanky black man, probably about fifty years old, standing by an old car with two police cars next to him, one on each side. Two policemen were handcuffing him. Upon my return to the pump, Dan looked me in the eye with a seriousness and urgency and repeated, "He really needs your prayers," then straight away drove off, headed for school, going to his mission and leaving me with mine. I knew Dan, who was strictly business. He had heard from the Holy Spirit, delivered the message, and now it was in my court, my shot to take. The Holy Spirit, through Dan, seemed to have given me responsibility for whatever was about to happen.

Since Dan had interrupted my gas pumping when the tank was about halfway full, I reverted to the "old man" response: finish filling my tank first. As I resumed pumping, the *Voice*, in a prodding manner, said, "How is he going to get your prayers with you down here pumping gas?"

"Right! Sure. Got it."

Quickly, I replaced the hose in the pump — it was time to get to plan A. By now, the policemen were putting the handcuffed man into the back seat of one of the police cruisers. My first mission appeared to be getting past the two policemen and to the man in their car — I didn't have a clue how to even start. As I began walking across the thirty yards of asphalt between us, the scene took on the distinct feeling of the movie, "High Noon." The policemen seemed to sense it, also, and they just tightened up and turned their full attention toward me. They already had one handcuffed and put away. What would be next?

I was learning that with any of these "in the Spirit" missions, we have to get outside ourselves — and outside the box — and rely totally on the Holy Spirit. And we usually needed to do it immediately.

The policemen were wondering what I was doing, and I was wondering even more what I was going to say. Come, Holy Spirit, it's up to you.

Walking with measured steps, the distance closed too fast, and it was time. The police were at full attention. It was obvious they were going to give me the first shot. In the most laid back, non-threatening manner that I could muster, I came out with the words,

"I noticed you putting the man in your car. Looks like his week is not getting off to a great start. I wonder if it would be okay if I prayed over him?" Hearing the words tumble out, they sounded preposterous even to me. I was sure they sounded equally absurd to them. Police have to see and deal with a lot, but this must have pushed the envelope.

Both of the officers were fairly young, in their late twenties or early thirties. The older of the two, clearly the senior, took the lead. With a voice full of authority and some degree of displeasure, he demanded, "Who are you?"

Motioning to my left, I just said, "I'm in the van down there at the pumps getting gas." That sounded totally unconvincing, even to me, and I quickly realized I would have to peddle hard. The lead policeman looked unimpressed, but the second policeman sensed that this was beyond his training and he quickly moved over to the empty police car and set up shop on the trunk, filling out reports. He was busy and looked like he was going to stay that way.

As the lead policeman stood glaring at me, I tried again, and with a sweeping motion pointed across the street to our school. "I'm also part of Alleluia Community."

Unmoved, he was now beginning to tire of the ordeal and was ready to send me packing. Then came one last chance. It was a gamble, it could go either way. I said, with some confidence, "I'm also a friend of Major Larry Deere—he's one of us." Larry was the third highest-ranked officer in the police department and also a member of Alleluia Community.

Somehow, that last effort seemed to keep the door cracked open just a little. With a somewhat milder tone, the policeman said, "This is not normal!" I wanted to shout out, "Amen, brother—you got that

275

right!" but I just quietly agreed and stayed patient. He continued, "He's under arrest. Once we arrest a person and put them in the car, we don't let anybody mess with them." In my most agreeable manner, I responded that I understood and all I wanted to do was to pray over him; I wouldn't create any problems.

Then I sensed the attitude of the policeman had changed. Just like that! I could see that he knew that this was supposed to happen. But how? Then, like two friends standing together, reasoning something out, he said, "Couldn't you just pray *for* him?" Wow, the Holy Spirit had really dealt with this policeman. He was acting like a new man, assisting in the mission.

"Pray for him, that's it, I can just pray for him," I said with enthusiasm. "Is it okay if I just lay hands on the police car? I won't mess with him."

Then, with a "whatever" shrug, he also headed toward the other police car, leaving me standing looking into the car, right at the handcuffed man.

Emboldened by this success through the Holy Spirit, it seemed fitting to complete the job, so I followed the lead policeman to the police car and asked, "And what is his name, so I'll be better able to pray for him?" Without missing a beat, he looked at his clipboard and just read off the name, Johnny Roosevelt Brown. Even I knew he wasn't supposed to disclose all that. Leaving the policeman to fill out his reports, I turned toward Johnny.

Johnny had no doubt been watching all this and wondering what in the world was happening. And who was this guy who'd been talking with the police? The demons resident in Johnny knew what was happening and didn't like it one bit. Johnny was sitting in the middle of the back seat with his arms pulled back and his hands cuffed behind him. He looked like no stranger to the back seat of a police car. As I looked intently at him, he was glowering at me as though with pent-up hatred. What a perfect time for a cross—but I didn't have one with me.

The distance between us was about twelve feet. It then dawned on me that of course I had a cross, and as I started to walk toward Johnny, I took my right hand and very deliberately "signed" him (in the air) with the cross. Instantly it looked as if he was being electrocuted—his whole body jerked back and his head and neck wrenched around (you could almost imagine hearing his bones cracking). His face contorted.

By now, I'm halfway to the car and I repeat the process with a second signing of the cross with my hand. The same thing happened again as Johnny was mercilessly wrenched around by the demons for the second time, straining against the handcuffs. It looked as though his entire body was being torqued almost out of joint. The cross and the demons were going at it! I continued to walk the last steps to the car, and for the third time, made a sign of the cross. Completing it as I reached the car, I then placed my hand flat on the back window of the cruiser.

Then it happened. Johnny's body was literally catapulted from the center of the seat right toward me, landing like a dead body up against the door, with his head resting against the glass—only the thickness of the glass separated my hand from his head. The power of the cross had reached Johnny.

At the prompting of the Holy Spirit, and in a compassionate and clear voice, I said, "Johnny, God has not given up on you. He has not given up on you!" I then told Johnny of God's great plan for his life, that what he was doing was wrong, but if he would change, this could be the best day of his life yet, and he could have a whole new beginning. Again, the Holy Spirit supplied the words—of course, He knew exactly what Johnny needed. The exhortation prayer probably took less than two minutes to deliver. All the while Johnny's body was curled in a fetal position with his head pressed against the glass. He hadn't moved at all.

When the prayer was completed, I withdrew my hand from the window. Johnny simultaneously moved his head back and looked up at me with the biggest, most grateful smile imaginable. His face was one of total peace at that moment. He then began to nod his head toward me—and to what he had been told in the prayer—as if in total agreement.

Walking past the policemen back toward my van, I had an "other world" feeling—just gratitude and awe. Drained and electrified at the same time. As I left the lot, I drove past the policeman and their cars. They were still filling out reports. I wondered how much they included. Looking into the back window of the cruiser, I could see that Johnny had somehow managed to turn his head and body all the way around facing the back and he repeated that great smile and nodding of his head. He had gotten it! Praise God!

Wow! Satan had Johnny bound in chains with a death grip, but on the third try, the power of the cross got through those chains. The words of truth and encouragement from the Holy Spirit gave Johnny a glimpse of freedom, and of what his life could look like. That depressing Monday morning start had taken on a new dimension for Johnny. If Johnny would allow it, the cross—the wondrous cross— could cut off all the chains in his life and forever keep them off.

For the story and message of the cross is sheer absurdity and folly to those who are perishing and on their way to perdition, but to us who are being saved it is the manifestation of the power of God. I Corinthians 1:18

Reflections and Conclusion

It is probably no surprise that I've pondered and prayed about this chapter more than any other in the book. How does the Holy Spirit want to conclude this book, which I truly believe is His? I've long since come to know that the hardest part of any challenging work is the completion. It is possible that He wants to personally deliver something to you, the reader.

How can we conclude a story that continues to unfold, with perhaps the best yet to come? The remainder of this journey may well be the most difficult to travel, but it will be the culmination of this great odyssey, the transformation, which is fraught with trials and replete with temptations. The goal we've been striving for is still beyond us; the Beautiful City looms up ahead but is nowhere yet in sight. The spirit responds to something beyond, like our senses do to rain in the distance before we can feel or see it. No one knows how far away this greatest of rewards is. We do know that if we stay on the *"narrow path that leads to life,"* one day we will arrive, the gates will swing open wide before us, and we'll be ushered in and given the welcome of a lifetime. That will be worth infinitely more than anything and everything it took to get there! Glory!

Like someone on an arduous trip up a long and high mountain road toward the summit, it's good to come aside for a few minutes and stop at an overlook. Just briefly, we need to reflect on where we have come from on our long, twisting route, with the stops, starts and turns that have brought us to this present place. We have committed everything to this trip and destination; we have purposed to give up pursuit of all else. What does the Spirit show us from this vantage point?

Looking down to the lowest level, I can see various points at which, while I was still an unbeliever, Satan either blinded my eyes to things he didn't want me to see, or magnified the things to which he wanted me to be drawn or attracted. Years earlier, I would have totally avoided some of these things to which he tempted me. I was enamored by and gradually pulled, little by little, into the prevailing culture—pulled into the quicksand of the love of the world. I was fascinated by its luxuries and pleasures, which I later learned are mostly just elusive dreams. While not acknowledging the fact, I had cut God out of my life, the worst and most dangerous choice possible. Now I can see that I had come to view church and the practice of faith as a "feel good" exercise intended for women and children, not necessary to the "real life." Though God had never withdrawn from me, He had allowed me to distance myself from Him—and finally to drop to a dangerously low point. It was purely by His amazing grace and mercy that I finally fell into His hands. There were so many deadly places I could have landed. Seen from this perspective, it's clear how perilous was the route I had traveled and how narrow my escape. My family was many times on the precipice, where I had taken us. How could I have been so blind and missed the treasure while pursuing the worthless—vainglory and fools' gold?

I have lived two vastly different lives—one spent exalting materialism and filled with spiritual darkness, the other spent exalting Jesus the Lord and filled with light and hope. Because my conversion was so "life and death" for me, that's the way I see it for everyone! It has clearly been life itself for me. The simplistic statement that "Jesus is the answer" seems almost too easy. But, there it is: God's only plan for rescue and restoration. From this vantage point, years and many miles later, that fact is so clear—but back in the madding crowd, it was anything but clear. Now even some of the worst "roads not taken," roads that were just one more bad choice or decision away, are coming into sharp focus. They are a chilling sight indeed, much like a near brush with death. The Spirit has plainly revealed some of the traps my family and I narrowly avoided and how we got safe passage. The angels, the signposts and the appointed helpers were like pinpoints of light in the darkness, placed there for us to discover and to show us the way—without them we couldn't possibly have made it to where we now are. There is hardly an hour that I don't feel an urgency to warn others of the impending dangers and perils that await them, much like someone who barely avoided a collapsing bridge.

From this well placed overlook, it is obvious that there is a myriad of ways that the Holy Spirit enables His people to traverse the Great Mountain. Watching carefully, I can see that no one is ascending above the lowlands on his or her own. There's much effort put into it, but like scaling a sheer wall, they need help. The Holy Spirit is the driving force and enabler for the ascent. The plan of God is far too great and difficult to accomplish without the Spirit's ongoing leading and assistance. It's no wonder that the Lord says it's His desire that all receive the Holy Spirit.

Considering my years of denial and neglect of the Lord, it hardly seems possible that Jesus would have sent the Holy Spirit to Nancy and me and our family to be our helper, our own personal counselor, and to give us peace in facing each day. That far surpassed any hope I could have ever had—but that's just what He did. As surely as the sun comes up each morning, the Holy Spirit is there, ready to help.

He not only forgave my sins, Scripture says He no longer even remembers them.

The awareness that He also desired to use us in His life-changing work with others, if we would be attuned and available, would have been too much to fathom before the empowering of the Holy Spirit. But, over time, I came to even anticipate and make space for plan A (His plan) and expect to be called upon at any time. His plan has become, for me, work at the very highest level. There's nothing as exhilarating as operating out of Holy Spirit direction and on His Schedule—living out divine appointments. Compared to anything that the world has to offer, that's like a glimpse of Glory! Even so, my salvation and early transformation are always near me. I remember it as though it was yesterday, being in the depths, at the bottom—but just as He didn't want me to stay there, He doesn't want others abandoned there, either. He wants none to be lost. As we were rescued, we must help rescue others.

Just as I was writing this chapter, suddenly the Spirit gave me a new clarity, a more definitive understanding of that wonderful Scripture in Matthew, chapter 6, *"Don't worry about anything—the Lord knows you need all these things. Seek first the Kingdom of God and His righteousness—and all other things will be added."* He revealed that *"All other things will be added"* is the actualizing of the Holy Spirit's provision; He leads, guides and assists us in carrying out all things. This means the practical, get-down areas of life, where the rubber really meets the road. Who doesn't need that? There's nothing needed that He can't help us accomplish or obtain—or He will supply it Himself, if need be. This seems to be His great plan: complete involvement in our everyday lives. I came to realize that having an independent spirit is no great help, and is sometimes even quite dangerous.

I began reflecting on the many practical ways the Holy Spirit enlightens and helps me in my work. I can no longer imagine embarking on any project without inviting His participation, and expecting His grace and assistance as needed. I can't help but smile as I remember how, from time to time, the Holy Spirit calls an audible (a play different from the one I had planned), telling me that this time, we're going to go about something another way. Invariably this "other way" works better, is surer, safer, cleaner or quicker (or all of these) than my old, proven way. Those moments, when His results begin to become clear, are truly some of the best "gotcha" moments. How great it is to work alongside the Holy Spirit with the strong sense that you're in this together and that He's watching out for your best interests.

I am mindful of the scores of good friends that I have, highly skilled in a variety of trades, vocations, professions and careers, from earthmoving to homemaking—they serve as contractors and educators, lawyers and physicians, leaders, and in many other capacities. They all rely on the Holy Spirit to carry them through the day and make their efforts successful. This is definitely no sign of weakness. Rather, they acknowledge their need for the Lord's ultimate equipping and provision. They are seeking first His kingdom and His righteousness, and other things are being added (their needs are being abundantly met).

As I draw toward the close of this work of reliving and recording these challenging, wonderful experiences, several thoughts come to mind. Looking back a decade or so, I surely didn't expect to be writing a book on our involvement with the Holy Spirit—no way.

Embarking on this daunting project, there were many times that I questioned my ability to write or to complete this work. (Satan tried hard to convince me that I am "just a woodworker," and definitely not a writer.) Sometimes I even questioned my motives for writing the book. Satan's accusations are to be expected if we seek to serve the Lord. The Holy Spirit continues to remind me that I am in good company, and that many individuals throughout the ages have suffered similar charges of unworthiness.

> *For simply consider your own call, brethren; not many of you were considered to be wise, according to human estimates and standards; not many influential and powerful, not many of high and noble birth.*

> *No, for God selected—deliberately chose—what in the world is foolish to put the wise to shame, and what the world calls weak to put the strong to shame. I Corinthians 1:26-27*

I fit right in with this description. Please use me, Lord.

I worked along for a few years, jotting down some of the stories, believing that they were to be recorded and preserved in order to strengthen various people's faith when they were discovered sometime later. Then the Lord seemed to call forth the book and put real anointing and energy on it. It was the fortieth year since my miraculous "seat belt" wreck. Forty seemed to have particular significance regarding the book. At Nancy's suggestion, I committed to write for one full day each week—and that soon became more. It was like sitting down and taking dictation from the Holy Spirit, and my memory for the events has been razor sharp all the while I have been writing. There has been as much grace on this endeavor as on any design or building project that I've had during my entire life—and that is a lot! It seemed that the Holy Spirit wanted these common and everyday events, which were transformed into Holy Spirit happenings before my eyes, to be shared among His people and to fan the flames of faith. Praise God! May it be so!

There's also another collection of Holy Spirit occurrences to be recorded in a second book—all are short stories. I think of them as Holy Spirit "flyovers" or "touch downs." Several are already written and others are in the memory bank ready to be put into words— some additional events in need of recording may have yet to happen! I feel duly energized, believing I've been given back fifteen or twenty years that the locust ate. My enthusiasm for building His kingdom has not waned one whit; I definitely don't want to squander this opportunity a second time. I am ever mindful that I have been given much—and much is expected.

By now, I hope you can see that this could be the story of *any* man or woman given over to the Holy Spirit. He wants to use each of us and use us to the full. You may have experienced far more than anything and everything recounted in this book. Praise His Name! May He use you even more! He appoints anyone He chooses, at anytime. And it's not nearly so much about our ability as about our *availability* to Him. The Lord desires to do great things through each of us. Hopefully He already is—but certainly, He wants to do so much more. Perhaps He wants to sharpen and put into His service a gift He gave you that has lain dormant or has rarely been used. Maybe you don't even know you have this gift and need to be made aware by someone else (the Holy Spirit may inspire someone to share that with you). Over the years, numerous people have told me that I needed to write a book about these experiences. I heard each one, and they each helped to prepare me to take action.

Let us each think higher, stretch further. One step at a time is all it takes, and trust is the key. When my work is finished here on this earth, should I get accepted into the Beautiful City, I hope to be allowed to work in the *sunrise and sunset shop*—where they are created! Wouldn't that be awesome—and for a former nonbeliever at forty! He tells us that *"If we live in Him, to ask what we will and it shall be done for us."*

With the out-of-control, downward-spiraling descent of the culture across America and the world, many believers anticipate and already sense a new wave of the Spirit moving across the land. This new wave may be unprecedented, with signs and wonders and challenges that will amaze us all. It might well be the worst of times to leave our wonderful Holy Spirit gifts unopened or dull and unusable, and yes, it may be the best of times to step out on behalf of the Lord like never before. For certain, we will need to be more "on duty" to the Holy Spirit and live with more trust and reliance on the Lord. As we count on Him, He also counts on us. *"The field is white and the workers are few."* Pray earnestly that the Lord will send us into this ripe field and help us to begin to gather in the harvest.

As you have been so gracious to allow me the time and opportunity—and your attention—so that I might deliver these thoughts and reflections, my prayer is that you allow the Lord to deliver His personal message to you, and to touch your heart anew and set you fully ablaze. He has more—a yet to be revealed "more"—for each of us, and that "more" can change the course and depth of our lives and the lives of so many others. If we err, let it be on the side of being overzealous—the Lord will certainly adjust that. Let us not come to the finish line grieving over what we failed to do, those tormenting sins of omission. *"For God did not give us a spirit of timidity but rather a spirit of power.*" Let us remember, "*What eye has not seen, and ear has not heard and has not entered into the heart of man, all that God has prepared—made and keeps ready—for those who love Him.*"

Our time set aside at the overlook to reflect has been meaningful and energizing, our vision has been sharpened, our hearts are grateful and filled to overflowing. But we must not tarry; it's time to get back on the road. Much is yet to be done and awaits us ahead. There are relationships to be tended, gorgeous woods to be worked, acts of service to be performed, crosses to be built, stories to be written, crucifixes to be sculpted and divine appointments to be kept—and the unknown awaits us, too. We must move onward and upward to be present for it all. Souls are in jeopardy—and our own shaping and molding is still in progress.

Let us each look for more ways to serve the Lord, reach out to the hurting, do what He asks of us, leave everyone in better shape than we found them, be available, put our whole heart, soul and being into this work, and "*press on for the prize, the upward call of Christ Jesus.*" May we put aside every encumbrance, fully die to self, and like a grain of wheat, go into the ground—and be raised up someday to hear those most desirable of words, "*Well done, my good and faithful servant.*"

I hope to meet you personally someday on the road—"*The Highway of Holiness, where the redeemed, the ransomed of the Lord go*" —and get to share some everlasting joy with you! If that's not to be, then may it be in the Beautiful City.

Now to Him who, by the power that is at work within us, is able to do superabundantly, far over and above all that we dare ask or think, infinitely beyond our highest prayers, desires hopes or dreams—to Him be Glory in the church and in Christ Jesus throughout all generations, forever and ever. Amen— so be it... Ephesians 3:20-21

CPSIA information can be obtained at www.ICGtesting.com
Printed in the USA
LVOW120815021012

301095LV00001B/3/P